C000108652

DE-INDUSTRI..........
AND
NEW INDUSTRIALISATION
IN
BRITAIN AND GERMANY

DE-INDUSTRIALISATION
AND
NEW INDUSTRIALISATION
IN
BRITAIN AND GERMANY

Edited by Trevor Wild and Philip Jones

A project of the
ANGLO-GERMAN FOUNDATION
FOR THE STUDY OF INDUSTRIAL SOCIETY

The Anglo-German Foundation for the Study of Industrial Society was established by an agreement between the British and German governments after a state visit to Britain by the late President Heinemann, and incorporated by Royal Charter in 1973. Funds were initially provided by the German government; since 1979 both governments have been contributing.

The Foundation aims to contribute to the knowledge and understanding of industrial society in the two countries and to promote contacts between them. It funds selected research projects and conferences in the industrial, economic and social policy area, designed to be of practical use to policymakers.

Cover: design by Bailey and Kenny

Printed in Great Britain by
Billing & Sons Ltd, Worcester

Anglo-German Foundation
for the Study of Industrial Society
17 Bloomsbury Square, London WC1A 2LP

Contents

Good qual.
state of the art

i

(handwritten annotations in margins)
Just a repeat placing
but seep. 267
Reconstruction only at end
Stress on R&D, technicians etc., p.193
Key point at p. 199-
Much familiar — pp 214/6/7 216/7 rural
H. quest- imp? of Manny.
The most innovative
Concn around Stuttgart
Brings out more common features than thought

List of Figures

List of Tables

Foreword

This volume originates from a symposium of British and German geographers held in Britain last year, at the universities of Hull and Cambridge, which followed up a similar one sponsored by the Foundation in Germany in 1978. It included several of the former participants, thus fostering continuity of contacts between policy experts in the two countries. This is important, as comparisons of national approaches to policy over the longer term can better separate out the effects of national institutions and structures from those of current government policy. The Foundation also values the opportunity to support the development of international policy communities, including academics, policy-makers, the 'social partners' and non-governmental organisations. This part of its original remit has grown in importance as Britain and Germany now have to seek common ground in policy at European Community level.

The book fits into the context of a broader initiative of the Foundation to help understand the role of industrial policy in both countries, the part played in this by local and regional development policies, identifying differences in policy and implementation, and indicating where lessons may be transferred from one country to the other. The British increasingly look to Germany for policy leads in the economic and environmental fields. However, with the problems of cleaning up and redeveloping the new states of the unified Germany, some of the British experiences (e.g. with privatisation, self-help in the voluntary sector, or even with protection of the countryside) may prove instructive for the management of this transition. Also, the inclusion of the new states in a larger Germany may, in the short term at least, make the overall national comparison between Britain and Germany more balanced.

The publication complements two recent books from the Foundation, one on the wider context of industrial policy in the two countries: *Industrial policy after 1992: an Anglo-German perspective* edited by Keith Cowling and Horst Tomann, 1990; and the other on local initiatives: *Local economic development in Britain and Germany* edited by Robert J. Bennett, Günter Krebs and Horst Zimmermann, 1990, as well as a pair of conferences funded by the Foundation and directed by Professor Huw Beynon, University of Manchester and Professor Martin Osterland, Universität Bremen, held in Bremen (1988) and Manchester (1989): 'De-industrialisation in the United Kingdom and the Federal Republic of Germany: company shutdowns and local economic and labour market policy' and 'New industries and new processes: patterns of change and development in the UK and the Federal Republic', which deal respectively with industrial and regional decline, and with prosperous regions and the rise of new industries and the manufacturing and service sector.

It remains for the Foundation to express its thanks to the organisers of a successful conference, in particular Trevor Wild, David Keeble and Heinz Heineberg; also to the editors of this volume, who have taken great care to make it accessible to policy-makers and the interested lay reader, as well as colleagues from their own discipline.

Dr Nicholas Watts
Projects Director
Anglo-German Foundation

List of participants

H. Acker	*Institut für Geographie, Universität Münster*
Prof G. Aymans	*Geographisches Institut, Universität Bonn*
Prof R. Bennett	*Dept. of Geography, London School of Economics*
Prof B. Butzin	*Institut für Geographie, Universität Münster*
Dr A. Champion	*Dept. of Geography, University of Newcastle*
P. Crowther	*Industrial Development Officer, Scunthorpe Borough Council*
Dr W. Dege	*Kommunalverband Ruhrgebiet, Essen*
P. Edwards	*Economic Development Officer, Glanford Borough Council*
Prof T. Elkins	*Hon. Professor, University of Sussex*
C. Ellger	*Institut für Anthropogeographie, Freie Universität Berlin*
K. Foster	*Glanford Borough Council, Dept. of Planning*
S. Fothergill	*Dept. of Economics, University of Reading*
Prof W. Gaebe	*Geographisches Institut, Universität Mannheim*
Dr A. Green	*Dept. of Town Planning, University of Wales College of Cardiff*
N. Guy	*Northern Ireland Economic Research Centre*
E. Hall	*Dean Clough Mills, Halifax*
J. Hall	*London Boroughs Association*
T. Hauff	*Institut für Geographie, Universität Münster*
Dr G. Haughton	*Dept. of Urban Planning, Leeds Polytechnic*
Prof H. Heineberg	*Institut für Geographie, Universität Münster*
Dr D. Keeble	*Dept. of Geography, University of Cambridge*
R. Kitchen	*Glanford Borough Council, Dept. of Planning*
Dr G. Krebs	*Dept. of Geography, London School of Economics*
Dr A. Jones	*Dept. of Geography, University College London*
Dr P. Jones	*Dept. of Geography, University of Hull*
C. Law	*Dept. of Geography, University of Salford*

Prof P. Lloyd	Dept. of Geography, University of Liverpool
A. Lyman	Chief Executive's Dept., Glanford Borough Council
J. North	Dept. of Geography, University of Hull
Prof H. Nuhn	Instituts für Geographie und Wirtschaftsgeographie, Universität Hamburg
Dr J. Oßenbrügge	Instituts für Geographie und Wirtschaftsgeographie, Universität Hamburg
Prof P. Roberts	Dept. of Urban Planning, Leeds Polytechnic
Dr G. Shaw	Dept. of Geography, University of Exeter
Dr D. Spooner	Dept. of Geography, University of Hull
H-U. Tappe	Institut für Geographie, Universität Münster
Dr G. Thieme	Geographisches Institut, Universität Bonn
Dr N. Watts	Anglo-German Foundation
Prof H-W. Wehling	Institut für Geographie, Universität Gesamthochschule, Essen
Dr H. Wiener	
Dr T. Wild	Dept. of Geography, University of Hull
Dr P. Wood	Dept. of Geography, University College London

Chapter I

Philip Jones (University of Hull) and Trevor Wild
(University of Hull)

Industrial restructuring and spatial change in Britain and West Germany

De-industrialisation and sectoral trends since 1970

The United Kingdom and West Germany both fit easily into the category of nation states which are often described as 'advanced industrialised societies'. They are also of a similar size and scale in terms of geographical area and population (areas, West Germany 249,000 km^2, United Kingdom 244,000 km^2; populations, West Germany 61.6 million, United Kingdom 56.0 million). However, there are salient differences in the basic economic structures of the two countries, as shown by Table 1.1. West Germany has a larger industrial base than the United Kingdom, whereas the converse is the case for the service sector. Between 1979 and 1986 the gap between the industrial component of the labour force in the two countries actually widened from 4.5 to 6.9 percentage points. On the other hand, there was a narrowing of the gap in the service sector, from 9.9 to 8.1 percentage points during these years. Even so, the balance of the employment structure in 1986 is far more heavily weighted towards manufacturing in West Germany, where this sector still employs 48% of the active population.

Such a broad comparison of the employment structures serves to emphasise that any consideration of de-industrialisation inevitably raises the issue of national perspectives. There is considerable debate within the economic and social sciences regarding the definition and measurement of 'de-industrialisation', but there is a general consensus that, amongst other negative trends, it involves a prolonged and persistent absolute decline in employment in the industrial sector within a national economy. Taking this proposition as a basic starting point, Table 1.2 illustrates that both countries conform to this description, albeit with markedly different intensities of development. Taking both the longer time span (1970-86), and the shorter and more recent time span (1979-86), it can be seen that industrial employment has declined in both countries. This decline has, however, been much more drastic in the United Kingdom, which has lost over 3 million industrial jobs between 1970-86, and has recorded a massive 25.4% loss since 1979. By comparison, the scale of job losses in the industrial sector in West Germany has been less severe; this is particularly evident in the more recent time period, where the rate of decline is less than one-third of that experienced in the United Kingdom (Table 1.2). Therefore, this immediately raises important comparative questions of the scale, intensity and timing of de-industrialisation within the two countries, with further implications for unemployment, national prosperity, and regional impacts.

Table 1.1: National employment in industry and services in the United Kingdom and West Germany, 1970-6

| country | employment in industry (in thousands) | | | | | |
| | 1970 | | 1979 | | 1986 | |
	numbers	%	numbers	%	numbers	%
West Germany	12,128	49.3	10,565	44.9	9,765	41.0
United Kingdom	10,475	44.8	9,139	44.8	6,821	34.1
	employment in services (thousands)					
West Germany	9,324	42.1	11,218	48.9	11,982	53.8
United Kingdom	11,528	52.0	13,578	58.4	14,443	61.9

Source: Eurostats. *Eurostat review, 1970-79; Eurostat review, 1977-86.*

2

Table 1.2 : Absolute and relative trends in industrial and service employment in the United Kingdom and West Germany, 1970-86

| country | industrial employment | | | |
| | change 1970-86 | | change 1979-86 | |
	numbers (000s)	%	numbers (000s)	%
West Germany	-2,363	-19.5	-800	-7.6
United Kingdom	-3,654	-34.9	-2,318	-25.4
	service employment			
West Germany	+2,568	+28.5	+764	+6.8
United Kingdom	+2,915	+20.2	+865	+6.0

Source: Eurostats. *Eurostat review, 1970-79; Eurostat review, 1977-86.*

Firstly, de-industrialisation has been much more severe in the United Kingdom. Secondly, the trend began earlier in the United Kingdom, where national industrial employment peaked in 1966 (Massey and Meegan, 1982). In West Germany employment in industry peaked in 1970 (Eurostat, 1970-79), following a phase of very strong industrial investment and reconstruction during the *'Wirtschaftswunder'* and the continuation of buoyant economic growth well into the 1960s. These significant differences suggest that de-industrialisation is not a simple, monolithic causal process, but is likely to embrace a number of causal trends, which may be interrelated, and which require further investigation in the following section of this chapter. For example, an important constituent of recent industrial change has been a shift away from mass production to specialised, 'made-to-order' products, with attendant implications for the inclusion of a higher value added content. As Gaebe (Chapter XI) points out, this is a particularly marked feature of the West German economy. Whilst a parallel expansion in service employment is observable in both countries, and indeed is to be expected within the context of the sectoral evolutionary model of advanced economies (Robinson and Eatwell, 1973), in neither country has the deficit in industrial jobs been numerically compensated, although the situation in West Germany does approach very closely a one-to-one replacement (Table 1.2). In the United Kingdom, however, despite much-vaunted claims to the contrary, the statistics reveal that there is a very large shortfall between loss of industrial jobs and growth of service jobs, over both the longer period and the recent post-1979 period. The relationship, therefore, between sectoral gains and losses in the two countries, has produced a very strong contrast in the overall employment market, with its attendant implications for unemployment. This largely explains why unemployment levels within the two countries differ substantially at the national and, as will be shown, at regional levels too. In 1970, 1979 and 1986 unemployment rates in the United Kingdom were substantially higher than in West Germany (Table 1.3); only very recently has there been a sharp reduction in the former, bringing the two countries, for the first time since the 1960s, into approximate parity. Moreover, as Keeble, Wood, Ellger and other contributors to this volume demonstrate, the service sector is itself a broad economic category and is not an entirely adequate diagnostic variable for the understanding of the evolution of modern society. Increasingly it is the so-called 'quaternary sector', incorporating the information-related activities, such as research and development, which acts as the driving force in the creation of new jobs of sufficient quality and international competitiveness. In particular, the regional consequences of the unequal growth of (and unequal access to) such information-oriented activities has become a crucial cornerstone of internal regional differences in both countries.

4

Table 1.3 : Comparative unemployment rates in the United Kingdom and West Germany, 1970-88

country	per cent unemployed			
	1970	1979	1986	1988
West Germany	0.6	3.4	7.1	8.1
United Kingdom	2.5	5.3	12.0	8.6

Sources: Eurostats. *Eurostatistics data, 1989, part 6; Eurostat review, 1970-79;* Commission of the European Communities. *Third periodic report on the social and economic situation of the regions of the Community, 1987.*

De-industrialisation: the underlying causes

De-industrialisation within advanced industrial societies should not be viewed in isolation, but as part of a wider process of economic restructuring. The arena for such economic restructuring is increasingly the international and global economy, which is subject both to cyclical oscillations and secular trends towards increased capital and managerial mobility (Wallerstein, 1974). Furthermore, within national territories, we can also observe at the same time, three interconnected processes of regional economic change:

- de-industrialisation,

- reindustrialisation,

- tertiarisation

(Keeble, Chapter II). Geographical scale is, therefore, a vital, but not an immutably-fixed property. The decline of some industries and the growth of others, within the same time-space context, belong to this underlying process of economic restructuring. What is more open to debate is the nature of the dynamic forces which create pronounced irregularities in historical, economic, and spatial development. In his contribution, Keeble draws our attention to three dominant theoretical frameworks which have been proposed to explain the recent wave of economic restructuring in western Europe, within which West Germany and Britain have special significance. For the sake of simplicity these will now be outlined briefly as individual entities, whereas in reality they are interconnected. The first theoretical framework postulates that industrial restructuring proceeds in a cyclical fashion, in which long waves of intense technical change and economic growth are separated by periods of relative stagnation and quiescence. For earlier phases of capitalist development, long waves in business activity were first identified by Kondratieff, but the actual causal linkages between these cyclical fluctuations and industrial innovation were specified by Schumpeter (Deane and Cole, 1962). According to Schumpeter, it is possible to identify a 'discontinuous process' of technological innovation, with recognisable temporal clusters of entrepreneurial activity; these clusters, or 'bunchings', acted as the basis for the upturns of the Kondratieff long waves (Schumpeter, 1939). In chronological order, the accepted Kondratieff and post-Kondratieff long waves are set out in Table 1.4.

There is controversy concerning the exact timing of the end of the fourth long wave. However, there is some agreement that recent years have seen the emergence of a powerful neo-Schumpeterian 'bunching' of innovations - in microelectronics, information technology, robotics and genetic engineering - which are establishing the foundations of the upswing phase of a new, fifth, long wave (Hall, 1985). It is this technological bunching which has underpinned industrial expansion in recent years. One of the fascinating aspects of this concept, which is explored by a number of contributors, particularly Butzin (Chapter IX), is the disassociation between the geographical concentrations of industries belonging to each Kondratieff wave. This can be linked to the 'blocking' power of old industries which have a markedly regional distribution. The tendency for each Kondratieff wave to generate its own spatial pattern of industrial activity also underlies the process of 'shifting industrialisation'. This creates a need for fresh regional locations for new industries, rather than the reuse of established industrial locations. It also focuses our attention on the importance of appreciating the significance of the chronology and technological maturity of individual branches of industry. As Hauff shows (Chapter X), it is salutary to reflect that the intense industrial specialisation of Gronau and west Münsterland remained essentially untouched from the middle of the nineteenth century to the middle of the twentieth.

The second theoretical framework places more emphasis on the *mode* of industrial production as the prime motivator of industrial restructuring, rather than Schumpeter's 'over-heroic and machine-dominated' interpretation of economic history (Mandel, 1975). From this point of view, the current phase of industrial restructuring in western Europe is part of a general transition from the system of industrial production which commonly goes under the description of 'Fordist', to one of greater flexibility. Fordist industrial production involves the use of standardised, mass-production, assembly-line techniques, which are characteristically associated with very large labour forces, utilised on inflexible lines, and with rigorous, unionised work principles. The immense factories characteristic of this form of industrial organisation are described by Gaebe in the Rhine-Neckar conurbation (Chapter XI). In contrast to this mode of production, flexible production theory proposes that new forms of industrial and service activity are characterised by the close integration of specialised production processes, smooth production flows and flexible labour practices, with a tendency for proportionately-reduced significance of labour costs to be accompanied by increasing development of labour skills (Wood, Chapter XIII). One manifestation of this change in the mode of production is the emergence of new spatial divisions of labour, whereby, with the help of 'just-in-time' deliveries, process subdivision and plant specialisation, production units can be strategically scattered to avoid over-concentration and vulnerability to organised labour pressures. This leaves the 'higher-quality' processes, such as research, product development and decision-making, to locate in different, usually more environmentally-attractive, regions.

The third theoretical framework places its emphasis upon the more integrating concept of the information economy, in which boundaries between manufacturing and services become indistinct, and in which the sale of information is viewed as more critical than the sale of manufactured goods. The epitome of such economic activity is to be seen in the dramatic expansion of financial services in central London and Docklands. The provision of business services and the swelling ranks of employees engaged in information-gathering and information-using activities are other manifestations of a growing trend, explored in Ellger's analysis of the 'Baden-Württemberg Effect' (Chapter XIV), which so impressed President Gorbachev on his State visit to West Germany in June 1989.

Table 1.4: Long waves of economic development

long wave	timing	main innovations
1st long wave	1789-1849 (upswing to 1814)	mechanisation of cotton spinning, and iron smelting
2nd long wave	1849-1896 (upswing to 1873)	generalisation of steam power, power-loom weaving, railways, Bessemer steel
3rd long wave	1896- approx.1930s (upswing to 1920)	electric power, chemicals, internal combustion engine as a means of transport
4th long wave	1940s-? (upswing to 1966)	electrical and light engineering, petro-chemicals, motor industry
5th long wave	?	electronics, information technology

Source: based on Massey, 1988.

Britain and West Germany: a comparative perspective of geography and government

The existence of significant differences in the experience of de-industrialisation between the two countries has already been demonstrated. Before we can make further progress in our analysis, however, certain major contrasts in national geographical and administrative configurations must be considered. These have an important bearing, both on problems and solutions.

The most obvious is the fundamental contrast in geography between Britain, an island nation, and West Germany, essentially a continental, land-based state, with a comparatively short maritime frontage restricted to the North and Baltic Seas. This largely land-locked position does, however, convey a supremely central geographical location to West Germany, which lies at the nodal points of major European transportation axes. In comparison, Britain's position is somewhat peripheral, particularly as far as the western and northern parts are concerned. West Germany, therefore, exists very much within the spatial core of the European Community, enjoying a centrality which Britain does not possess. The continental location of West Germany also conveys a more immediate concern and awareness of international issues (especially those involving the environment) than the insular perspectives derived from an island situation.

These contrasts in geographical configuration are matched by salient differences in internal political and administrative structures. The United Kingdom has a very long historical continuity as a highly-centralised nation state, and the tendency towards increasing central government power and control in recent years is a notable recurrent theme amongst the British contributions in this volume. The Federal Republic of Germany, whose constitutional status is embodied in the Basic Law of 1949, is western Europe's most recently-formed nation state. Under the Basic Law an administrative framework was established which was deliberately designed to avoid

9

the centralised control, or *Einheitsstaat,* of the Nazi period. Most important was the devolution of political control and administration into three fundamental tiers:

- firstly, the Federal level, based at the provisional capital of Bonn;

- secondly, the *Länder,* or Federal states, such as Baden-Württemberg or Bavaria;

- finally, at the most local level, the *Gemeinden,* or local authorities.

A further aspect of this deliberate decentralisation of administration, which has a considerable bearing on contemporary patterns, was the dispersion of Federal Government functions. This has avoided the centralising administrative paralysis which is latent in the British context; for example, the Federal Labour Office is in Nuremberg, and the Federal Judiciary is in Karlsruhe. This dispersion of public bodies has many parallels in the wider distribution of control functions in the private sector, such as financial institutions and the headquarters of major industrial companies (Strickland and Aiken, 1984).

A cumulative effect of these structures in West Germany is to convey much greater strength to 'localism', and 'locality', and to local government and private inputs into economic decision-making. The case for a strong regional and local-scale involvement in economic development is argued by Roberts and Haughton (Chapter III). They also highlight the weaknesses of British local authorities and the de facto absence of a true regional tier of government in the United Kingdom. These deficiencies are in marked contrast to the powers and autonomy of the West German *Gemeinden* and *Länder.* At the same time, the degree of decentralisation within West Germany does pose certain problems in detail, as Gaebe indicates for the Rhine-Neckar conurbation (Chapter XI). In this case, physical planning is handicapped by the juxtaposition of three *Land* boundaries.

Figure 1.1: Regional patterns of unemployment levels in the United Kingdom and West Germany (FRG), 1986

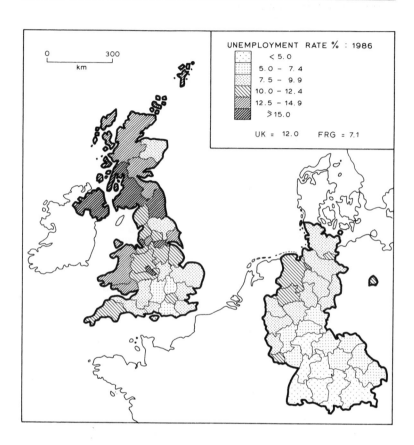

Figure 1.2: Regional unemployment levels and 'synthetic index' in the United Kingdom and West Germany (FRG), 1986: dispersion diagrams

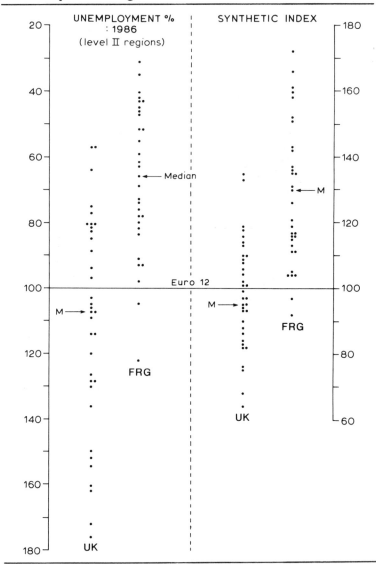

Source: Eurostats, *Eurostatistics data, 1989, part 6.*

De-industrialisation in Britain and West Germany: the spatial outcomes

The de-industrialisation trend in both countries has had profound regional impacts, which are graphically summarised in the term 'north-south divide'. In a general sense this description is applicable to both countries, but again it is different in its intensity. It is also important to stress that not all contributions in this volume subscribe to the simplicity inherent in such a conceptualisation. Roberts and Haughton, in particular, emphasise the multidimensional nature of spatial inequalities in the 'classic' indicators of unemployment, job creation, and regional economic production, which in their view create a highly-variegated mosaic, rather than a simple macroscale regional division. We shall now place the two countries in a comparative framework, both from the point of view of macrodivides, and of introducing further dimensions of spatial inequalities.

Figure 1.1 confirms the existence of important north-south divides in both countries, taking unemployment rates as a critical indicator. In the case of the United Kingdom, the divide runs approximately from the Wash to the Severn estuary, although Cornwall and Devon in the extreme south-west have higher rates than all regions to the south of this line, with the exception of Greater London. Indeed, the performance of Greater London reminds us that these divides, however significant they may be as perceptions in the minds of the public and of policy-makers, are geographical generalisations. In West Germany, as in Britain, the so-called 'north-south divide' (*Nord-Süd Gefälle*), strictly speaking, takes on a north-east to south-west trend. It is drawn quite sinuously from the Saarland, in the south-west, across the *Mittelgebirge*, or Central Uplands, to the frontier with East Germany near Kassel. The contrasts in unemployment rates on either side of this divide are both sharp and homogenous. Unemployment falls to its lowest levels in the booming triangle of Baden-Württemberg, southern Bavaria and western Hesse, but is also quite low in some of the south's older industrial areas, such as the Rhine-Neckar region and Upper Franconia.

Nevertheless, Figure 1.1 reveals inescapable national differences in regional intensities of unemployment. No British region has a rate as low as the 12 best performers in West Germany, whilst no West German region has a rate as high as the worst 12 performers in the United Kingdom. The statistical dispersion diagrams of regional unemployment levels (Figure 1.2; [left]) emphasise that, whilst there is some overlap, there are very marked differences in the extremes of regional performance within the two countries. These diagrams also indicate that the 'spread' of unemployment rates in the United Kingdom is almost double that in West Germany. Unemployment, as Thieme (Chapter V) argues, is only one of several possible indicators with which inequalities can be measured. In recognition of this, the Commission of the European Communities (CEC) has devised a 'synthetic index' which measures regional economic health in terms of a combination of unemployment rates, labour force expansion, regional economic output, and regional economic prosperity (CEC, 1987). The statistical dispersion of regional performances on this index in the United Kingdom and West Germany is shown in Figure 1.2 [right]. Once again, there are clear differences between the two countries: West Germany's 10 best performers outrank the top British region; conversely Britain's 11 poorest regions are all below West Germany's worst. Pertinently, the median values for each country are a huge 35 points apart on the index. This evidence demonstrates that the 'north-south divides' in both countries, although different in scale, are realities and not just perceptions. The validity of the divides is also confirmed by other contributors to this volume. Thieme's analysis of the West German situation (Chapter V) is particularly apposite, since he uses indicators other than strictly economic ones, demonstrating that the divide here has only in recent years become firmly established in the minds of the West German public and media. Within the British context, Green (Chapter XII) illustrates the markedly uneven regional north-south performances in the growth of high-

14

tech industries and services. Regional population trends, which are very much responses to differences in economic performance, neatly pick out the sharp re-emergence of the north-south divide after some quiescence in the 1960s (Champion, Chapter IV). Indeed, this reactivation of the north-south divide in Britain serves to emphasise its general longevity in time; its roots can be traced as far back as the interwar period (Law, 1981). In the West German experience, the emergence of the north-south divide has displaced the 'Rhine axis' phenomenon as a dominant feature in the country's economic geography.

Despite the clarity of the north-south divides, other dimensions of inequality also have an important bearing on the development of regional economic disparities. Urban/rural contrasts were formerly particularly significant in West Germany, leading to what Thieme (Chapter V) describes as the 'classic polarity' of dynamic core cities and stagnating or declining rural regions. This polarity was especially strong in the 1940s and 1950s. In Britain, substantial deconcentration of population and economic activities commenced earlier. In West Germany the situation is now rapidly changing, as a 'catching-up' process is under way.

A further vital difference exists between the acute regional concentration of metropolitan functions in Britain, with its strongly primate city-size distribution, and what Ardagh (1987) describes as a 'diversity of dominant cities' in West Germany. Greater London accounts for 14% of the UK population, whereas Hamburg, West Germany's largest city, (excluding West Berlin as a special case) accounts for only 2.7% of the national population. The mass of functional concentration represented by London in the British case is spread over a plurality of large cities in West Germany, which are distributed fairly evenly across the national territory. This dispersal of activities within the West German city system provides an inherently more balanced pattern of regional growth, but there is some concern that in the more recent wave of growth associated with the tertiarisation process (Keeble, Chapter II), many of the cities in northern Germany appear to be falling behind. This is especially true of the cities of North Rhine-Westphalia, which are so closely interconnected and have to compete strongly with each other.

A further major dimension of spatial inequalities within the two countries is the contrast between the declining traditional industrial regions, of varying sizes, and the brash, burgeoning and fast-expanding new industrial spaces. By and large, these are situated in different portions of each country's national territory. Within West Germany and Britain, regions with a heavy dependence on resource endowments of coal and ironstone, port-linked industries or textiles, all redolent of nineteenth century patterns of industrialisation, dominate the locations of decline. As Spooner (Chapter VI) describes, all three types of region are present within a compact space in northern England. Wehling, Nuhn, and Hauff, among the German contributors, provide parallel case studies of industrial decay in north-west Germany, focusing respectively on steel and coal in the Ruhr, shipbuilding in Hamburg, and textiles in west Münsterland. In the case of the Ruhr, the sheer scale of this European giant amongst industrial regions has led to the historical emergence of significant internal differentiation in development, which, as Butzin shows (Chapter IX), has important implications for present-day problems and planning.

New industrial spaces in Britain and West Germany are also distributed unevenly, reflecting the attraction of industries such as electronics and computers to different types of location factors. There is, however, a broad contrast between the two countries. In the British case, a broad 'macrospace' has emerged in south-east England, containing within it intense concentrations such as the M4 Corridor of 'sunrise' industries and the explosion of high-tech industries in the Cambridge subregion (the so-called 'Cambridge Phenomenon'). In West Germany there is no region of comparable dominance for such activities, but several major cities, such as Stuttgart, Munich, Frankfurt, Düsseldorf and Hamburg have important concentrations. The three southern complexes of Frankfurt, Stuttgart and Munich, however, are probably the most dynamic and rapidly expanding.

Spatial uneveness is even more pronounced in the tertiarisation process, whereby the fast-expanding activities associated with the circulation of capital and information are heavily concentrated in selected cities at the top of the urban hierarchy. Although this process is now creating new inequalities between the cities of West Germany, the prime example is unquestionably London. As indicated by Wood (Chapter XIII), the extraordinary concentration here of all kinds of international financial services, coupled with the huge impetus provided by deregulation in 1986, has led to an enormous boom in property development and employment, with immense social and economic consequences for London and the south-east in general, and areas like London Docklands in particular.

It would appear, therefore, that the broad results of these new spatially-uneven trends are to create more intense gradients of relative prosperity and more homogeneous regional spaces in the national territory of Britain. This partly reflects the unique presence of London, and partly the high degree of centralisation of all aspects of national economic, social, and political life. In West Germany, there is undoubtedly a broadly similar trend reflecting a divorce between old and new activities, but the gradients are not so steep, and the contrasts are moderated by the deep-rooted traditions of dispersion, localism, and Federal decentralisation.

This is not to suggest that these broader regional inequalities are the only manifestations of changing economic structures. Even within Britain, studies such as the *Northern Lights* (Breheny, Hall and Hart, 1987), based on smaller-scale administrative districts, show that there are several localised pockets of high affluence and quality of life within some of the regions north of the divide; instances include Harrogate, Ripon and York in Yorkshire, and north-east Cheshire in the north-west. Conversely, there are localised black spots to the south of the divide, such as east Kent (with its coalfield) the southern dockyard towns, and many inner London boroughs (Fothergill and Vincent, 1985).

New industrialisation

Whilst de-industrialisation is one pervasive trend in advanced industrial economies, 'new industrialisation' is another. In the transformed technological and organisational environment of the late twentieth century, the boundaries between traditionally-defined sectors are becoming increasingly indistinct. In using the term 'new industrialisation', we include not only new forms of manufacturing industry as such, but also the rapidly-emerging field of information technology, which includes components from manufacturing and services. Indeed, as Ellger points out (Chapter XIV), it is fruitful to consider a new, information-led, 'quaternary' economic sector, which is now the pacemaker of employment generation in advanced societies. We are, therefore, concerned here with three interrelated processes of economic development, each having its own locational logic and spatial expression.

- First, there is the creation of new industrial spaces through the medium of new types of manufacturing industries;

- secondly, there is the application of new industrial investment to foster the reindustrialisation of old industrial regions;

- thirdly, a rather different type of economic development is associated with the immense pressures for change, generated by the increased tertiarisation of the economies of selected major cities.

This third trend is essentially market-led in both countries, and is not commonly directed wholly on the initiative of public bodies. However, attempts at partnerships of public and private capital are now being pursued, in order to encourage this momentum in diverse circumstances, as Wehling (Chapter XVII), for the Ruhr, and Law (Chapter XVI), for Manchester-Salford, point out.

The requirements of new industries: a general appraisal

Before turning to the spatial patterns produced by new industrialisation, we must first of all consider the special locational needs of the new forms of economic activities.

Each mode of production has its own blend of locational requirements, and new industrialisation in Britain and West Germany is no exception. Location in relation to fixed or imported raw materials, and dependence on inflexible labour skills, were the mainsprings of past technological eras. Indeed, in the Schumpeterian notion of 'creative destruction', these old locational attractions can act as obstacles to modern forms of economic activity. Hence there is a tendency in Britain and West Germany for 'shifting industrialisation' to occur, in which old industrial regions are discarded and suffer from underinvestment, while new industrial spaces are established elsewhere. The needs of new industries are markedly different from those of the old, and are epitomised by the high-tech and information industries described by Green (Chapter XII) and Ellger (Chapter XIV). They make minimal demands upon materials and transportation, but maximum demands upon technological innovation, scientific and professional resources, and accessibility to increasingly complex and highly-differentiated markets. The fundamental problem, therefore, revolves around the question of where such demands are likely to be best satisfied. Nor can we automatically confine considerations of modern technological inputs to ostensibly new industries, such as electronics. This is because an inevitable consequence of rapid technological change is the adoption of such inputs to older industrial processes and products, as is happening in some 'declining' industries, such as clothing, ceramics, iron and steel. However, there is a very important distinction to be made between technological innovations which are used to create new products, and those which revolutionise existing processes, in order to make them economically and technically more efficient and profitable. As many contributors point out, the consequences for jobs are strikingly different. For

19

example, Spooner (Chapter VI) and Butzin (Chapter IX) comment on the severe reductions in employment in the iron and steel industries of Scunthorpe and the Ruhr's Emscher zone, following huge investments in their process technology. In contrast, it is also pertinent to emphasise that many of the new industries create jobs of very different qualities. Some of them tend to maintain sharp functional and geographical contrasts between the more innovative and creative branches, but at the same time, others produce standardised consumer products which have a.1 increasingly rapid product life cycle. Such a distinction is amplified by Green (Chapter XII) in the case of the British electronics industry. In the following discussion of spatial patterns of new industrialisation, it is important to bear in mind the real-world complexities inherent in the process of industrial change. It is not simply a contrast between two homogenous categories of 'old' and 'new'; we must also incorporate the role of concepts such as the product life cycle, and the vital distinctions between product innovation and price innovation, because these processes influence the quantity and quality of new employment.

Patterns of new industrialisation

The formation of new industrial spaces

New industrial spaces are characterised by their concentrations of new industries and new products. Whilst no official definition of the range of industrial activities involved has been constructed, the list of high-tech industries, produced by Butchart (1987) and adopted by Green (Chapter XII), is a reasonable approximation. It includes industries related to electronics in various forms, precision engineering, telecommunications and computing, and advanced branches of more established industries such as aerospace equipment and pharmaceuticals. Besides incorporating advanced technology, these new industries also share, to varying degrees, other characteristics, including strong product innovation, vigorous small- and medium-firm formation (often as a result of entrepreneurial spin-off), research and development facilities, and a high degree of interdependence with advanced service activities. The strong regional agglomeration of these activities is, indeed, a vital factor in their success.

The essential requisites of new industrial spaces, as revealed by some chapters in this volume, are multifaceted. One of the most salient, if difficult to measure, is what Thieme (Chapter V) describes as the 'soft' locational factors. Basically, these are attributes which constitute an idealised high quality of life for the elite segment in the labour force of industrial and other organisations. Both south-east England and southern Germany satisfy these particular attributes to a large extent: attractive rural landscapes for both leisure and residence; small- to medium-sized urban centres with strong historic qualities, such as cathedral towns or picturesque market centres; a lack of past industrial despoilation; varied and high-quality housing provision; and lastly, easy access to large cities for higher-order cultural and other facilities, including education, shopping and entertainment. Given such a combination of soft environmental factors, firms experience few difficulties in attracting and retaining the qualified technical and scientific staff which they vitally require.

A more specific set of advantages, favourable to the establishment and growth of new industries, is based upon the accumulation of links with scientific research and development facilities. These include government research establishments and laboratories, universities possessing strong scientific faculties, and firms or organisations with a heavy involvement in military contracts. Examples include the 'Cambridge Phenomenon' in Britain and the 'M4 Corridor' in south-east England, and the environs of several university cities in West Germany (for example, Tübingen, Erlangen and Konstanz). The net effect is to create thriving agglomerations of science-based activities and an information-rich environment for the rapid exchange of ideas and exploitation of technological developments in these advantageous locations. Here there is not only a tendency for new industries to agglomerate further, but they also push out established economic activities which are less able to compete in the local labour market.

An interesting example is the Stuttgart conurbation (Ellger, Chapter XIV), where the city is increasing its concentration of quaternary functions, such as the headquarters of national and international companies (including Bosch and Daimler-Benz), while the conurbation fringe retains its predominantly manufacturing base.

From the point of view of policy-makers, the critical question is whether these types of advantages are self-reinforcing and hence cumulative, or whether they can be replicated in other types of location. If they are self-reinforcing, then the nascent new industrial spaces will be further consolidated. Both Green (Chapter XII) and Ellger (Chapter XIV) indicate that there is an entrenchment of such comparative advantages, especially as the critical bonds are those which are provided by human knowledge and control, rather than by the physical factors of transport or industrial infrastructure. If their assessments are correct, then the task of policy-makers in declining areas becomes even more difficult.

Trends in the old industrial regions

The old industrial regions continue to suffer from the steep de-industrialisation trend. They are also handicapped by the predilection of new industries to select other types of locations. While, in some cases, considerable progress has been made towards economic restructuring, it is nonetheless true that in both countries the typical image of old industrial regions is still dominated by that of the 'rust belt': a composite image of ugly, smoke-blackened factories, outdated infrastructure, mean and monotonous housing of substandard quality, a very limited range of leisure and cultural facilities, and a physical environment polluted and scarred by the industrialisation of the past. Whatever the realities, this stereotyped perception is not only widely held, but extremely difficult to overcome, as Dege (Chapter XV) explains. Moreover, a concomitant product of their past industrial evolution was the growth of a particular social formation, dominated by work-dependent, monolithic working-class communities, with just a leavening of middle-class social flexibility. An essential component of this social structure was the high profile of large industrial companies and cartels confronting powerful labour unions. As Butzin shows (Chapter IX), the former were able to stifle other locally-based initiatives in the Ruhr by such practices as retaining extensive 'land banks' with development potential and exercising control over local human capital by virtue of their immense size and economic dominance. The unions, in turn, have been accused of maintaining social traditions rooted in inflexible labour practices, which are inappropriate in the new era of flexible production. As such, this combination unfortunately constrains the restructuring process in two main respects:

- firstly, it causes an inadequate rate of generation of local businesses, especially in the high-tech and information spheres;

- secondly, it imposes checks upon the types of industrial enterprises which these regions are able to attract.

The pattern of industrial activity in old industrial regions is therefore distinctively different from that in the new industrial spaces. First of all, it contains the shrinking residue of earlier types and forms of industrial production, ranging from textiles to iron and steel, coal-mining, shipbuilding and heavy engineering industries. All of these are in the declining, late-mature stage of the product life cycle. Secondly, their mode of production is dominated by very large, Fordist plants, as exemplified in the cities of the Rhine-Neckar region, which have enormous factories belonging to giant companies such as BASF, Daimler-Benz and Brown-Boveri (Gaebe, Chapter XI). Moreover, even when new industries are present, usually as a result of government regional policies, they have this mode of labour organisation in common. Very typical are the large branch plants established in old industrial regions by multinational corporations or national companies possessing multiplant operating characteristics (Fothergill and Guy, Chapter VII).

23

A third feature which is characteristic of old industrial regions is a high degree of dependence on external ownership, as Fothergill and Guy also demonstrate. This results in a lack of local input into decision-making in vital areas, a paucity of high-quality senior white-collar jobs, a comparative lack of fundamental research and development work leading to product innovation, and a general prevalence of low-order production and processing plants. This scenario is further demonstrated by Green's analysis of the British electronics industry (Chapter XII), in which there is a sharp contrast between the typical factories of the south-east, on the one hand, and the old industrial localities in the Development Areas, on the other.

There is, therefore, a tendency for recent industrial growth in old industrial regions to perpetuate older modes of industrial organisation, because they are attracting particular types of new factories exploiting a new spatial division of labour. The old industrial regions find that their traditional labour skills are no longer in demand for incoming industry, which is now seeking unskilled or semiskilled workers, often female. The situation is epitomised by the industrial estates in British Development Areas (Spooner, Chapter VI), and in the new industries of north German industrial areas, such as the Emscher zone of the Ruhr (Wehling, Chapter XVII) and the west Münsterland textiles district (Hauff, Chapter X). This pattern of reindustrialisation does not form a sufficient platform for the economic regeneration of the 'rust belts' of either country and, as we shall see, policy initiatives have been particularly concerned with widening their appeal, in order to attract new types of firm formation.

The tertiarisation of major cities

The 'tertiarisation process' describes the shift in the employment structure from industry to services - from the secondary to the tertiary (including quaternary) sector - which characterises the post-industrial period. Although a dynamic process in both countries, it is much more locationally-specific than the formation of new industrial spaces. It is also highly selective in its choice of cities for its most advanced forms of development and, equally important from a social and economic viewpoint, the process involves very small geographical spaces within these urban areas. Tertiarisation, in recent years, has to be viewed in the overall context of spatial change in metropolitan areas, especially the decentralisation of economic activity and population in the past two to three decades, which has drained away the vitality of large inner-urban districts. This decentralisation trend, with its adverse socioeconomic impacts on local populations, has been undoubtedly more severe in the British experience. Law (Chapter XVI) maintains that the intensity of decline in inner-urban areas in Britain is more comparable to the situation in the United States, rather than western Europe. He presents figures which show that the population of inner Manchester-Salford has declined hugely from 620,000 in 1951 to 297,000 in 1981, and that the number of jobs has fallen from 402,000 in 1971 to 298,000 in 1984 within the same locality. The outstanding component of the decline in jobs was the contraction of manufacturing employment, especially in the Trafford Park Industrial Estate, so highlighting the significance of inner-urban de-industrialisation. Although Nuhn (Chapter VIII) cites a one-third decline in traditional port-linked industrial employment in Hamburg between 1970 and 1985, evidence suggests that the vacuum left by inner-city economic decline is less severe in West Germany. Indeed, much of the activity which has been lost to the inner city here has been transferred into the 'outer city', which, given West Germany's superior and cheaper urban public transport facilities, remains reasonably accessible in cost and time to inner-city residents.

Over recent years there has been a vigorous, but nevertheless selective and patchy, recovery and regeneration of British inner cities, in which three factors are particularly apparent:

- the cardinal role of property-led development schemes;

- the pivotal role of service-based activities in the employment field;

- the dominance of private capital and entrepreneurship.

All of these factors reach their full fruition in the extraordinarily rapid expansion of financial and producer services in the City of London, and the closely-associated London Docklands developments (Spooner, Chapter VI). Wood (Chapter XIII) emphasises the uniqueness of this 'London phenomenon', which is a reflection of the city's function as Europe's primary financial base, and the centre of its finance circulation. Its dominance has been enhanced not only by its dense pool of skilled labour, expertise and specialist information, but also by a sympathetic government which has shown itself willing to create an economic climate of maximum flexibility, openness and financial deregulation.

Whilst the scale of tertiary-led development in London is, by general agreement, unmatched elsewhere, there are scaled-down versions in other major cities, both in Britain and in West Germany. For the most part, these developments reflect the emergence of spontaneous market-led forces, by which the expanding service sector generates a demand for office and other property construction in central locations. However, such has been the publicised success of the London Docklands experience, in which enormous expansionary pressures were deliberately diverted into hitherto discarded and neglected former port and industrial land in London's East End, that this has acted as a model for replication in broadly similar situations elsewhere. The Salford Docks redevelopment scheme examined by Law (Chapter XVI), in which we find typical property-led projects embracing the construction of offices, leisure-oriented services (such as multiple cinemas and luxury hotels), and a substantial housing input, is one of many such schemes which have blossomed during the 1980s in Britain. As Wehling demonstrates, the basic concept is being adopted by some cities in West Germany (Chapter XVII). He describes the economic decline of Ruhr cities, where the availability of abandoned industrial land has attracted such ambitious property-based regeneration schemes as the Canadian 'Triple Five' Corporation's Euro-Mall scheme at Oberhausen, which, when completed, will incorporate about 800 shops, together with a casino, cinemas, sports facilities, restaurants and marina, all to be built on a 100 ha^2 derelict industrial site.

A notable and controversial aspect of the tertiarisation process, and of property development schemes in particular, is the acute juxtaposition which they create between glittering affluence and modernity on the one hand and, on the other, the continuing social malaise of the local communities which are still locked into their cycle of decline. Characteristically, there is only a very limited degree of interaction between the 'post-construction' supply of new jobs, new housing and other new facilities, and the needs of the local populations and communities, amongst which the new projects are rising, phoenix-like. By and large, the *direct* beneficiaries of the tertiarisation process are different populations from the victims of the preceding de-industrialisation. In the West German city, tertiarisation, apart from schemes such as those described by Wehling (Chapter XVII), has tended to be a more diffuse development. It can be seen in the deliberate creation of office parks in the suburban districts of most major cities, but also more controversially, in the continual creeping outwards of commercial functions from city centres to adjoining inner-city residential quarters (Wild, 1983). This latter erosion of inner residential space in West German cities has given rise to much criticism, and occasional outbursts of physical conflict (*Der Spiegel*, 1981).

Policy initiatives

Introduction
These three trends - the formation of new industrial spaces, the reindustrialisation of old industrial regions, and the tertiarisation of major cities - have posed acute problems for policy-makers and planners in both countries. Before considering the range of policy initiatives currently in use, it is necessary to turn to certain common issues which emerge as being of particular importance in planning intervention in both old and new industrial regions and cities.

One key issue is the selection of an appropriate model of development. Is it to be dominantly 'top-down', in which the direction, impulses and mechanisms are imposed from above, and therefore inevitably from outside? Or is it to be 'bottom-up', relying essentially on the mobilisation and supplementation of local initiatives, ideas and resources? As Butzin stresses in the case of the Ruhr (Chapter IX), achieving an appropriate blend is difficult. Moreover, a major theme of recent developments in British planning intervention has been the necessity to adopt planning devices which will activate local enterprise within the general context of the market mechanism. A surfeit of top-down mechanisms arguably creates a stultifying weight of bureaucracy. Equally, a total reliance on bottom-up, individual enterprise embodies the risk of not being able achieve longer-term objectives and fuller use of resources.

A second issue that emerges from the contributions is the sometimes conflicting roles of economic and social objectives in development policy. At its starkest, this can be seen in the recent spate of dominantly economic-directed policy initiatives which are being brought to bear on the regeneration of inner-urban areas in Britain, involving the creation of Enterprise Zones and Urban Development Corporations, but also showing a comparative neglect of social considerations, such as the creation of commensurate public transport investments and adequate training and job-creation for the local labour force (Spooner, Chapter VI; Law, Chapter XVI). Conversely, German contributors emphasise the continued importance in West Germany of a balanced approach to national, regional and local development, within the framework of legal obligations to safeguard social interests. In its widest sense, this is embodied in the concept of the 'social market economy', which expresses an essential responsibility of government to protect social values within an economic system which is fundamentally market-driven.

The third issue, which is rapidly assuming a much greater importance, due to increased public concern and publicity, has arisen from the adverse impact of modern economic development on the environment. The crucial question here, is whether the much-desired goal of responsible environmental protection can be achieved in today's political climate of decreasing regulations and an overriding objective of promoting economic efficiency and sustained profitability. Concerning this, contributions to this volume identify a major divergence between West Germany and Britain, the two countries apparently pursuing very different paths. Within the British context, the past decade has been one of a general trend towards economic deregulation, as seen in the weakening of many physical planning controls, the easing of constraints on transport operations, and a steadfast reluctance to deal adequately with the emissions of electricity generating stations burning fossil fuels. West Germany, although it recognises that there is a latent conflict between the needs of an efficient economy and a diversified ecology has, nevertheless, the most environmentally-conscious society in the European Community. As Oßenbrügge (Chapter XIX) points out, as many as one in three West Germans belong to consumer groups in which consciousness of environmental influences is a major consideration in their purchases and, as a consequence of the electoral system of proportional representation, the ecological political lobby is correspondingly powerful. This has been one of the main factors behind West Germany's 'green' public transport policy, in which environmentally-clean and quiet rail transport and urban rapid transit systems are heavily subsidised at the expense of road travel and haulage (North, 1983). Furthermore, the commitment to the construction of environmental protection policies has been enhanced in recent years by the passing of new legislation, designed to limit the quantities of atmospheric pollution; in particular the *Immissionsschutzgesetz* and the *Technische Anleitung Luft* (Oßenbrügge, Chapter XIX). At the same time, the increasing legislation is backed up by the establishment of overseeing environmental ministries at Federal and *Land* levels. Oßenbrügge argues that, far from reducing employment and economic efficiency, responsible environmental protection can actually act as a job creator, in what he describes as the 'environmental industry'. The force of this argument has made much less progress in Britain, although recent estimates suggest that the manufacture of emission control plant for Britain's electricity generating industry could generate a potential market of £1.6 billion over the next few years (*Sunday Times*, 1989). It is possible, therefore, that attitudes may change, particularly in the light of recent advances by the British Green Party, mounting media publicity, and pressure from the European Commission itself.

Policy initiatives within new industrial spaces

The new industrial spaces which have emerged in parts of Britain and West Germany have not been created as part of conscious public planning policy at a regional level. However, their growth has been encouraged in some cases by particular partnerships of people and interested bodies, who have had the foresight to anticipate, firstly, the significance of the swing to high-tech industries and the quaternary sector and, secondly, the potentials of specific locations to profit from this trend. A key ingredient in the encouragement of new enterprises in these situations has been the establishment of appropriate infrastructures and the design of prepared space. This places a high priority on the creation of an environment conducive to maintaining a high degree of interaction and exchange between occupiers, and also a very flexibile system of space and accommodation modules which can be rapidly adjusted to the growth curves of the new tenants. As Dr Bolton, Director of the St John's Innovation Centre in Cambridge, emphasised to the Symposium, the key role of the Innovation Centre is to act as an incubator within which small enterprises can develop marketable products within a relatively limited period of time. When this stage has been reached, the firm must then move out into larger accommodation, either in the Science Park itself, or in some other, less specifically-equipped location. These types of development, as epitomised by the Cambridge Science Park, the St John's Science Park and the Innovation Centre (Spooner, Chapter VI), provide attractive locations in small- to medium-sized towns outside the main metropolitan London labour market in south-east England. In West Germany too, considerable interest is now being shown in the 'Science Park' concept, which has been adopted, for example, in the Hamburg Region (Nuhn, Chapter VIII) and in Dortmund (Wehling, Chapter XVII) in northern Germany. However, the evidence of Ellger's analysis for Baden-Württemberg (Chapter XIV) indicates that the quaternary sector in West Germany continues to concentrate mainly in and immediately around the major urban agglomerations, rather than form large new industrial spaces. It is, in fact, only just possible to perceive signs of a nascent south German 'sun belt' of quaternary activities in the south Baden-Lake Constance area.

Policy initiatives for old industrial regions

In both countries the bedrock of policy initiatives to revitalise old industrial regions has been the set of measures generally grouped under the heading of 'regional industrial policy', designed to attract mobile industry and to stimulate the expansion of existing industry. In Britain the definitions of assisted areas have always been geared essentially to prevailing unemployment rates. This practice has had the effect of excluding some old industrial regions from enjoying the benefits of maximum regional aid. Spooner (Chapter VI) notes, for example, that the Calderdale district of the West Yorkshire textiles region has been consistently excluded from full 'development area' status, mainly as a consequence of heavy out-migration (which reduces local unemployment levels) and a very large female component in the traditional industries. With this proviso, it can be seen (Figure 1.3) that Britain's assisted areas are now essentially concentrated in a group of old industrial regions to the north of the north-south divide. In West Germany, the framework of the present development areas was laid out in the 1969 'Joint Task: improvement of regional economic structures'. Figure 1.3 shows its pattern of development regions (Regional Action Programmes) after the modification in 1983. The map demonstrates that a much larger proportion of West Germany (about 50%) is included in designated Federal development regions, reflecting the broader interpretation and method of defining problem areas. The indicators used in West Germany embrace not just unemployment, but also other variables, such as out-migration, local occupational structures and accessibility to major employment centres. A north-south contrast in assisted and non-assisted regions is less apparent than in Britain, since problem rural areas are given a broadly similar weighting as declining industrial areas. The 'border zone' (*Zonenrandgebiet*), in particular, cuts right across the north-south divide; in fact, its first designation preceded the Joint Task by 16 years.

In view of the many detailed economic, fiscal and geographical modifications which occur through time, it is difficult to make a precise comparison of the two respective national regional policy frameworks. However, during the 1980s, there has been a pronounced divergence between the two countries in the degree of political and financial commitment to regional policies. In West Germany the system has continued unchanged in major respects, and the level and extent of intervention has continued to be high. In Britain there has been a major redirection of policy, involving a dramatic reduction in the geographical and financial commitment to regional industrial policy in its traditional forms, paralleled by the introduction of new policy initiatives designed to be more cost-effective and more specifically targeted. From a geographical point of view, this has involved the replacement of a broader regional perspective by more localised initiatives in particular. Indeed, such has been the transformation of British regional policy that regional assistance is no longer automatically available, even in the remaining full Development Areas. However, today the retention of Assisted Area status is essential for the fulfillment of the European Community Regional Policy directives, especially the assistance which is now available for designated 'steel closure' and 'textiles closure' areas. The extra financial support available under these schemes has been a material factor in the progress

Figure 1.3: Assisted areas in the United Kingdom and West Germany (FRG)

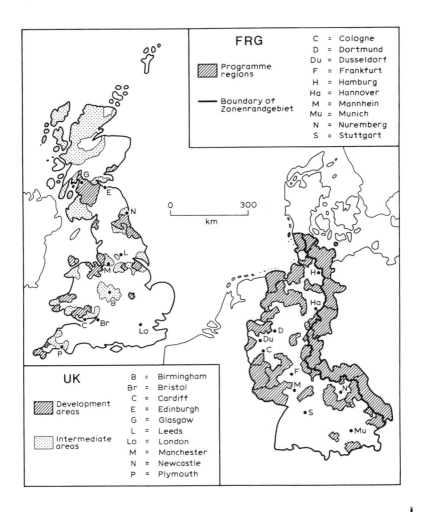

FRG

◨ Programme regions

— Boundary of Zonenrandgebiet

C = Cologne
D = Dortmund
Du = Dusseldorf
F = Frankfurt
H = Hamburg
Ha = Hannover
M = Mannhein
Mu = Munich
N = Nuremberg
S = Stuttgart

UK

◨ Development areas

▧ Intermediate areas

B = Birmingham
Br = Bristol
C = Cardiff
E = Edinburgh
G = Glasgow
L = Leeds
Lo = London
M = Manchester
N = Newcastle
P = Plymouth

towards restructuring a number of local economies in Britain, including the Scunthorpe area described by Spooner (Chapter VI).

A further impetus for regional economic development in West Germany is provided by groupings (*Verbände*) of local authorities for such purposes as land use, environmental and transport planning, publicity, and strategic and infrastructural integration, where the tasks would be beyond the resources of individual administrative districts, especially those which have increasing municipal debts (Bennett, Chapter XVIII). The contribution of the *Kommunal Verband Ruhrgebiet* (KVR) to the improvement of the regional image, attitudes, and perceptions of the problematic Ruhr region since 1984, is outlined by Dege (Chapter XV). Another example is the *Rhein-Neckar Verband*, which was established to combat the inherent problems of this agglomeration's position astride the boundaries of the three *Länder* of Hesse, Baden-Württemberg, and Rhineland-Palatinate, (Gaebe, Chapter XI). With the major exceptions of the Welsh and Scottish Development Agencies, there is no parallel in Britain to this regional tier of intervention and organisation. In fact, the dismantling of such bodies as the Greater London Council demonstrates that this level of regional co-operation has no part to play here in current policy thinking.

During the last decade, one of the most distinctive trends in the development of regional policy in Britain has been the increasing stress on fostering enterprise-led, economic-oriented initiatives, within a general framework of deregulation. A cardinal motivator of these measures has been the desire, on the part of central government, to bypass existing and long-established channels of local authority control. This involves two significant and controversial processes:

- firstly, cutting through what private developers often see as obstructive, time-consuming and bureaucratic planning procedures;

- secondly, the reduction in the influence of traditional, democratically-elected institutions, especially District Councils.

The most important new government initiatives in Britain are Enterprise Zones and Urban Development Corporations, both introduced on a limited scale in 1981 and subsequently applied more extensively. In Enterprise Zones, the intention is to speed up the regeneration of specific areas, either in declining industrial regions or in inner-city districts, by using a mix of short-term financial subsidies (such as de-rating of property and tax concessions) and simplified planning procedures. In the case of Urban Development Corporations, government-appointed boards are set up for a limited length of time; they have centrally-provided funding, to help them act as promoters of economic regeneration in designated localities within those urban areas where it is considered that the progress of regeneration has been inadequate. The membership of the boards strongly reflects the primacy of economic objectives over social priorities, and is dominated by individuals with prominent business backgrounds, including involvement in property development, finance and industry. Ordinary local government writ is removed from these designated spaces, and complete control, including powers to purchase land and grant planning permission, is vested in the Corporations. In both cases, because of the existence of huge tracts of abandoned buildings and derelict industrial land, the use of Derelict Land Grants to support initial site clearance and preparation, has been a prominent feature.

Undoubtedly these 'top-down' initiatives in Britain, which circumvent local authority involvement and the local democratic process, have achieved some spectacularly rapid results. Nowhere is this more apparent than in the example of the London Docklands Development Corporation, where 36,000 jobs have been created between 1983 and 1988 (Keeble, Chapter II). Whilst the total central government expenditure has been estimated at £456 million, proponents of the concept will point to the pump-priming role, in that subsequent private capital investments have been of the order of £4.4 *billion*: a ten-to-one leverage. Nevertheless, in London Docklands and in other Development Corporations and Enterprise Zones, disquiet has been expressed at certain features of the resulting pattern of development. The overriding criticism, as Law (Chapter XVI) indicates for inner Manchester-Salford, is that land and property development has sup-planted the original objective of enhancing employment for local people. The free play given to the operation of market forces within Urban Development Corporations (indeed, which they have a statutory requirement to foster), has turned out in favour of massive investments in office construction, hotels, leisure complexes and similar schemes, which do not match the needs of the local labour market. Even in the case of Enterprise Zones in highly industrial towns, such as Scunthorpe, many of the new occupiers of land are retail establishments or warehouse and distribution depots, rather than manufacturing plants (Spooner, Chapter VI). Other criticisms, particularly of the Urban Development Corporation concept, revolve around:

- firstly, the massive daily stress imposed upon local communications infrastructures in the absence of integrated city-wide planning;

- secondly, the adverse impact on the urban landscape of new constructions which are technically subject to less stringent planning controls within EZ boundaries.

Over and above all the detailed shortcomings, there is the general observation that these schemes are, in effect, not entirely coherent within the overall city structure, since they are deliberately excluded and divorced from the normal evolutionary sequences of urban development.

These types of policy simply have no parallel in West Germany, where there is continued strength of local democratic involvement, and where it is generally accepted that social and economic objectives have to be pursued in a balanced manner within a tightly-regulated environment. This does not exclude the development of constructive partnerships beween private developers and public agencies, as Wehling (Chapter XVII) demonstrates, with reference to the immense problem of reclaiming and preparing derelict land in the Ruhr. This process also emphasises that derelict land reclamation in West Germany has incorporated much more rigorous monitoring of potential environmental hazards. Concern was expressed by the West German partcipants at the apparent haste and insensitivity with which former industrial land in Britain was being recycled. Moreover, as Gaebe (Chapter XI) illustrates, in the case of the Rhine-Neckar region, the autonomous resources which local authorities in West Germany can bring to bear upon economic regeneration, are very considerable. They involve the comprehensive improvement of the local technical, recreational and communications infrastructure, and also inner-city renovation of built environments, preparation of industrial land, and encouragement of new economic enterprises by means of loans, technical advice centres, and enterprise parks. Ironically, under this system, local authorities in West Germany which face problems of heavy unemployment, also incur high levels of fiscal indebtedness, due to their large social security and welfare payments. These can affect their ability to give full support to the economic regeneration process.

References

Ardagh, J., *Germany and the Germans*, Penguin, London, pp. 30-49, 1987.

Breheny, M., Hall, P. and Hart, D., *Northern Lights: a development agenda for the north in the 1990s*, Derrick Wade and Partners, Preston, 1987.

Butchart, R.L., 'A new definition of the high technology industries' in: *Economic Trends*, Vol. 400, pp. 82-88, 1987.

Commission of the European Communities (CEC), *Third periodic report on the social and economic situation of the regions of the Community*, European Community, Brussels, 1987.

Deane, P. and Cole, W.A., *British economic growth 1688-1959*, Cambridge University Press, Cambridge, 1962.

Der Spiegel, 'Neue Wohnungsnot', in: *Der Spiegel*, Special Issue, 12 January 1981.

Fothergill, S. and Vincent, J., *The state of the nation*, Heinemann, London, 1985.

Hall, P., 'Geography of the fifth Kondratieff cycle', in: Hall, P. and Markusen, A. (eds.), *Silicon landscapes*, Allen and Unwin, London, pp. 1-19, 1985.

Law, C., *British regional development since World War I*, Methuen, London, 1981.

Mandel, E., *Late capitalism*, New Left Books, London, 1975.

Massey, D., 'What's happening to UK manufacturing?', Chapter II in: Allen, J. and Massey, D., *The economy in question*, Sage Publications, London, p. 83, 1988.

Massey, D. and Meegan, R., *The anatomy of job loss*, Methuen, London, 1982.

North, J., 'Developments in transport', in: Wild, M.T. (ed.), *Urban and rural change in West Germany*, Croom Helm, Beckenham, pp. 130-60, 1983.

Robinson, J. and Eatwell, J., *An introduction to modern economics*, Mcgraw Hill, London, 1973.

Schumpeter, J.A., *Business cycles: a theoretical, historical and statistical analysis of the capitalist process*, Vol. 1, Mcgraw Hill, London and New York, 1939.

Strickland, D. and Aiken, M., 'Corporate influence and the German urban system: headquarters locations of German industrial corporations 1950-82', in: *Economic Geography*, Vol. 60, pp. 38-54, 1984.

The Sunday Times, 'King thinks big in Babcock spin-off', in: *The Sunday Times*, 2 July 1989.

Wallerstein, I., *The modern world-system*, Academic Press, New York, 1974.

Wild, M.T., 'Residential environments in West German inner cities', in: Wild, M.T. (ed.), *Urban and rural change in West Germany*, Croom Helm, Beckenham, pp. 40-70, 1983.

Chapter II

David Keeble (University of Cambridge)

De-industrialisation, new industrialisation processes and regional restructuring in the European Community

Introduction: processes and theories

Since the mid-1970s, the countries of the European Community have been experiencing a period of remarkable industrial and economic turbulence involving acute recession, the rapid decline of the traditional nineteenth-century industries and the growth of radical new process technologies, research-based industries and advanced services. These changes are having a major impact upon Europe's cities and regions, especially those of northern Europe, on which this chapter focuses as a framework for subsequent case studies of urban and regional industrial change in Britain and West Germany.

The complexity and variety of economic forces currently at work in the regions of northern Europe are too great to be encompassed by any single, all-embracing theory of economic change. Moreover, their spatial outcomes are contingent upon many factors, not least the social and political responses to these forces by local communities, institutions and governments. This said, however, it can be argued that the most important contemporary processes of regional economic change are those set out in Table 2.1; and that these processes can be understood by reference to three types of evolving theoretical framework (Table 2.2), namely: long-wave theory, flexible-production theory, and information-economy theory. These theoretical frameworks are by no means rigidly defined or universally accepted constructs. They comprise, rather, foci of vigorous contemporary debate and elaboration, which overlap at various points. But the concepts and propositions on which they centre do have great

relevance to understanding contemporary regional economic restructuring in the highly affluent, technologically-advanced capitalist
economies of the European Community.

Table 2.1: Key processes of European regional economic restructuring in the 1980s

De-industrialisation:	Substantial manufacturing decline, especially of employment, focused on nineteenth-century 'smokestack' industries (steel, ship-building, heavy engineering, textiles) and old industrial regions.
Reindustrialisation:	Small firm/new firm resurgence, often in new, less-industrialised regions. Rapid growth of 'high technology' industry, especially based on microelectronics. Widespread adoption of new computer-based technologies by existing industries. Surge of new, inward multinational investment (Japanese, American) to serve European Community markets.
Tertiarisation:	(including): growth of tourism, recreation and leisure industries, as a direct result of rising real incomes: impact on 'sun belt' and peripheral regions. Growth of producer services (finance, banking, business and information services), especially in Europe's major capital cities.

Source: Keeble, 1989b.

Table 2.2: Theoretical frameworks and European economic change

Long-wave theory (Schumpeter, Mensch, Freemann, Hall)

- High-technology industry, research-based products, vital role of highly-qualified workers and entrepreneurs.

- New process technology in existing industries: dispersion or reconcentration of industrial production.

Flexible production theory (Aglietta, Piore and Sabel, Schoenberger)

- Growing 'customisation', specialisation, and volatility of market demand.

- Development of flexible process technologies and work organisation.

- Flexible use of labour, including part-time working, home-working and self-employment.

- Growth of small and new firms, large-firm fragmentation: key role in development of 'new industrial spaces'?

Information economy theory (Bell, Gershunny, Illeris)

- Continuing absolute and relative growth of service employment and output.

- Growth of professional and managerial occupations, and of producer services (finance and business services).

- Growth of personal consumer services (leisure, tourism) and of part-time female employment.

Thus, for example, 'neo-Schumpeterian' long-wave theory stresses the key role of major technological innovations in generating entirely new products and industries, revolutionising process technology in existing industries, and directly modifying household and domestic behaviour. Freeman (1986) argues convincingly that microelectronics are, indeed, capable of engendering a technological revolution in these fields, but with differential and contingent impacts on different sectors, regions and continents, with Europe lagging behind Japan and the United States.

Equally, the rapidly-burgeoning debate over flexible-production theory (Schoenberger, 1988 and 1989; Gertler, 1988 and 1989; Scott, 1988), whether deriving from Marxian perspectives (Aglietta, 1979) or non-Marxist conceptualisations (Piore and Sabel, 1984), focuses attention on the impact of current radical changes in production organisation in many manufacturing and service industries, aimed at increasing the flexibility, and hence competitiveness, of their operations (Milne, 1989a and 1989b). These changes are being enforced by new market imperatives from increasingly affluent and discriminating consumers, and are enabled by new technology in a context of intensified global competition. Within Europe, these and other forces are also promoting a substantial increase in new firm formation and small-firm development (Keeble and Wever, 1986), small firms possessing many advantages with respect to flexibility of production and market sensitivity.

Finally, the seemingly inexorable shift in employment and output in western Europe towards tertiary activities is addressed by information-economy theory, with writers such as Marshall (1988) and Illeris (1989) demonstrating that one of the most important components in this shift is the remarkable growth of producer services. Such services, usually defined as including financial, insurance, accountancy, legal and business services of many kinds, employ an above-average share of highly-qualified professional staff and are growing rapidly, for a variety of reasons. Not the least of these are:

- the increasing demand for specialised business information in the context of intensified global competition;

- increasing complexity of economic and political organisation;

- rapidly-changing technological and market opportunities (Illeris, 1989). In the British case, the business-service sector has been the country's fastest-growing industry in employment terms since 1981, with an expansion of no less than 620,000 jobs, representing a 73% increase, by March 1989.

De-industrialisation and reindustrialisation of traditional industrial regions

The spatial outcomes of the processes identified in Table 2.1, within the theoretical context provided by long-wave, flexible-production and information-economy frameworks, are complex and debatable. However, it is clear that one major consequence of long-wave recession and industrial restructuring in Europe since 1970 is severe economic decline in those older industrial regions, traditionally specialising in nineteenth-century branches of industry, such as iron and steel, coal, heavy engineering, textiles and shipbuilding. This decline is a product of static or declining demand, increasing competition from low-cost producers outside Europe, and heavy job losses, due to investment in new technology. Thus, for example, between 1974 and 1988, British Steel was forced to close nearly 100 small iron- and steelworks in Britain and to cut its workforce by 175,000, or 78%. These were by far the most severe job losses in the EC steel industry. The widespread regional impact of 'de-industrialisation' (Martin and Rowthorn, 1986) is clearly evident in the 1989 designation by the European Commission of no less than 132 Community regions, containing 50 million people, as being eligible for aid under Objective 2 of the 1988 reform of the EC's structural funds (Commission of the European Communities, 1989). This objective is

44

aimed specifically at helping regions which are 'hard-hit by industrial decline' and are characterised by job losses and high unemployment. Nearly all of these areas are in the northern countries of the European Community, with 27 in West Germany and 33 in the United Kingdom.

However, de-industrialisation is not the whole story. In certain cases, heavy investment in new technology and radical restructuring of production organisation is having a major effect on the economic fortunes of traditional industries and the regions in which they are located, as is illustrated by the case of British Steel (Table 2.3). The social costs of these changes, in terms of acute unemployment in local communities (for example, Consett, Ebbw Vale and Corby), has been enormous. But computer-controlled technology, and the transformation of this company into a high-technology, market-sensitive and flexible producer, has revolutionised its economic fortunes in a space of less than 10 years. Such examples offer some hope of renewed economic viability and stability to traditional industries and old industrial regions, notwithstanding recent acute de-industrialisation.

An alternative 'reindustrialisation' process, affecting some older European industrial regions, is 'inward' manufacturing investment in new sectors, often by foreign-owned companies, stimulated primarily by government regional policy incentives and agencies. This process is having a significant effect upon such older UK regions as south Wales, where recent Japanese investment in industries such as consumer electronics (Milne, 1989a and 1989b) is a major reason for a better 1980s Welsh manufacturing employment performance (Table 2.4) than that of any other region in the United Kingdom. The Nissan car assembly and Fujitsu semiconductor plants in north-east England, and the Toyota car assembly plant announced in April 1989 for Derbyshire, are further dramatic examples of this trend, which is particularly evident in Britain. While this process raises many questions, not least its impact upon the quality and durability of job opportunities in the context of a 'spatial division of labour' between peripheral and core regions (Massey, 1984; Keeble and Kelly, 1988), there is no doubt of its importance. Foreign inward manufacturing investment to Britain in 1988, for example, totalled well over £5 billion in 320 projects. This represented a 20% increase on the 1987 figure, with the majority of the projects locating in the traditional industrial regions (Beresford, 1989). The role of foreign investment is much less evident in West Germany (Nuhn and Sinz, 1988), but is of growing importance in France, where the old industrial region of Lorraine ranked fourth (27.7%, after Alsace, Picardie and Centre) amongst French regions in 1986, in terms of proportion of industrial employment in foreign-owned firms (Datar, 1989).

Table 2.3: The British Steel Corporation's productivity and profitability revolution, 1979-89

	1979-80	1981-2	1983-4	1985-6	1986-7	1987-8	1988-9
turnover (£'000m)	3.11	3.44	3.36	3.74	3.46	4.12	4.91
profit/loss (£m)	-1,784	-504	-256	+38	+178	+410	+593
employees ('000s)	166.4	103.7	71.1	54.2	52.0	51.6	55.0
man-hours (per tonne)	13.2	9.4	7.1	6.3	6.2	5.0	4.7
deliveries (m. tonnes)	10.5	10.7	10.4	10.7	10.3	12.1	13.1

Source: British Steel Corporation. *Annual accounts.*

Table 2.4: Regional manufacturing employment change in the United Kingdom, 1981-9

	manufacturing employment 1989 (March) (thousands)	manufacturing employment change 1981-9	
		(thousands)	%
Wales	238	-2	-0.8
East Anglia	180	-5	-2.7
South-west	369	-28	-7.1
East Midlands	488	-44	-8.3
Rest of south-east	878	-120	-12.0
Northern Ireland	105	-18	-14.6
North-west	674	-136	-16.8
Yorks & Humber	485	-98	-16.8
North	280	-59	-17.4
West Midlands	667	-150	-18.4
Scotland	415	-95	-18.6
Greater London	431	-255	-37.2
UNITED KINGDOM	5,210	-1,010	-16.2

Source: Employment Gazette.

New industrial spaces and the role of SMEs and high-technology industry

Since at least the mid-1970s, the northern countries of the European Community have been experiencing two arguably novel and, to some extent, overlapping processes of industrial change. These are a significant growth in numbers of small- and medium-sized firms and enterprises (SMEs: see Keeble and Wever, 1986; Giaoutzi, Nijkamp and Storey, 1988) and of research and development-based industries producing new technologically-advanced products (Ayda-lot and Keeble, 1988). At the same time, the geography of industrial activity as a whole has been undergoing quite dramatic changes, simultaneously involving a shift from urban to rural areas (Keeble, Owens and Thompson, 1983; Keeble, 1988a) and the growth of new industrial regions, often situated in scenic and climatically-attractive 'sun belt' locations at some distance from traditional industrial cities. Examples of the latter change include Provence-Alpes, Côte d'Azur, Languedoc-Roussillon and Midi-Pyrenees, Bavaria and Baden-Württemberg, East Anglia and south-west England (Table 2.4). To what extent are these spatial and industrial changes linked?

The urban-rural manufacturing shift is characteristic of a wide range of sectors, not just high-technology industries, while large-firm investment (for example, Siemens in Bavaria and IBM at Montpellier and La Gaude), often in research and development and technologically-advanced production facilities, is an important process in the growth of new industrial regions (Keeble and Kelly, forthcoming). This said, SME- and high-technology industrial development do seem to be particularly important processes in current rural and regional industrialisation. High rates of creation and growth of SMEs are characteristic of many rural areas of northern Europe, as well as of new industrial regions, such as those in southern France (Aydalot, 1986) and East Anglia (Keeble, 1989b). This association undoubtedly reflects a variety of sociocultural and economic influences (Keeble and Wever, 1986), but one important process appears to be the longer-term impact of environmentally-stimulated selective migration of higher-income, more-skilled and professionally-qualified individuals and their families to smaller settlements and to 'sun belt' regions. This migration, for which much recent evidence exists (Aydalot, 1984; Jones, Caird and Ford, 1984), is itself a product of widening choice of residential location in Europe because of rising real incomes, mass car-ownership, and greatly improved communications. In turn, environment-influenced migration has been shown by empirical surveys to be directly linked to high rates of new business formation in areas such as East Anglia and the Scottish Highlands (Keeble and Gould, 1985; Jones, Caird and Ford, 1984), with migrants subsequently or simultaneously setting up small businesses in the areas where they have chosen to live for environmental reasons. Environmentally-favoured regions are also increasingly attracting retirement migrants, second-home owners and tourism development, all of which further help to stimulate SME development by expanding local market demand.

The general significance and impact of SMEs for regional and national economic development is, of course, a matter of considerable local debate. But there is much evidence to suggest that they are of growing importance in the Europe of the late-1980s, especially in rural and newly-industrialising regions. Thus, in the United Kingdom, new and surviving businesses created perhaps 1.3 million jobs between 1980 and 1987 (Keeble, 1989b) and, in France, accounted for over 40% of all businesses and 23% of all employment in new 'sun belt' regions such as Provence-Alpes, Côte-D'Azur and Languedoc-Roussillon (Datar, 1987).

The growth of technologically-advanced manufacturing and service industry is a further important component in the industrialisation process currently under way in a number of new industrial spaces in northern Europe (Scott, 1988). The regions most affected are all what Illeris (forthcoming) calls 'prestige environments', characterised by a high perceived quality of life and a marked occupational bias towards highly-qualified workers. Two types of high-technology 'prestige environment' can be identified (Keeble, 1988b):

- one comprises formerly less-industrialised 'sun belt' and 'ski belt' regions, such as the French Riviera, Montpellier, Grenoble, the Lake Constance area of Baden-Württemberg, and perhaps also East Anglia, especially Cambridge (Keeble, 1989d). These regions are characterised by small- or medium-sized towns, which sometimes, but not always, contain universities or scientific research institutions.

- The second category of prestige environments comprises the selected outer zones of Europe's major capital cities and certain other metropolitan agglomerations. Important examples are the 'science city' of Paris-Sud towards Orsay, the north-eastern zone of the Milan metropolitan area towards Vimercate, and the Berkshire 'M4 Corridor' to the west of London. Each of these contains hundreds of high-technology companies, engaged in sectors such as computers and dataprocessing, information technology and microelectronics, aerospace, scientific instruments, pharmaceuticals and research and development consultancy.

While the history and processes involved in the evolution of these high-technology prestige environments undoubtedly vary, a key and common underlying influence of great importance is the local availability of highly-qualified professionals, research scientists and engineers. Such workers are of growing and crucial significance in all high-technology industries because of the key role of R & D and technological innovation in competitive success in these sectors (Kelly and Keeble, 1988). Moreover, Green's (Chapter XII of this volume) striking recent finding of an 80% increase in the numbers of professional engineers employed in the British electronics industry from 1978 to 1987 (set within a 20% decrease in overall employment in this industry), powerfully supports this view. Locationally, however, the exceptional availability of such workers in the prestige environments reflects not only special historic factors, the presence of major scientific universities, such as Cambridge or Grenoble, or the decentralisation of high-technology firms from congested cities (as, for example, with Paris-Sud), but also their perceived environmental and residential attractiveness. Highly-qualified and high-income professionals are arguably particularly selective in this respect. The deliberate location by firms of major research and development laboratories, as well as high 'birth rates' of small technology-based firms set up by 'boffin entrepreneurs' in these areas, are rooted in the 'psychic income' and quality of life which they afford to highly-qualified individuals and their families.

This also helps explain the more general pattern of an urban-rural shift of high-technology industry throughout much of northern Europe. This is clearly illustrated for Britain by Figure 2.1 and Table 2.5, using a definition of high-technology activity based upon R & D intensity and including both manufacturing and service industries (Keeble, 1988c). All Britain's large cities have lost high-technology employment in the 1980s; growth being confined to less-industrialised counties such as Norfolk, Cambridgeshire, Devon, Gwent, Shropshire and Cumbria. Small, often new, companies appear to be playing an important role in this growth, a phenomenon which is also evident in West Germany, where there is an above-average relative concentration of technologically-innovative SMEs throughout much of the rural south, especially in Bavaria and Baden-Württemberg (Meyer-Krahmer, 1985).

Table 2.5: Urban-rural variations in high-technology employment change in Great Britain, 1981-4

	numbers employed 1981	employment change, numbers	1981-4 %
conurbations (8)	462,152	-36,799	-8.0
more urbanised counties (14)	309,918	-32,608	-10.5
less urbanised counties (21)	365,177	+14,806	+4.1
rural counties (20)	91,319	+4,156	+4.6

Source: Unpublished Census of Employment statistics. The classification of areas according to degree of urbanisation is from Keeble (1980). The figures in brackets are of the actual numbers of areas represented in each category.

Figure 2.1: The geography of growth and decline in high-technology industry in Britain, 1981-4

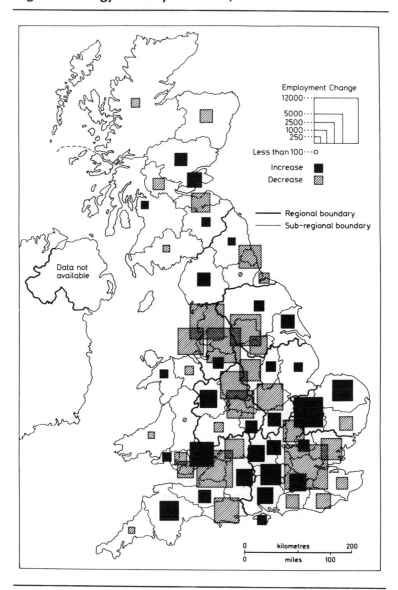

Source: Keeble (1988c), p. 78.

Tertiarisation, manufacturing decline and the reurbanisation of Europe's 'national' cities

The striking urban-rural shift of all sectors of manufacturing industry, which has been proceeding throughout Europe since the 1960s (Keeble, Owens and Thompson, 1983), is one major component in the pronounced 1970s' 'counterurbanisation' of population and employment in many north European countries (Illeris, forthcoming). This 1970s' counterurbanisation, as charted, for example, by Champion (1988; 1989) for Britain, involved exceptional rates of population emigration and manufacturing-employment loss in western Europe's largest cities, but growth of population and employment in small towns and rural settlements, including some rural areas.

Very rapid decline of manufacturing employment appears to have continued in Europe's largest cities in the 1980s (see Table 2.7 for the Greater London case). On this evidence, manufacturing industry seems destined for virtual extinction, as far as north Europe's congested giant cities are concerned. The reasons for this are complex, but certainly include the powerful inhibiting effect of constrained urban sites and severe space shortages for investment in new, more space-demanding, production technology (Keeble, Owens and Thompson, 1983; Fothergill, Kitson and Monk, 1985). This has major implications, both for physical relocation outside cities, and for the long-term competitiveness of residual urban firms. In addition, however, environmentally-determined population migration from cities has substantially diminished the available pool of manufacturing entrepreneurs, managers and qualified workers, during a period when the structure of manufacturing is shifting rapidly towards those sectors and smaller firms which are particularly dependent on such human resources. This is, of course, the converse of the argument presented earlier about the reasons for industrial growth in less urbanised locations.

Table 2.6: The changing occupational structure of employment in the United Kingdom, 1981-5

	actual change 1981-7 (thousands)	forecast change 1987-95 (thousands)
Management and administration	+234	+163
Professional and related occupations	+1,093	+1,027
Clerical and secretarial	-76	+219
Personal service and sales	+457	+402
Craft and skilled manual	-347	+214
Labourers and unskilled manual	-706	-310
All occupations	+652	+1,716

Source: Warwick University Institute for Employment Research, *Occupational update,* August 1988.

Table 2.7: Financial and business services growth and manufacturing decline in Greater London, 1981-8

	employment (thousands) 1981	1988	employment change thousands	%
Banking, insurance financial and business services	568	743	+175	+31
manufacturing	686	477	-209	-34

Source: Employment Gazette.

Continuing manufacturing decline is, however, only part of the story. For, as Illeris (forthcoming) demonstrates, in the 1980s certain large European cities have experienced a significant change in their demographic evolution, with the cessation, and even reversal, of previous population losses. Thus, Greater London's population, which had fallen by 88,000 per annum during the early 1970s, actually grew, for the first time since World War II, by 6,000 a year between 1983 and 1986 (Champion and Congdon, 1987). Reurbanisation, in terms of a cessation of population decline and even renewed population growth, is also evident in Copenhagen, Oslo, Stockholm and, to a lesser extent, the 'Randstad' (Amsterdam, Utrecht, Rotterdam and the Hague: see Illeris, forthcoming; and Jobse, 1988). Population losses still, however, characterise Greater Paris and the larger cities of West Germany, where counterurbanisation has, if anything, intensified in the 1980s (Kontuly and Vogelsang, 1988). Reurbanisation is also not apparent in Europe's old nineteenth-century manufacturing cities.

The causes of demographic reurbanisation, where it has occurred, and its possible links with metropolitan economic restructuring, are a matter of debate. However, it seems very probable that one, if not the major, influence is a fundamental structural shift in European economic organisation in the 1980s, involving a 'transition from a predominantly mass-producing industrial society to a service, or information, society' (Illeris, forthcoming). The latter is characterised by a large and ever-increasing share of service activities, engaged in the production, processing and exchange of information of many kinds, often in smaller, more flexible, firms. The very dramatic trends in occupational structure which this shift (along with de-industrialisation and a growth of income-led consumer services) entails, are illustrated for the United Kingdom in Table 2.6. This shows the remarkable growth in the 1980s of jobs in relatively highly-qualified 'professional and related occupations' (a net growth of over one million), nearly all of which are in the service sector, especially information-intensive services. A further one million professional jobs are forecast for the period 1987 to 1995. In striking contrast, labouring and unskilled manual employment declined by 700,000 during the years 1981-7. Further decline in these jobs is expected in the 1990s, many of them being in manufacturing and production-orientated sectors.

The geographical significance of the growth of the 'information economy' (Table 2.2), and of new information technologies and telecommunications systems, is seen by Illeris (forthcoming) as enabling a wider choice of location for economic activity than had been the case previously. While this is almost certainly true, Europe's existing 'national' administrative capitals and dominant financial centres have benefited substantially from these trends in recent years. This reflects the special advantages they offer of close functional and information linkages, exceptional national and international communications, and unique access to very large professional labour markets.

These factors remain of great importance for competitive success in many financial and business-service activities (especially accountancy, property management, market research, advertising and legal services) which serve national and, increasingly, international markets. Thus, the continuing rise of London, with deregulation and the 1984 'Big Bang', as one of the capitalist world's three dominant financial control centres, is a major cause of its massive growth in financial and business service jobs (Table 2.7). Since 1980, the number of Japanese banks and security houses operating in London, for example, has risen very substantially (to as many as 72 by 1988), as has the number of Japanese professionals and their families - an increase from 11,700 in 1981 to 25,200 by 1987 (*The Independent*, 1988). This example, therefore, demonstrates the existence of a direct link between tertiarisation and demographic reurbanisation. Similar trends may well characterise other buoyant European administrative and financial cities, such as Amsterdam, Frankfurt and Milan. These cities are also benefiting from their dominant roles as national cultural, entertainment and media centres, in an age of increasing leisure time and personal incomes.

Finally, the process of reurbanisation has, of course, been assisted in a number of European cities by deliberate government policies of urban physical redevelopment, aimed at revitalising derelict industrial or port areas. This is true in the Netherlands (Jobse, 1987), the Ruhr (Wehling, Chapter XVII) and Britain (Law, Chapter XVI). In Britain, government-appointed 'Urban Development Corporations' (Figure 2.2), all established since 1981, are now actively redeveloping derelict areas in 12 different British cities. Though it is the target of much local and ideological criticism, the London Docklands Development Corporation, the most publicised case, has undoubtedly been a major catalyst behind the extraordinary economic and demographic restructuring of its inner-city area. Between 1983 and 1988, London Docklands' employment rose by 46% to 36,400, while government infrastructure expenditure of £456 million here attracted £4.4 billion of private-sector investment. By 1988, 11.1 million square feet of commercial and industrial floorspace was completed or under construction, along with 15,000 new dwellings. Government policies are therefore playing a part in the reurbanisation of some European cities, although the extent to which these are likely to be successful within declining nineteenth-century industrial cities, such as Newcastle or Essen, is more debatable.

Figure 2.2: Urban Development Corporations in Britain, 1989

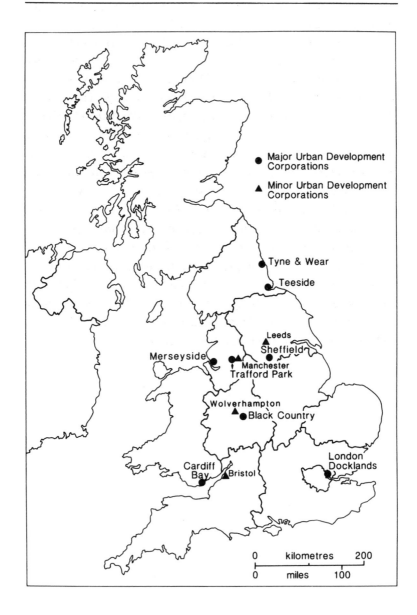

Major Urban Development Corporations

Minor Urban Development Corporations

Tyne & Wear

Teeside

Leeds

Sheffield

Merseyside

Manchester
Trafford Park

Wolverhampton

Black Country

Cardiff Bay

Bristol

London Docklands

0   kilometres   200

0   miles   100

Conclusions

This brief review of the nature and causes of contemporary regional restructuring in Europe is inevitably somewhat partial, focusing, as it does, solely upon the key processes affecting manufacturing and producer services in the northern countries of the European Community. Sectors such as agriculture, energy and tourism are, of course, also very important for regional economic change, especially in Europe's more peripheral, low-income regions (Keeble, Offord and Walker, 1988; Keeble, 1989a). This said, however, the processes which have been outlined in this chapter - regionally-selective de-industrialisation, SMEs and high-technology development in new industrial areas, and radical metropolitan restructuring from manufacturing to producer services - are of fundamental importance, both to academic understanding, and to effective government regional-policy intervention in north European countries during a period of turbulent economic and technological change. This chapter, it is hoped, therefore provides a conceptual framework for the more detailed and policy-focused case studies of regional economic change in Britain and West Germany which are presented in the following chapters of this volume.

References

Aglietta, M., *A theory of capitalist regulation*, New Left Books, New York, 1979.

Aydalot, P., 'Note sur les migrations interregionales en France 1975-1982', in: *Dossiers du Centre Economie Espace Environment*, Universitie de Paris, 1 Pantheon Sorbonne, Vol. 40, pp. 1-16, 1984.

Aydalot, P., 'The location of new firm creation: the French case', in: Keeble, D. and Wever, E. (eds.), *New firms and regional development in Europe*, Croom Helm, London, pp. 105-23, 1986.

Aydalot, P. and Keeble, D., 'High-technology industry and innovative environments in Europe: an overview', in Aydalot, P. and Keeble, D. (eds.), *High-technology industry and innovative environments: the European experience*, Routledge, London, pp. 1-21, 1988.

Beresford, P., 'Foreign firms sink record £5bn in Britain', *The Sunday Times*, 2 April 1989.

Commission of the European Communities (CEC), 'Good news for the regions', in: *Information Memo*, 8 March 1989.

Champion, A.G., 'Counterurbanization: the British experience', in: *Geographical Perspectives*, 1988.

Champion, A.G., 'Counterurbanization in Britain', in: *Geographical Journal*, Vol. 155, pp. 52-59, 1989.

Champion, A.G. and Congdon, P., 'An analysis of the recovery of London's population change rate', in: *Built Environment*, Vol.13, pp. 193-211, 1987.

Datar, 'Creations d'entreprises et dynamique de l'emploi', in: *La Lettre de la DATAR*, Vol. 111, Novembre, supplement, pp. 1-4, 1987.

Datar, 'La France est-elle attirante pour les investissements étrangers?', in: *La Lettre de la DATAR*, Vol. 122, Avril, pp. 1-12, 1989.

Fothergill, S., Kitson, M. and Monk, S., *Urban industrial change: the causes of the urban-rural contrast in manufacturing employment trends*, HMSO for the Departments of the Environment and Trade and Industry, London, 1985.

Freeman, C., 'The role of technical change in national economic development', in: Amin, A. and Goddard, J.B. (eds.), *Technological change, industrial restructuring and regional development*, Allen and Unwin, London, pp. 100-14, 1986.

Gertler, M.S., 'The limits to flexibility: comments on the post-Fordist vision of production and its geography', in: *Transactions Institute of British Geographers, New Series*, Vol. 13, pp. 419-32, 1988.

Gertler, M.S., 'Resurrecting flexibility? A reply to Schoenberger', in: *Transactions Institute of British Geographers, New Series*, Vol. 14, pp. 109-12, 1989.

Geographical Journal, 'Counterurbanization in Europe', in: *The Geographical Journal*, Vol. 155, pp. 52-80, 1989.

Giaoutzi, M., Nijkamp, P. and Storey, D.J. (eds.), *Small and medium size enterprises and regional development*, Routledge, London, 1988.

Illeris, S., 'Counter-urbanisation revisited: the new map of population distribution in central and north-western Europe', in: Bannon, M., Bourne, L. and Sinclair, R. (eds.), *Urbanisation and urban development*, University College, Dublin, forthcoming.

The Independent, 'Japan and Britain', in: *The Independent,* 3 May 1988.

Jobse, R.J., 'The restructuring of Dutch cities', in: *Tijdschrift voor Economische en Sociale Geografie,* Vol. 78, pp. 305-11, 1987.

Jones, H., Caird, J. and Ford, N., 'A home in the Highlands', in: *Town and Country Planning,* Vol. 53, pp. 326-27, 1984.

Keeble, D., *The economic context for information technology and telecommunications strategy in the rural areas of the northern European Community: final report to the European Commission*, Department of Geography, University of Cambridge, 1988a.

Keeble, D., 'High tech in pastures new', in: *The Geographical Magazine,* Analysis, pp. 4-7, January 1988b.

Keeble, D., 'High-technology industry and local environments in the United Kingdom', in: Aydalot, P. and Keeble, D. (eds.), *High-technology industry and innovative environments: the European experience,* Routledge, London, pp. 65-98, 1988c.

Keeble, D., 'Core-periphery disparities, recession and new regional dynamisms in the European Community', in: *Geography,* Vol. 74, pp. 1-11, 1989a.

Keeble, D., 'New firms and regional economic development: the implications for the 1980s', in: *Cambridge Regional Review,* Vol. 1, 1989b.

Keeble, D., 'The dynamics of European industrial counterurbanization in the 1980s: corporate restructuring or indigenous growth?', in: *The Geographical Journal*, Vol. 155, pp. 70-74, 1989c.

Keeble, D., 'High-technology industry and regional development in Britain: the case of the Cambridge Phenomenon', in: *Environment and Planning C: Government and Policy*, Vol. 7, pp. 153-72, 1989d.

Keeble, D. and Gould, A., 'Entrepreneurship and manufacturing firm formation in rural regions: the East Anglian case', in: Healy, M.J. and Ilberry, B.W. (eds.), *Industrialization of the countryside*, Geobooks, Norwich, pp. 197-220, 1985.

Keeble, D. Offord, J. and Walker, S., *Peripheral regions in a Community of twelve member states*, Commission of the European Communities, Luxembourg, 1988.

Keeble, D. Owens, P.L. and Thompson, C., 'The urban-rural manufacturing shift in the European Community', in: *Urban Studies*, Vol. 20, pp. 405-18, 1988.

Keeble, D. and Kelly, T., 'New firms and high-technology industry in the United Kingdom: the case of computer electronics', in: Keeble, D. and Wever, E. (eds.), *New firms and regional development in Europe*, Croom Helm, London, pp. 75-104, 1986.

Keeble, D. and Wever, E., 'Introduction', in; Keeble, D. and Wever, E. (eds.), *New firms and regional development in Europe*, Croom Helm, London, pp. 1-34, 1986.

Kelly, T. and Keeble, D., 'Locational change and corporate organisation in high-technology industry: computer electronics in Great Britain', in: *Tijdschrift voor Economische en Sociale Geografie*, Vol. 79, pp. 2-15, 1988.

Kelly, T. and Keeble, D., 'The corporate chamelon: a geography of IBM in Europe', in: De Smidt, M. and Wever, E. (eds.), *A geography of enterprise*, Routledge, London, forthcoming.

Kontuly, T. and Vogelsang, R., 'Explanations for the intensification of counterurbanisation in the Federal Republic of Germany', in: *Professional Geographer,* Vol. 40, pp. 42-54, 1988.

Marshall, J.N., *Services and uneven development,* Oxford University Press, Oxford, 1988.

Martin R. and Rowthorn, R., *The geography of de-industrialisation,* MacMillan, London, 1986.

Massey, D., *Spatial divisions of labour: social structures and the geography of production,* MacMillan, London, 1984.

Meyer-Krahmer, F., 'Innovation behaviour and regional indigenous potential', in: *Regional Studies,* Vol. 19, pp. 523-34, 1985.

Milne, S.S., *New forms of manufacturing and their spatial implications: the case of the UK electronic consumer goods, high fidelity audio and domestic electrical appliance industries,* unpublished Ph.D. thesis, Department of Geography, University of Cambridge, 1989a.

Milne, S.S., 'New forms of manufacturing and their spatial implications: the case of the UK consumer electronics industry', in: *Environment and Planning A,* Vol. 21, 1989b.

Nuhn, H. and Sinz, M., 'Industrial change and employment trends in the Federal Republic of Germany', in *Geographische Rundschau,* Heft. S3211E, pp. 68-78, 1988.

Piore, M.J. and Sabel, C.F., *The second industrial divide: possibilities for prosperity*, Basic Books, New York, 1984.

Schoenberger, E., 'From Fordism to flexible accumulation: technology, competitive strategies and international location', in: *Environment and Planning D: Society and Space*, Vol. 6, pp. 245-62, 1988.

Schoenberger, E., 'Thinking about flexibility: a response to Gertler', in: *Transactions Institute of British Geographers, New Series*, Vol. 14, pp. 98-108, 1989.

Scott, A.J., *New industrial spaces: flexible production organisation and regional development in North America and western Europe*, Pion, London, 1988.

Chapter III

Peter Roberts (Leeds Polytechnic) and
Graham Haughton (Leeds Polytechnic)

Cities in regions and regions in Europe: unravelling some aspects of the British regional problem

Introduction

Renewed interest in the British regional problem has emerged as the very selective nature of the beginnings of post-recession recovery has been uncovered, appearing to manifest itself in a sharpened north-south divide (Martin, 1988). At the same time, a number of studies have emerged which attempt to identify the scale of the problem and its precise regional and urban manifestations, using composite national indicators of regional economic health. In this chapter we look at how the problem has been gauged in terms of both its spatial dimensions and the types of indicators used to assess the nature and scale of the problem. In particular, we look at the question of whether it is ever meaningful to conduct an analysis of the regional problem using a common notion of 'problem' for every region or area. We also consider whether the regional problem is really an urban problem which has regional manifestations, or whether it is more of a manifestation of Britain's positioning within the European Community. We then move on to reflect on how this affects our view of the undoubtedly complex mosaic of regional and local economic health which currently exists in Britain.

In recent years, much of the academic debate on spatial problems and policy has shifted its scale of focus within the British economy, away from the regional/subregional dimension and increasingly towards the role of the locality within the national and global economies (Urry, 1981; Massey, 1985). This has been accompanied by a reassessment of the view that local and regional distinctiveness has been diminished, succumbing to a uniformity imposed by the rigours of trading in increasingly open national and global markets. If anything, the opposite view now prevails, that local distinctiveness has increased in importance (albeit possibly diminished in absolute terms), as a factor in attracting mobile capital. Running parallel to this trend has been the emerging tendency within government policy to relegate in importance the regional dimension of spatial inequality, preferring instead to target a diminishing overall level of resources more closely on problem urban areas.

It is doubtful whether this switch in emphasis away from the regional scale will be a long-term trend. Warnings have already been sounded in academic debates about the dangers of concentrating on the global and the local, if this is at the expense of the intervening regional level, since it is here where many social, economic, political and cultural dynamics are still being shaped (Haughton, 1989a; 1989b). In policy terms, the imminence of 1992, and the changes already made to the structural and regional funding mechanisms of the European Community, look certain to involve a shift in resources away from addressing urban problems and towards the regional scale. The problem, however, is that we are still uncertain of the regional dimensions of economic problems and, equally importantly, regional potentials.

It could, of course, be a classic case of how, by shaping our structures, we allow them eventually to shape ourselves. Britain is almost unique in the European Community in having no official tier of regional or subregional government, the only exceptions being the regional administrations in Wales and Scotland (and some might claim also in Northern Ireland). The demise of the metropolitan counties and the Greater London Council has left a vacuum in the management of urban regions in England. This is unlikely to be filled adequately by vague notions of regional strategic guidance, and it is also unlikely that we shall see, in the near future, the establishment of regional authorities with full executive powers. In this political and administrative vacuum, city-cum-district authorities have gained substantial political power in the past and have accelerated the shift of policy and expenditure away from the region and towards the locality. Again, the main exceptions to this general demise of the region as the natural arena for policy (aimed at economic restructuring), are to be found in Scotland and Wales, where the region or, perhaps more importantly, the subregional dimension in policy and its implementation continue to be relatively important (Wannop et al., 1986).

This regional/subregional gap in the political geography of England is apparent in the way in which regional policy issues are (mis)managed vis-à-vis the European Community's structural funds. To date, European Regional Development Fund programme submissions lack any real feeling for regional or subregional needs and potentials; instead they reflect the concern of central government with maintaining the established departmental - often spatially divisive - structure of administration. It is, therefore, not only the occurrence of regional problems that have been marginalised, but also the political case for regional government and administration. However, the regional issue is now back on the agenda, for the technical reason of gaining European funding, and also due to the renewed interest which has been expressed in regional strategic management and, possibly, regional government. This renewal of interest in regional issues reflects both the private sector's desire to achieve some degree of order in making its long-term investment decisions, and also the government's desire to hold off the political challenge of nationalism.

REALLY?

It is in this context that we set our analysis of the north-south divide.

Identifying the regional problem

There are four major approaches to studies which seek to analyse the nature and extent of the north-south divide:

- firstly, the political-economy approach of Martin (1988);

- secondly, the use of functional regions by Champion and Green (1987; 1988);

- thirdly, the quality-of-life approach of Rogerson et al. (1987; 1988a; 1988b);

- lastly, the identification of *Northern Lights* by Breheny, Hall and Hart (1987). In reviewing these approaches briefly, we are less concerned with the specifics of their conclusions, but rather more with the underlying assumptions which have guided their work. We should also stress that, whilst all of these studies have some problems, none are without considerable merit in improving the overall quality of the current regional debate.

A political-economy approach

Martin adopts a political-economy approach, which largely relies for empirical evidence on data using the ten standard regions of mainland Britain, plus, in a few cases, counties. The data cover sectoral changes in employment, the labour market, occupational details, the organisation of labour (unionisation and strike rates), new firm formation, the distribution of wealth, and the political map itself. The analysis which accompanies this is telling, but lacking in local detail, inevitably tending to imply a degree of regional homogeneity which quite simply does not exist. It comprises broad 'brush strokes', which hide an equally interesting, much more finely-detailed, picture. As with Massey's (1988) treatment, the value of Martin's work lies in its political awareness in attempting to unravel the causal processes at work in creating and re-creating various dimensions of the north-south divide.

Functional regions approach

Champion and Green provide an analysis which is conducted at a much finer level: the University of Newcastle CURDS (Centre for Urban and Regional Development Studies) framework of functional regions. Overall, their work is illuminating and valuable, but it does need to be scrutinised closely. Functional regions are based on a notion of self-containment in travel-to-work patterns. Surprisingly, the two authors appear happy to accept this delimitation somewhat uncritically, and to dismiss the use of administrative boundaries. In contrast, we would argue that functional regions are misleading in terms of the regional problem. They imply limited areas of job-search on the lines of these commuting patterns. The emerging '*Gastarbeiter* culture', which sees as many as 10,000 northern migrants heading to London at the start of each week, gives the lie to this (Hogarth and Daniel, 1988). More worrying still, the use of functional regions ignores the importance of labour market segmentation, and the impact which this can have on travel-to-work and job-search activities (Peck, 1989). Male white-collar workers define the outermost limits of functional regions, but people confined to less fortunate labour market segments, for instance single mothers, display very different spatial boundaries. Self-containment of labour markets is much more ambiguous than might at first appear: the limits are usually arbitrarily drawn and their relevance as to how regional health is created and shared is dubious. Functional regions inherently tend to underplay local variations in economic health, and in addition, they are overtly economistic, ahistorical and acultural. As Norris (1978) points out, in the increasingly few cases where work is still the thing which most evidently draws a community together, the 'dominated' local labour market still rarely emerges as its own functional region or travel-to-work area; a classic example being the industrial town of St Helens, where the Pilkingtons glass-manufacturing company dominates, and which is part of the Liverpool 'travel-to-work area'.

To dismiss administrative boundaries is to be a little suspect. Administrative boundaries are quintessentially functional, albeit con-

70

sumer-service, rather than labour market orientated. Moreover, many people do regard themselves in some sense in relation to a particular administrative area. Even in the controversial authority of Humberside, those rebelling against the new county only want to revert to as far back as their traditional county identities, in this case Lincolnshire and the East Riding of Yorkshire.

The range of data available to Champion and Green was limited by their preoccupation with functional regions. Interestingly, in their later publication (Champion and Green, 1988) they do manage to increase the scope of their data, though they remain ambiguous about what exactly each set of data is either meant, or likely, to indicate. For instance, population change is less meaningful when not disaggregated down to fine spatial units and social classes. An example of this is the Isle of Dogs in London Docklands, the scene of huge demographic changes, which displays at least two important trends: the in-movement of well-off migrants, and the displacement of original residents. Laudably, Champion and Green progress to incorporate more indicators of change, but their choice of variables makes it inevitable that discussion can only take place on recent apparent changes in terms of outcomes, not processes, of change. Essentially, their variables appear to be selected for pragmatic reasons, relating to data availability for analysis of functional regions, rather than being grounded in any theoretical framework which seeks to identify causal relationships in differential regional health. The contrast here with Martin's work is sharp: he introduces variables, such as strike rates, precisely because he is looking as much at processes as he is at product. Champion and Green are much more concerned with discerning patterns, rather than processes, and this is reflected in their choice of variables, and the adoption of a descriptive, rather than an analytical approach.

The quality-of-life approach
The third approach to interpreting the north-south divide stems from the work of Rogerson and his colleagues in Glasgow (Rogerson, Fin-

dlay and Morris, 1987; 1988a; 1988b). Restricting themselves to the major city regions of mainland Britain, they provide one of the most useful critiques of area-health and quality-of-life measurements, and also the most rigorously-developed system for choosing variables and weighting them to arrive at a composite indicator. In brief, they used a national survey to determine those characteristics which individuals themselves most valued in assessing the quality of their urban life. The key variables that emerged from this survey were then used, after being weighted according to their findings, to assess the 'liveability' of 38 British urban areas. However, there are some considerable problems in using this information. London, for instance, is treated as a single entity, which says nothing for the huge diversity within our capital city. A similar criticism is valid for other major cities, especially Manchester and Birmingham (the latter being the least desirable city in Britain, according to this analysis). The analysis also suffers from taking dimensions of human well-being, which are based on personal perceptions, but ignore business perceptions (which are arguably essential to understanding variations in economic performance and potentials). This is especially true in the service sector, where Birmingham has recently become a favourite location for office investments (Roberts et al., 1988).

Northern Lights

Finally, there has been the much-cited work of Breheny, Hall and Hart (1987), on identifying what they describe as 'Northern Lights': that is, 10 northern areas with strong growth potential. These were identified by using three key dimensions:

- a prosperity index, using variables such as proportions of people with a higher education qualification, owner-occupation housing status, and more than one car;

- a quality index, using counts of such facilities as local golf courses, antique shops and restaurants in the *Good Food Guide;*

- lastly, a service index, based on such measurements as distance from a major urban centre and distance to motorway.

This work has the merit of combining indicators of both potential and problems, spanning environmental and social, as well as economic, variables. Whilst the concept is undoubtedly rather idiosyncratic in its choice of variables (which vary greatly in what they can tell us), *Northern Lights* is the first major work to begin to turn traditional views of the north-south divide on their heads, and to investigate the many undoubtedly positive attributes of northern areas. Where it suffers most is with its inherent tendency, caused by its choice of variables and use of local authority boundaries, to pick out gentrifying, or gentrified, towns and suburbs just outside city boundaries. For example, to the south of Manchester, Congleton emerges as a 'Northern Light', rather than nearby, more prosperous, Altrincham, because it is free-standing as a local authority. Recognising this as a major failing of the analysis, it becomes important to consider the whole range of other towns which have been 'passed over' because of this methodological bias. In the Pennines, Ilkley to the north of Bradford, Saddleworth to the east of Oldham, and Holmfirth to the south of Huddersfield, are all examples of this. In addition, it could be said that the Breheny, Hall and Hart analysis suffers from its utilisation of middle-class values, rather than measures which reflect other forms of potential for development.

Finally, in this section of our chapter, it is important to note that the four approaches which have just been discussed all focus their attention mainly on the north-south divide as it is manifest in mainland Britain. Although they represent a major contribution to our understanding of the occurrence of spatial inequalities within Britain, they ignore the increasingly-important context of the European Community. It is ever more important, in studying spatial inequality, to consider not only the national significance of regional problems, but also their severity when measured against a European yardstick. This is especially the case when resources for intervention are limited and the causes of the regional problem are, in some large part, transnational in origin. It is not intended to review the literature on European regional problems here; rather, it is our purpose to highlight the need for analysis and policy formulation to emphasise the European dimension. This is essential for achieving a better understanding of the changing factors which explain the occurrence of regional problems and set the scope for resolving them. Academic studies have demonstrated the changes that have occurred in the relative accessibility of regions and the effects of such changes upon their economic potential (Keeble, Owens and Thompson, 1982). These studies, when translated into policy proposals (Kowalski, 1989), indicate the need to move away from approaches which utilise a comparative static framework of analysis, and the need to move towards a research model which places emphasis upon the identification of potential and the generation of appropriate policies for positive change.

Key dimensons

Our review of these major geographical contributions to the north-south debate highlights four key areas for further detailed consideration in devising methodologies for, first of all, coming to terms with the nature and extent of this divide, and then for the formulation of appropriate regional policies for the 1990s.

Problems and potentials

In examining the north-south divide, it is important to address the question of what might be done to alleviate spatial imbalances, to divert pressure away from congested areas and to encourage the growth of lagging areas. This was central to the investigation, conducted some 20 years ago, by the Hunt Committee (Hunt, 1969). Yet many of the important messages from that investigation have still not fully penetrated the British public policy system. At the heart of the Hunt Committee's analysis was the assumption that regional policy should not only be concerned with reacting to the occurrence of

74

problems, but also with their anticipation and avoidance. In order to achieve such objectives, it is important to set problems against potentials, and possible future success against past failures.

This is, perhaps, the most important, yet underinvestigated, dimension of the regional problem. We have evolved various levels of understanding of how regional imbalances emerge; what we have not even begun to investigate fully is how areas and regions manage to 'turn themselves around', or at least manage to contain potential decline. The term 'problem area' needs to be much more carefully constructed and used. Problems should not be seen in isolation, either from each other or from other, more positive, attributes. As areas such as Hull, for example, recognised in the 1960s and early 1970s, designation of problem area status can, in fact, exacerbate problems through stigmatisation. Problems and potential are very much interrelated and need to be studied as such.

Whilst the work of Breheny, Hall and Hart, and also of Rogerson and his colleagues, do provide some valuable moves in the direction of identifying indicators of potential, the value of their investigations lies much more in helping to redirect the research agenda, than in reformulating it. This is largely because, like much of the current debate, there is a tendency to collect and analyse data in a theoretical vacuum. What is needed is a much clearer understanding of how areas, regions and cities are able to regenerate and reverse their fortunes. Such little work as there has been on examining aspects of economic 'turnaround' in areas of Britain during the 1980s, fails to address the theoretical need. In consequence it appears tame and lacklustre, and descriptive rather than analytical (Department of Environment, 1988). Whilst such studies attempt to examine the characteristics of individual areas, they tend towards an approach which places undue emphasis upon the analysis of the factors which indicate the dimensions of change, rather than upon the processes or dynamics which actually bring about change. It may be timely to return to the regional development texts of the 1960s, in order to refresh our memories of the purposes of analysis and of the need to relate it more directly to policy formulation and its implementation (see, for example, Boudeville, 1966).

The changing spatial mosaic

One thing which all commentators are increasingly in agreement about, is the diversity of economic health between individual localities within broadly-defined regions (Breheny, Hall and Hart, 1987; Champion and Green, 1988). What remains to be done is to make an understanding of this the focus of analysis, rather than a by-product. In particular, we need to acknowledge not only the existence of a *mosaic* of regional economic health, but also the interrelatedness of the poorer and more prosperous areas, and how changes in one area transmit a range of beneficial and deleterious effects to other areas. Small shifts in one area's well-being will have knock-on effects for other areas which, in turn, can affect the whole picture of regional health.

Such change could be said to be kaleidoscopic in nature, since, by altering the elements that are considered in analysis, not only are they themselves rearranged, but also new patterns emerge. Thus, for example, by adopting a different ideological perspective towards spatial policy intervention, a new and perhaps more pleasing pattern may be perceived. This suggests that changes in spatial patterns may be brought about through many different forms of policy action, and that the results of these may be the outcomes of a complex process of spatial sorting. What this suggests is that whilst a locally-dominated scale of analysis may reveal the detail of the major elements which influence change, it may fail to recognise the underlying circumstances which cause change to occur. Equally, a national level of analysis may understand the circumstances of change, but only have a vague notion of the elements relevant to a local area. In formulating the future research agenda and applying it to the needs of practice, we therefore advocate the use of the 'development from above and below model' (Stohr and Taylor, 1981). This offers the opportunity to

construct regional and subregional policies which are more relevant
to the areas to which they are applied.

Convenience containers

We have also expressed some concern about the scale of analysis
appropriate to studies of the regional problem. In reality, the north-
south divide covers a tremendous variability in regional well-being.
Whilst one would not argue in general terms against the existence of
such a divide, what should be emphasised is the different nature of
the mix of regional and urban problems faced in the north and the
south of the country. It has often been said that the problem of the
north is essentially one of the high number of large Victorian towns
and cities whose outdated industrial bases have faced decline. Parts
of London, too, have suffered from high shares of older industries
facing structural decline. The problem of the north is one of complete
industrial urbanised regions, whilst that of the south is connected to
the more locationally-specific difficulties of intrametropolitan industrial decline.

This leads us to an important pair of conclusions. Firstly, an appropriate scale for analysis and policy intervention cannot be one
which is centrally determined and then imposed on the whole *Cf.*
country - in one area it may be the standard region which is the most *Liberab*
appropriate scale for analysis and intervention, in another it might
be the neighbourhood. Secondly, the regional problem can be best
approached by using a mixture of scales for analysis and action (from
the local through to the regional, and from the transnational down
to the regional), building up to a composite view, rather than looking
for an elusive, and often virtually impossible to define, average or
common denominator. In many cases it seems that the appropriate
scale for detailed analysis may be the local, whilst the appropriate
scale for policy intervention may be regional. There is no necessary
contradiction in this. Sensitively applied, a true regionally-co-ordi-
nated delivery of national urban policy might overcome many of the
oversights and other shortcomings of the current situation (Haughton

and Roberts, 1989). More than this, the effective policy divide for dealing with regional and urban problems seems inherently illogical and wasteful of public resources. The two scales are strongly related and must be treated as such in policy implementation.

Composite indices

Indices of an area's well-being always stand prone to criticisms of being reductivist and mechanistic. None of the studies which have been discussed here are immune to these problems. Moreover, there is another, still larger, question which needs to be addressed much more fully than hitherto. The 'top-down' imposition of national indices of regional economic and social health diminishes the sensitivity of the indicators to local needs. We would argue very strongly that local well-being can only be meaningfully gauged in relation to local conditions and local needs. The needs of people in rural areas differ significantly from those of residents of the inner city: for instance, consider the questions of access to services and the incidence of pollution. The notion of a composite indicator, meaningful to all areas, is evidently difficult, if not impossible: the diversity of local and regional needs and potentials ought to be reflected in the variables chosen. This, in turn, implies the need for a much better-developed feel for, and understanding of, individual places, than is apparent in most studies of the north-south divide to date.

Summary

In this paper we have deliberately set out to take a critical and detached assessment of the growing literature on north-south divide in Britain in the 1980s and, more broadly, of the most recent empirical work on the nature of regional inequality in Britain. What emerges is a view that, whilst one can understand considerably more about the geographical manifestations of regional inequality, we have yet to improve our understanding of the actual *causes* of regional inequality significantly. We put this down, in part, to the blinkered view of the British regional problem which ignores the European dimension. In addition, we question the preoccupation of researchers with problem indicators, to the virtual exclusion of indicators of potential. Identifying what turns an area around in terms of its economic and social health, be it a neighbourhood or a standard region, is the most important new avenue for debate. Identifying and explaining the emergence of problems is only one part of a much broader debate which we need to engage in if we are to get to grips with effective policy for combatting both regional and urban problems. We might, in our future research, concern ourselves much more with the possible application of the techniques for strategic analysis and the understanding of economic potential that are offered by business and management science (Roberts, 1989).

Finally, we are heavily critical of the 'spatial fetishism' which appears to have led to an undue separation of regional and urban problems and, following from this, regional and urban policies. Both scales are simultaneously relevant to the needs of individual areas; government policy needs to be much more aware of this. Most tellingly, the administrative structures for implementing spatial policies (and, indeed, the many related policy areas), require a much more strongly-devolved administrative structure; quite probably one which operates at either regional or subregional levels. Such an approach to analysis and administration would help to ensure that more effective and appropriate policy is constructed and implemented, in order that problems might be alleviated and potentials more fully utilised.

References

Boudeville, J., *Problems of regional economic planning*, Edinburgh University Press, Edinburgh, 1966.

Breheny, M., Hall, P. and Hart, D., *Northern Lights: a development agenda for the north in the 1990s*, Derrick Wade and Partners, Preston, 1987.

Champion, A. and Green, A., 'The booming towns of Britain: the geography of economic performance in the 1980s', in: *Geography*, Vol. 72, pp. 97-108, 1987.

Champion, A. and Green, A., *Local prosperity and the north-south divide: winners and losers in 1980s Britain*, Institute for Employment Research, University of Warwick, Coventry, 1988.

Department of the Environment, *Kirklees, Wakefield and Doncaster: co-ordination report*, prepared for the Department of the Environment by the Centre for Urban and Regional Development Studies (CURDS), University of Newcastle, HMSO, London, 1988.

Haughton, G., 'Community and industrial restructuring in the Illawarra region of Australia', in: *Environment and Planning A*, Vol. 21, pp. 233-247, 1989a.

Haughton, G., 'Manufacturing recession? BHP and the recession in Wollongong', in: *International Journal of Urban and Regional Research*, forthcoming, 1989b.

Haughton, G. and Roberts, P., 'Government urban economic policy in England, 1979-89: problems and potential', in: Campbell, M., *Local economic development*, Cassel, London, forthcoming.

Hogarth, T. and Daniel, W., *Britain's new industrial gypsies*, Policy Studies Institute, London, 1988.

Hunt, Sir J., *The intermediate areas*, HMSO, London, 1969.

Keeble, D., Owens, P. and Thompson, C., 'Regional accessibility and economic potential in the European Community', in: *Regional Studies*, Vol. 16, pp. 419-431, 1982.

Kowalski, L., 'Major current and future regional issues in the enlarged Community', in: Albrechts, L. et al. (eds.), *Regional policy at the crossroads*, Jessica Kingsley Publishers, London, 1989.

Martin, R., 'The political economy of Britain's north-south divide', in: *Transactions Institute of British Geographers, New Series*, Vol. 13, pp. 389-418, 1988.

Massey, D., 'New directions in space', in: Gregory, D. and Urry, J. (eds.), *Social relations and spatial structures*, Macmillan, London, pp. 9-19, 1985.

Massey, D., 'A new class of geography', in: *Marxism Today*, pp. 12-17, May 1988.

Norris, G., 'Industrialist paternalist capitalism and local labour markets', in: *Sociology*, Vol. 12, pp. 469-89, 1978.

Peck, J.A., 'Reconceptualising the local labour market: space segmentation and the state', in: *Progress in human geography*, forthcoming 1989.

Roberts, P. et al., *Future trends in office development*, ECOTEC, Birmingham, 1988.

Roberts, P., *Strategic vision and the management of the UK land resource*, Strategic Planning Society, London, 1988.

Rogerson, R., Findlay, A. and Morris, A., 'The geography of the quality of life', in: *Occasional Paper Series*, Department of Geography, University of Glasgow, 1987.

Rogerson, R., Findlay, A. and Morris, A., *A report on the quality of life in British cities*, Department of Geography, University of Glasgow, 1988a.

Rogerson, R., Findlay, A. and Morris, A., 'The best cities to live in', in: *Town and Country Planning*, Vol. 5, pp. 270-273, 1988b.

Stohr, W. and Taylor, D., *Development from above or below*, International Institute of Research, Vienna, 1981.

Urry, J., 'Localities, regions and social class', in: *International Journal of Urban and Regional Research*, Vol. 5, pp. 455-74, 1981.

Wannop, U. et al., *Strategic planning for regional potential*, Royal Town Planning Institute, London, 1986.

Chapter IV

Tony Champion (University of Newcastle)

City revival and rural growth: Britain in the 1980s

Introduction

The last two decades have witnessed a major transformation in the geography of population change in most of the advanced Western world. The general tendency has been a significant reduction in the rate of population growth in the major cities and national core regions, together with a parallel recovery in smaller settlements and more rural and remote zones of national territory. In several countries this trend went so far in the 1970s that it led to a reversal of net migration flows, away from traditional urbanisation patterns and towards the repopulation of long-declining areas (Vining and Kontuly, 1978; Fielding, 1982). More recently, however, evidence has emerged of renewed growth of larger cities and core regions, suggesting that a 'back to the city' movement is underway and that the turnaround of metropolitan migration and the associated counterurbanisation trend of the 1970s may have been a temporary anomaly, rather than the harbinger of a new post-industrial settlement pattern (Cochrane and Vining, 1986).

Both Britain and West Germany have felt the effects of urban deconcentration and 'peripheral' growth during the past two decades, but their experiences have differed considerably in detail. Counterurbanisation, when defined as a negative relationship between rate of population change and size of city region (or functional urban region), was already strongly developed in Britain before the end of the 1960s and peaked in the early-1970s (Champion, 1987); whereas in West Germany this phenomenon did not become a dominant element of population change patterns until the mid-1970s, and has subsequently intensified (Kontuly and Vogelsang, 1989). On the other hand, the latest information (provided by the official population estimates for local authority areas in England and Wales) indicates that, while the recovery of London's population change rate has been maintained into the latter half of the 1980s, population growth is again accelerating in rural Britain and is now not far short of the peak levels attained during the period of most rapid counterurbanisation in the early-1970s (Britton, 1986; OPCS, 1988).

This chapter concentrates on recent population trends for Britain (i.e. excluding Northern Ireland), and some of the data relate only to England and Wales. It is planned that a comparative analysis of British and West German trends will be carried out over the next two years. The key issue, in the British case, is the co-existence of 'back to the city' and 'back to the country' movements in the 1980s; basically, how is it that both London and rural Britain can be performing so strongly in comparison with recent past experience? The answer to this apparent paradox requires an investigation of the population trends, not only in these two types of area, but also for other settlement types which have presumably declined in their aggregate attractiveness since the 1970s.

Back to the countryside and back to the city in the same decade

'Back to the countryside and back to the city in the same decade' was the title of a perceptive paper by Larry H. Long (Long, 1980). It referred to the American scene in the 1970s, which began with the recognition of the reversal of migration flows between metropolitan and non-metropolitan areas, and ended with increasing attention being paid to the revitalisation of city neighbourhoods through gentrification. This was very similar to the British experience of the 1970s, during which the fortunes of rural areas formed a mirror image of population trends in the larger cities. In 1980s' Britain, however, the available data seem to show that the 'back to the countryside' and 'back to the city' movements were taking place simultaneously, breaking the previously inverse relationship.

The evidence for this assertion is presented in Figure 4.1, which shows the population change rate, relative to the national average for the two extremes of the settlement system in England and Wales. This is based on annual population estimates for local authority districts, distinguishing the performance of the 13 inner London boroughs with that of a group of 78 districts, classified as 'remoter, largely rural, districts' by the Office of Population Censuses and Surveys (OPCS, 1981), following Webber and Craig (1980). The graph in Figure 4.1 clearly shows the inverse relationship between the two types of areas in the 1960s and 1970s, as the rate of population loss from inner London first accelerated and then subsided steadily after 1970-1, and as the gains for 'more rural' areas peaked in 1972-4. Figure 4.1 also shows that the rate of growth for the rural category, relative to the national rate, reached a low point in 1980-1 but, thereafter, accelerated back towards the level of the early-1970s. The turning point at the beginning of the 1980s was, however, accompanied not by a new surge of population loss from inner London, but by a further sharp reduction in losses. This recovery has been maintained into the mid-1980s, seemingly unaffected by the acceleration in rural growth.

The context of the wider settlement system

The direct answer to the paradox of lower population losses in London, and more rapid growth in rural areas, must be sought in the relative deterioration in the population growth performance of other parts of the settlement system. Table 4.1 gives a complete picture of population trends during the period 1961-87, for a total of 10 types of districts, as identified by the OPCS in 1981. It shows the actual rate of population change (expressed as an annual rate per 1,000 people), rather than in terms of differences from the national rate.

Figure 4.1: Population change (annual percentages) in inner London and 'remoter, largely rural, districts' of England and Wales, 1961-87

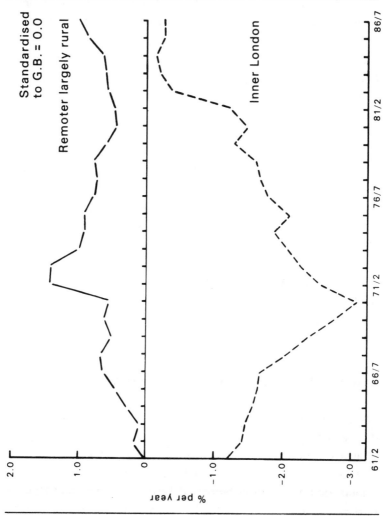

* the values on the graph are expressed as deviations from the national change rate.

Source: Champion, A.G. (ed.), *Counterurbanization,* Edward Arnold, forthcoming.

Table 4.1: England and Wales: average annual population change rates, 1961-87, by type of district (annual rate per 1,000 people)

type of district	1961 -66	1966 -71	1971 -74	1974 -77	1977 -81	1981 -84	1984 -87
GREATER LONDON BOROUGHS	-4	-9	-12	-12	-7	-2	+1
inner London	-8	-19	-21	-19	-15	-5	0
outer London	-1	-2	-6	-7	-3	-1	+1
METROPOLITAN DISTRICTS	+2	0	-4	-5	-4	-4	-3
principal cities	-8	-8	-11	-10	-8	-5	-4
other districts	+7	+4	-1	0	-3	-3	-2
NON-METROPOLITAN DISTRICTS	+13	+10	+8	+4	+5	+3	+6
cities	+1	-2	-2	-4	-3	-3	-4
industrial	+8	+7	+7	+1	+2	-1	+1
with New Towns	+23	+19	+16	+14	+14	+8	+9
resort, port and retirement	+14	+10	+9	+5	+5	+7	+13
other urban, etc.*	+23	+17	+9	+6	+7	+5	+7
remoter, largely rural	+8	+10	+15	+9	+7	+6	+11
ENGLAND AND WALES	+6	+4	+2	0	+1	+1	+3

*Note: 'other urban, etc.' refers to 'other urban, mixed urban-rural and more accessible rural'.
Source: calculated from OPCS mid-year population estimates. To be published in Champion, A.G. (ed.), *Counterurbanization*, Edward Arnold, London, forthcoming.

It shows even more clearly the marked upward shift in change rate since 1981-4 for both inner London and the 'remoter, largely rural, districts', but this partly reflects the rise in the national rate of growth.

Looking at Table 4.1 as a whole, the most immediate impression is the reduction in population growth which took place during the 1970s in the so-called 'non-metropolitan districts'. In the case of 'cities' and 'industrial districts', the changes did no more than to parallel the national trend; but, for the three other types of districts (besides 'remoter, largely rural'), there was a much more substantial cutback in growth rate between the 1960s and the 1970s than occurred at national level. The Table also confirms the distinctiveness of the 'remoter, largely rural, districts' in being the only category which experienced faster growth in the early-1970s than in the 1960s: in doing so it moved against the national tendency. It would appear that the greater prominence of 'remoter, rural growth' at this time, was associated with a decline in the capacity of intermediate accessible levels of the settlement hierarchy to absorb the large scale of population losses from Greater London and the principal metropolitan cities.

Turning to the 1980s, Table 4.1 suggests that the principal feature of 1981-4 was a convergence in change rates, with rates of gains and losses, if they moved at all, both shifting back towards zero. The only exception to this was the 'resort, port and retirement', category. This, however, also accelerated in its growth rate between 1981-4 and between 1984-7, so, in fact, three of the 10 categories (the other two were inner London and the 'remoter, largely rural, districts'), recorded notably stronger upward shifts in population change rate during the 1980s. Judging from the evidence of Table 4.1, the reason why this was possible lies in the below-average resilience of the six metropolitan counties in aggregate (West Midlands, Greater Manchester, Merseyside, Tyne and Wear, and West and South Yorkshire) and of the non-metropolitan cities and districts with New Towns. It is also noteworthy that the 'industrial' and 'other urban' districts changed only in line with the national rate; in the 1980s they were performing at about the same level as in the 1970s, relative to the national average.

There is, therefore, some evidence here to support the assertion made by Fielding (1986), that deconcentration from larger to smaller settlements (also clearly documented for the early-1970s) was no longer the dominant feature of population redistribution by the beginning of the 1980s. While this counterurbanisation process may have been proceeding at a lower level, it was being accompanied by the effects of economic restructuring, which adversely affected the larger metropolitan centres and other industrial areas heavily reliant on traditional manufacturing activities. The process also involved the growth of settlement in areas possessing environmental attractions, such as resorts and countryside. There is evidence, too, that the more traditional destinations of metropolitan out-migration, notably the New Towns and 'other urban' category, have come up against capacity problems, particularly given the tight planning controls imposed on physical urban expansion.

The re-emergence of the north-south divide

At least part of the explanation for, firstly, the upswing in the population change rate for London and the remoter, rural areas and secondly, the relative downswing of several of the intermediate categories in the settlement hierarchy, can be found in the greater divergence between north and south which occurred in the 1980s. Indeed, Table 4.2 indicates that the differential in annual rate of growth per 1,000 people widened progressively from 3.8 points in 1977-81, to 4.9 points in 1981-4 and 6.2 in 1984-7. Between these last two periods, East Anglia, the East Midlands and the south-west have all recorded substantial rises in growth rate, with the south-west's renewed acceleration dating back to the beginning of the decade. No less dramatic, particularly in terms of absolute numbers of people, has been the turnaround of the south-east, from a high rate of loss in 1974-7 (only the north-west showed a faster rate of population decline), to a strong gain in the mid-1980s, exceeded only by the other three southern regions. In the 'north', only Wales managed to outpace the national upturn in growth rate between the early and mid-1980s, while Scotland, the northern region of England, and Yorkshire and Humberside were distinct 'laggards'.

Table 4.2: Great Britain; population change, 1971-87, by standard region (annual rate per 1,000 people)

region	1971-4	1974-7	1977-81	1981-4	1984-7
GREAT BRITAIN	+2.0	-0.3	+0.7	+0.6	+2.7
East Anglia	+16.1	+9.9	+9.3	+7.9	+12.7
South-west	+9.5	+5.5	+4.7	+6.1	+9.5
East Midlands	+8.4	+3.7	+4.3	+1.9	+5.9
South-east	-1.1	-2.4	+1.0	+2.0	+4.0
SOUTH TOTAL	+1.0	-1.1	-1.2	-1.8	-0.4
Wales	+5.4	+1.8	+1.1	-0.7	+3.4
West Midlands	+2.7	-0.8	+0.6	-0.7	+1.4
Yorkshire & Humberside	+1.7	-0.4	-0.1	-1.0	-0.3
North-west	-1.7	-3.2	-3.0	-3.3	-1.3
Northern	+0.2	-0.5	-2.5	-2.5	-1.8
Scotland	+0.3	-0.9	-2.2	-2.2	-2.2
NORTH TOTAL	+1.0	-1.1	-1.2	-1.8	-0.4
Difference between south and north	+2.0	+1.6	+3.8	+4.9	+6.2

Note: the regions are ranked in order of 1984-7 population change rate.

Source: calculated from mid-year estimates. To be published in Champion, A.G. and Townsend, A.R., *Contemporary Britain: a geographical perspective*, Edward Arnold, London, forthcoming.

Table 4.3: Great Britain; population change, 1981-5, by north/south and LLMA size categories

LLMA category	population 1981 (thousands)	population change 1981-5 (thousands)	rate*
	GREAT BRITAIN		
Large dominants	15,553.3	-171.9	-2.8
Cities	16,934.0	+111.7	+1.7
Towns	17,582.7	+235.6	+2.3
Rural areas	3,480.5	+69.1	+5.0
TOTAL	53,550.6	+244.5	+1.2
	NORTH		
Large dominants	7,736.1	-126.1	-4.1
Cities	10,430.2	-57.9	-1.4
Towns	9,764.5	+9.7	+0.3
Rural areas	1,739.8	+20.9	+3.0
TOTAL	29,670.6	-153.4	-1.3
	SOUTH		
Large dominants	7,817.2	-45.8	-1.5
Cities	6,503.7	+169.6	+6.5
Towns	7,818.3	+225.8	+7.2
Rural areas	1,740.8	+48.3	+6.9
TOTAL	23,800.0	+398.0	+4.2

*annual rate per 1,000 people.

Source: calculated from data supplied by CACI Market Analysis.

The significance of the reopening of the north-south divide lies in the relative importance of the two parts of the country for the types of settlement identified in Table 4.1 and Figure 4.1. Several of the intermediate categories, such as 'cities' and 'industrial districts', have a stronger representation of northern areas in their populations than do the 'remoter, largely rural,' and the 'resorts, ports and retirement' districts. Whatever the cause-effect relationship, the acceleration in growth rate for the two latter categories can be associated with their more southerly orientation. Moreover, by definition, Greater London is located in the south, whereas the six metropolitan counties and their principal cities lie north of the north-south line which, since the early-1980s, has been considered to stretch broadly from the Wash to the Severn estuary.

The relative importance of north-south and urban-rural dimensions

The relative importance of the two main dimensions of population redistribution in the 1980s can be established most accurately by reference to a special tabulation of population data for Local Labour Market Areas (LLMAs). These are functionally-defined areas, based on commuting hinterlands around urban concentrations of employment and retail floorspace. They were produced by the Centre for Urban and Regional Development Studies at Newcastle University, specifically for the analysis of urban and regional change in Britain. In Table 4.3 the 280 LLMAs of Great Britain are grouped according to population size/urban status in 1971, and by broad location north or south of the Wash-Severn Estuary line.

Table 4.3 highlights two particular points in relation to the discussion so far. First, it demonstrates very clearly that both dimensions of population change were operating in the first half of the 1980s. The annual growth rate for the south during this time was 4.2 per 1,000 people, whereas for the north it was declining by 1.3 per 1,000; a difference of 5.5 points. Meanwhile, a clear overall relationship is

92

found between smaller (in terms of population numbers) LLMA size and stronger population growth, with 7.8 points separating the change rates of the small 'rural' LLMAs from the 'large dominants', comprising London, Birmingham, Glasgow, Manchester, Liverpool and Newcastle-upon-Tyne. Secondly, Table 4.3 reveals a broad difference between north and south in the importance of the urban-rural dimension. Counterurbanisation appears to be more fully developed in the north, where there exists a regular progression in change rate between the largest and the smallest LLMAs. In the south, however, the only clear-cut distinction is the decline of London, with all the other size categories growing at a similar pace. The three non-London categories of the south are clearly benefiting, both from the continuing decline of London (albeit now on a small scale compared with the previous two decades), and from the depopulation of the north; their population growth can be seen to have been spread evenly across the size categories in proportion to their original population shares.

Underlying factors

Several factors appear to have contributed to the regional and urban differences in population change rate found in 1980s' Britain, and to the progression which these represent from the patterns of the 1960s and 1970s. They can most easily be described by reference to the broad framework of LLMA categories used in Table 4.3.

As has been noted by Salt and Flowerdew (1980), London constitutes the primary motor of migration flows in Britain, operating in net terms to draw in people from the northern half of the country and to disperse people outwards to other parts of the south. The reduction in population losses from London since the early-1970s can be related primarily to a reduction in gross out-migration to the rest of the south, resulting from a combination of the winding up of the New, and Expanded, Towns programme, the general scarcity of sites with permission for housebuilding, and the more difficult economic climate of the late-1970s. The trend was reinforced by a rise in net in-migration to London from the north during the main recessionary years of 1979-82 and also by an increase in net international immigration into London in 1983-6. This can be related to a major recovery in London's employment, with particularly strong growth of jobs in financial and related services, involving both domestic and international labour (Champion and Congdon, 1988a; 1988b).

The reduction in the rate of population growth of the rest of the south during the 1970s can be explained principally in terms of the fall in the level of net out-migration from the London area at this time. Its subsequent acceleration is only partly the result of a further increase in the rate of exodus from London to these areas: it has more to do with the general widening of the economic divide between north and south. The rest of the south has 'benefited' considerably from proximity to the strong London economy, not only through an increase in long-distance commuting to central London, but also because of the decentralisation of more routine 'back-office' work. Moreover, as outlined by Fielding (1989), a further element of the restructuring of production has involved the growth of 'prestige areas', with attractive natural and cultural environments, which are popular with highly-qualified staff involved in research and other specialised activities. This would account for the rapid population growth in traditional resorts and retirement areas, noted earlier in this chapter. It would also explain the reinforcement of growth in the rural areas, either through their inherent features, or their lower levels of development pressure.

Finally, the patterns of population growth in the north tend to reflect the negative aspects of the recent round of economic restructuring. Its clear counterurbanisation pattern of population change in the 1980s is due more to the differential effects of restructuring than it is to the inherent attractiveness of the towns and rural areas. Basically, the rural areas had fewest traditional manufacturing jobs to lose in the major contraction of the early-1980s. Moreover, the larger northern cities have found it hard to attract, or even retain, jobs in the strongly-growing financial and producer-services sector which has become increasingly concentrated in the London region. It is also the case that urban deconcentration did not get under way in the north as early as it did in the south. Although the process slowed in the late-1970s, it has maintained considerable momentum in the 1980s, no doubt spurred on by the deterioration of conditions in the conurbations and by the low level of development pressures, compared with rural areas in the south.

Summary and conclusions

According to the most recent population estimates, the population growth of rural Britain, following a decade of more modest growth, is accelerating towards the peak rates recorded in the early-1970s. At the same time, London is now broadly maintaining its recovery from the massive levels of population loss which it sustained in the 1960s and 1970s. This chapter has examined the background to this apparent contradiction of the counterurbanisation model.

It has been found that the population geography of 1980s' Britain is dominated by the reopening of the north-south divide, together with some resurgence of urban deconcentration after the main period of economic recession in 1979-82. While all large cities experienced some reduction in net out-migration during the late-1970s, the slowdown was most dramatic for London. The capital city also benefited disproportionately from a rise in net international migration into the United Kingdom in 1983-6.

The relatively strong performance of rural Britain can be attributed to the wide spread of rapid population growth in the south, which has affected its rural areas as much as its larger towns and cities. In the north, rural areas have not grown as rapidly as their southern counterparts but, nevertheless, with a distinct negative correlation between settlement size and population growth rate here, they have certainly been much more dynamic than the north's urban areas.

These broader regional developments can be linked to the continued restructuring of the British economy away from traditional manufacturing and particularly towards financial and related services. This process is primarily a response to the changing international market, but has been reinforced by government policies in economic management and regional policy. The renewed intensity of rural population growth, particularly in southern Britain, can be related to the build-up of urban development pressures in more accessible areas, as well as to further improvements in transport and communications and a general increase in mobility, due to the economic recovery.

References

Britton, M., 'Recent population changes in perspective', in: *Population Trends,* Vol. 44, pp. 33-41, 1986.

Champion, A.G., 'Recent changes in the pace of population deconcentration in Britain', in: *Geoforum,* Vol. 18, pp. 379-401, 1987.

Champion, A.G., 'United Kingdom: population deconcentration as a cyclic phenomenon', in Champion, A.G. (ed.), *Counterurbanization,* Edward Arnold, London, forthcoming.

Champion, A.G. and Congdon, P.D., 'Recent trends in Greater London's population', in: *Population Trends,* Vol. 53, pp. 11-17, 1988a.

Champion, A.G. and Congdon, P.D., 'An analysis of the recovery of London's population change rate', in: *Built Environment,* Vol. 13, pp. 193-211, 1988b.

Cochrane, S.G. and Vining, D.R., 'Recent trends in migration between core and peripheral regions in developed and advanced developing countries', in: *Working papers in regional science and transportation,* Regional Science Department, University of Pennsylvania, Vol. 108, 1986.

Fielding, A.J., 'Counterurbanization in western Europe', in: *Progress in Planning,* Vol. 17, pp. 1-52, 1982.

Fielding, A.J., 'Counterurbanisation', in: Pacione, M. (ed.), *Population geography: progress and prospects,* Croom Helm, London, pp. 224-56, 1986.

Fielding, A.J., 'Migration and urbanization in western Europe since 1950', in: *The Geographical Journal*, Vol: 153, pp. 56-61, 1989.

Kontuly, T. and Vogelsang, R., 'Federal Republic of Germany: the intensification of the turnaround', in: Champion, A.G. (ed.), *Counter-urbanization*, Edward Arnold, London, forthcoming.

Long, L.H., 'Back to the countryside and back to the city in the same decade', in: Laska, S.B. and Spain, D. (eds.), *Back to the city: issues in neighbourhood renovation*, Pergamon, New York, pp. 6l-76, 1980.

OPCS, *Census 1981*, preliminary report, England and Wales, HMSO, London, 1981.

OPCS, *Population estimates for local authorities and health authorities, mid-1987*, Office of Population Censuses and Surveys, London, Monitor PP1 88/1, 1988.

Salt, J. and Flowerdew, R., 'Labour migration from London', in: *The London Journal*, Vol. 6, pp. 36-50, 1980.

Vining, D.R. and Kontuly, T., 'Population dispersal from major metropolitan regions: an international comparison', in: *International Regional Science Review*, Vol. 3, pp. 49-73, 1978.

Webber, R. and Craig, J., 'Which local authorities are alike?', in: *Population Trends*, Vol. 5, pp. 13-19, 1980.

Chapter V

Günter Thieme (Universität Bonn)

Spatial aspects of socioeconomic disparities in West Germany: a comparison of indicators

While both Britain and West Germany are certainly well to the fore amongst the world's developed industrial countries, they both have striking regional inequalities and imbalances. On the one hand, these have a socioeconomic component; the slogans of the 'two nations' and the 'two-thirds society' illustrate this very clearly. On the other hand, in close connection with the social disparities, yet by no means identical to them, distinct regional structures have developed in both countries. These have not only become common objects of study in economics and social science, puzzling regional planners, but have also become important issues for the media and the general public.

Particularly notable trends in the patterning of regional differences in West Germany are the declining classical contrasts between town and country, between urban agglomerations and rural areas, and between industrialised and predominantly agricultural regions. Indeed, it becomes more and more evident today that major spatial disparities exist, not so much between urban and rural areas themselves, but actually within these two very basic types of space. This means that it is now necessary to distinguish between old industrial and service-orientated urban agglomerations, and between agricultural, early industrialised and tourist-orientated rural areas (Sinz and Strubelt, 1986). However, in the eyes of the media and the public, these specific regional structures are superseded by what is now frequently referred to as the 'Nord-Süd Gefälle', or north-south divide. Regardless of how much this is a myth or a reality - the answer depends largely on which indicators are chosen - the concept of a macro-scaled regional divide is now firmly established in West Germany, as well as in Britain (Champion et al., 1987). It is all the more important, therefore, to avoid the use of clichés and stereotypes; a danger that is particularly imminent because the north-south economic contrast in West Germany also has a political component. Until recently the electoral geography of this country showed a pattern of a predominantly Social-Democratic north and an overwhelmingly Conservative-voting south. This has a striking parallel to the situation in Britain. The question: 'does it matter where I live?' is now entering into discussions of such issues as differential mortality and life expectancy in the United Kingdom (Howe, 1986). But this debate can only be rhetoric, since regional disparities are, of course, of great importance, because they influence the living conditions and life chances of populations and social groups within differently-equipped parts of the country (Taubmann, 1980).

The choice of indicators is crucial in measuring degrees and spatial patterns of regional disparities. Accordingly, it is worth making a few comments on the theoretical background of indicators and indicator systems before presenting empirical results. An initial problem is the question of the scale of spatial units. Several studies on the north-south divide in West Germany are based on the very unsatisfactory spatial level of the *Bundesländer*, or Federal states (Kiesewetter, 1986; Körber-Weik and Wied-Nebbeling, 1986). Some of the results of these studies have been quite instructive, but the use of these far too generalised spatial units masks very important internal variations within the various *Länder*. Much more satisfactory, for the purpose of measuring regional disparities, is West Germany's spatial framework of 344 *Kreise*, or 'county districts' (these include 91 *Kreisfreiestädte*, or autonomous cities).

A second issue revolves around the point that any analysis of regional imbalances must call into question its ultimate point of reference. Should it be the economic strength of regions that matters the most, or should it be the quality of human living conditions, whichever way they are defined? Must economic variables exclusively be used for regional analysis, or should a wider field of spheres of life

100

be included, according to the ideas of the geography of social well-being? Is the selection of indicators to be based on objective indicators, or on the subjective perception of problem fields? (Pacione, 1982; Thieme, 1985). Depending upon the answer to such conceptual questions, the emphasis of analysis will be placed on quite different aspects of social life and different spatial patterns. Bearing this in mind, we can now consider a number of economic and social indicators, and then proceed to examine their spatial representation.

In West Germany the most important spatial contrast used to be the traditional one, between urban industrialised areas and rural agricultural areas. Until fairly recently, all frameworks for regional development and regional policy in West Germany indicated extensive rural regions as 'depressed areas', 'retarded areas', and areas with specific deficits in employment and/or infrastructure. Very typical of this identification of many rural parts of the country as the nation's main problem areas is a well-known paper by Gatzweiler (1979), carrying the English title of *Rural areas - handicapped forever?* Opinions like this were usually derived from indicators of economic strength and income levels. Measures such as gross domestic product or gross value added per capita are, indeed, still among the most popular indicators of regional economic 'health' and status. There are good reasons, however, for the view that these conventional measurements are of very limited validity, especially if the objective of analysis is to assess the actual living standards of regional populations. In fact, measurements like gross domestic product and gross value added only serve to emphasise economic achievements. Accordingly, they tend to highlight the places of production and neglect the actual utilisation of these economic achievements in the places where people live.

Figure 5.1: West Germany; regional pattern of gross value-added indicator, 1982 (DM per inhabitant)

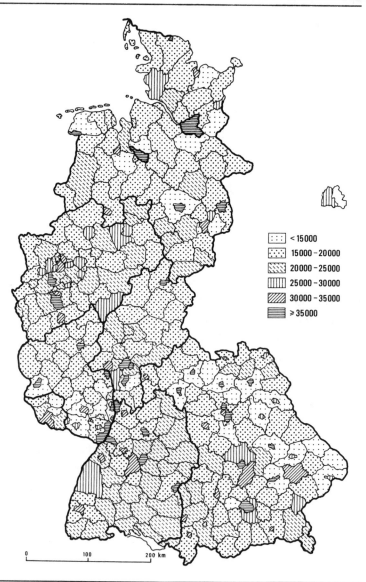

Legend:
- `< 15000`
- `15000 – 20000`
- `20000 – 25000`
- `25000 – 30000`
- `30000 – 35000`
- `≥ 35000`

0   100   200 km

Source: after Böltken et al., 1987.

When one views the spatial distribution of the gross value-added economic indicator (Figure 5.1), it is the central cities of the main agglomeration areas that stand out with the highest values. Apart from these, and several other towns and cities, only a small number of areas, mostly representing manufacturing districts, have high values. Interestingly, suburban districts around the agglomeration areas show quite low values, even though they are normally considered to be prosperous and privileged in many repects. This anomaly is due to the statistical fact that the gross value-added of each *Kreis* district is divided by its number of inhabitants. This procedure does not take into account the intensive commuter flows between the central cities and the agglomeration fringes. Macroscaled disparities of economic strength, such as the north-south divide, are difficult to assess on the basis of this indicator: for example, only the comparatively low figures for the Ruhr area provide something of a hint of the present problematic situation of this northern regional giant.

Much more convincing are the figures of average per capita income calculated by the *Gesellschaft für Konsum-, Markt- und Absatzforschung* (GFK). This measurement of regional differences in purchasing power is based on income tax statistics. It also includes weightings for transfer payments by the state (unemployment benefits, child allowances, rent rebates and public assistance), and untaxed agricultural incomes (Fischer, 1983). These tend to moderate rural-urban contrasts. Unfortunately, however, this index of purchasing power is not readily available for all parts of the country; it is only possible to present the values for *Kreise* within Baden-Württemberg, Bavaria and parts of Rhineland-Palatinate (Figure 5.2). The two most important agglomeration areas in southern Germany, Munich and Stuttgart, with their particularly high figures of medium per capita incomes, contrast markedly with the much lower values of the rural agricultural areas and the peripheral regions of northern Bavaria, especially those which adjoin the borders of East Germany and Czechoslovakia.

Figure 5.2: Southern Germany; regional pattern of average per capita income, 1986

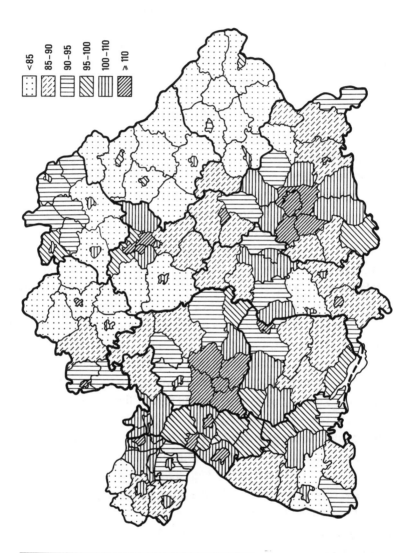

* index, national average = 100.
Source: Kaufkraftkennziffern der GFK, 1987.

Figure 5.3: West Germany; regional pattern of unemployment, September 1986

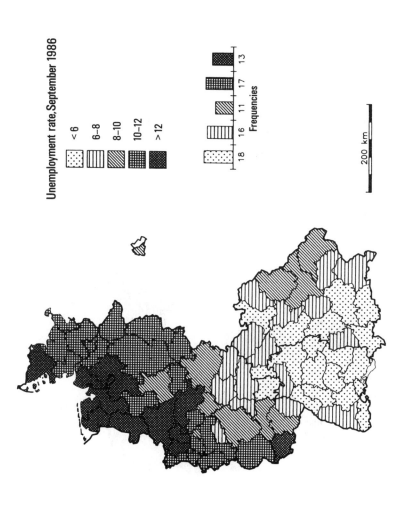

Source: after Böltken et al., 1987.

Figure 5.4: West Germany; regional pattern of long-term unemployment, September 1986

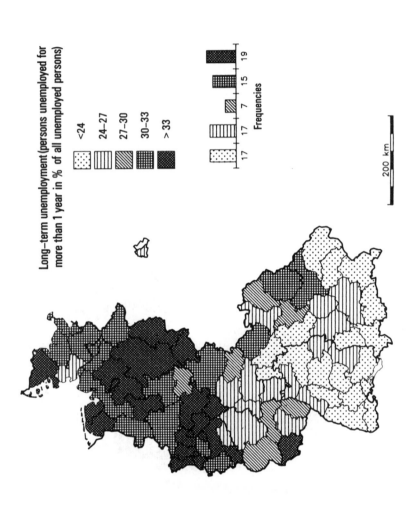

Source: after Böltken et al., 1987.

Figure 5.5: West Germany; north-south transect of unemployment rates, 1980 and 1986

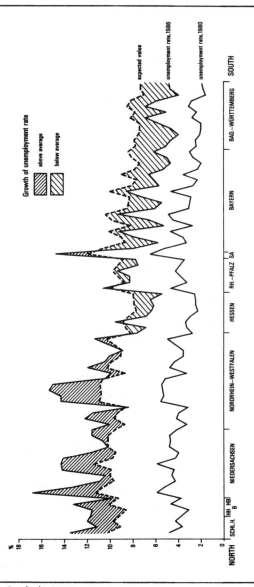

Source: after Strubelt, 1986.

Up to this point in our discussion, the regional imbalances which have been measured are those which are largely orientated along the lines of the classical polarities of regional policy. However, when we consider indicators from the spheres of occupation and unemployment, a much different type of regional picture, now dominated by north-south differences, becomes clearly evident. We can turn, first of all, to two indicators of unemployment - the unemployment rate of September 1986 (Figure 5.3) and the proportion of this which is classified as long-term unemployment (Figure 5.4). Mapped out on the basis of official regional units (*Regionen*), the general pattern is quite similar in both cases: regions with high unemployment rates and, at the same time, a high share of long-term unemployed, are most frequently found in northern Germany. In contrast, the regions of Baden-Württemberg tend to have very low unemployment rates: in the Stuttgart area in 1986, they were as low as the 4% level. The belt of low unemployment in southern Germany extends well into western and southern Bavaria. In this once very rural part of the country, it is interesting to observe also that some of the most easterly-lying *Kreise* (which little more than a decade ago had featured amongst West Germany's worst unemployment blackspots) have improved their position considerably, and only show moderate levels in the two maps.

The next map, Figure 5.5, illustrates a transect across the country, from the extreme north to the far south, showing unemployment rates at the median points of all regions and cities along this line. The graph clearly demonstrates that the south, almost without exception, has improved its position in the labour market. Proceeding from the national unemployment rate of the earlier year (1980), a scenario for 1986 was calculated, under the assumption that the degree of change in each of the represented regions and places was the same average trend. During the short period of 1980-6, there was an overall increase in unemployment in West Germany, from around 4% to 7%. In reality, most of the north German locations can be seen to have exceeded the projected figures significantly at the latter date; on the other hand, most of the southern locations were able to record unemployment rates well below the expected levels.

Likewise, the south is favoured by the job balance (Figure 5.6). Of those regions that were able to experience job creation in sufficient numbers to compensate for (or even to exceed) the loss of traditional sources of employment, the large majority are to be found in southern Germany, especially in Baden-Württemberg and Bavaria. In addition to the distinct north-south contrast in the job-balance map, it should be noticed that the strongest gains in numbers of workplaces tend to occur in suburban and, not uncommonly, even in rural areas. This is clearly reflective of the suburbanisation and centrifugal trend in the location of new economic activity and related job creation.

Below-average labour market trends and above-average unemployment rates are bound to exert serious social effects on the afflicted cities and other urban centres. From 1970 to 1985 the numbers of recipients of social welfare benefits in West Germany grew by a huge 88% (*Statistisches Bundesamt*, 1987), with much the larger share of this increase coming from the ranks of urban dwellers. Even in times of generally-growing affluence, poverty has by no means disappeared. Moreover, the phenomenon of poverty in West Germany today, is no longer restricted to social fringe groups. The major recipients of public assistance are unemployed people who, even after being provided with their statutory benefits, qualify for additional public assistance to provide an adequate living.

Looking at the spatial pattern of social benefits distribution (Figure 5.7), the north-south divide is again clearly visible. A strong urban-rural contrast is also evident. Moreover, different levels of prosperity between major cities are also represented: for example, compare the low showing (therefore high prosperity) of Stuttgart and Munich with the much higher proportions (therefore low prosperity) of social welfare recipients in the northern cities of Hamburg, Bremen, West Berlin and several of the Ruhr cities.

Figure 5.6: West Germany; regional pattern of employment growth and decline, 1980-5

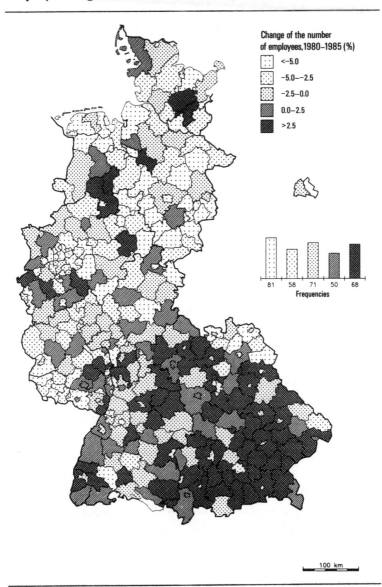

Change of the number
of employees,1980–1985 (%)

- <-5.0
- -5.0--2.5
- -2.5-0.0
- 0.0-2.5
- >2.5

81 58 71 50 68
Frequencies

100 km

Source: after Böltken et al., 1987.

110

Figure 5.7: West Germany; regional pattern of social benefits distribution, 1985

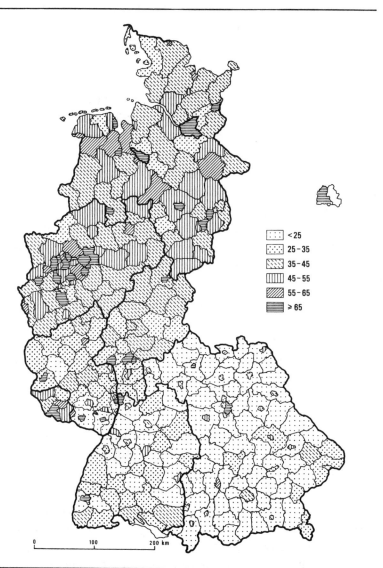

`:::`	< 25
`:::`	25 – 35
`\\\\`	35 – 45
`||||`	45 – 55
`///`	55 – 65
`≡`	≥ 65

0   100   200 km

the values are recipients of social benefits per 1,000 population.
Source: after Böltken et al., 1987.

On the causes and the background of the north-south divide, there is a substantial body of literature available, both for the British, and for the West German case. It is not the purpose of this chapter to discuss this in detail, but rather to cast doubts upon some preconceptions and to present a few hypotheses. The north-south divide in West Germany cannot primarily, or even exclusively, be ascribed to different regional branch structures of industry. Of course, the coastal regions of northern Germany, for example, do suffer acutely from the problems of their ailing shipbuilding industries, and the Ruhr and Saar areas have to endure the burdens of their declining coal, iron and steel industries. However, the south possesses a sizeable share of West Germany's recessive industrial branches too: for example, textiles and clothing manufactures, which are to be found in southern Baden-Württemberg and several parts of Bavaria. Moreover, the north, despite its economic problems, does, in fact, have a somewhat higher level of occupational involvement in the generally-prosperous service sector. The deciding differences of productivity are not to be found *between* industrial branches, but *within* them (Sinz and Strubelt,1986), with a strong growth component in favour of the south. Concentration on specialised high-quality production, heavy involvement in research and development activities, and strong investment in appropriate product and process innovations, are now crucial factors effecting the leading positions of the main southern agglomerations of Frankfurt, Stuttgart and Munich.

Among other attempts at explaining the north-south divide in West Germany, of particular interest are those which stress the historical dimension, especially the studies which incorporate Veblen's (1915) long-established theory of the 'advantage of backwardness'. During the late-nineteenth century the southern states and provinces of the German Empire were very much 'latecomers' to mechanised forms of industrialisation. However, this very lateness eventually proved to be a long-term advantage, because, compared with many northern regions, southern Germany was (and still is) less conditioned by, and less committed to, traditional industrial structures. The example of

Württemberg, especially the Stuttgart area, shows how an initial pattern of trade and industry, characterised by a diverse branch structure, close ties between agriculture and manufacturing, proximity of residence to place of work, and high levels of female participation, could adapt quite easily and flexibly to changing economic requirements. In particular, the high levels of female employment, which were, and are, so typical of this part of West Germany, ease problems in the labour markets and also have the positive effect of increasing the purchasing power of local families and, through this, improving their material living standards. Two additional comments concerning the north-south contrast should be made:

- firstly, its appearance in West Germany can, to some extent, be viewed as a consequence of deliberate government (Federal and *Land*) regional development policy, not the least in decisions on the locations of military industrial plants;

- secondly, the importance of so-called 'soft' locational factors, such as recreational value and quality of environment, must now be stressed. These factors are gaining in significance today, especially in the recruitment of key executive and managerial staff.

Figure 5.8: West Germany; regional pattern of net internal migration rate, 1983-5

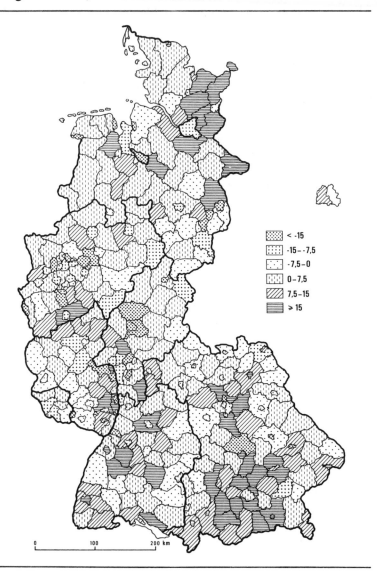

Legend:
- < -15
- -15 – -7,5
- -7,5 – 0
- 0 – 7,5
- 7,5 – 15
- ≥ 15

0   100   200 km

* the values are net migration rate per 1,000 population.
Source: after Böltken et al., 1987.

Figure 5.9: West Germany; regional pattern of average life expectancy index

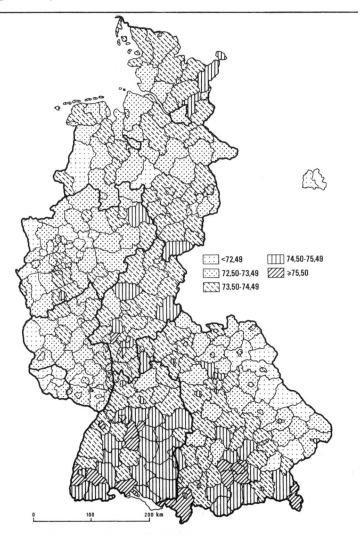

Legend:
- ⬚ <72,49
- ⬚ 72,50-73,49
- ⬚ 73,50-74,49
- ⬚ 74,50-75,49
- ⬚ ⩾75,50

0   100   200 km

---

* the values are averages of life expectancy at birth, taken over the years 1979-81.
Source: Bundesforschungsanstalt für Landeskunde und Raumordnung, Bad Godesberg, unpublished material.

115

Other important social indicators are regional figures of the net-migration trend and of life expectancy. These, however, do not produce a very pronounced north-south divide. In theory, migration flows are supposed to follow patterns of economic disparities, but, as can be seen in Figure 5.8, the real pattern of internal migration in West Germany is not so straightforward. Viewed in broad terms, there is something of a general north-south difference here, with southern Germany having a substantially higher proportion of *Kreise* receiving in-migration during the years 1983-5, and the north having a much lower proportion. But there are also quite extensive areas in the north which did record sizeable gains: for example, the north-western parts of Lower Saxony which, despite recording some of West Germany's highest unemployment rates, received significant inflows of people. Important, too, in Figure 5.8, is the contrast between cities and their suburbanised fringes; most of the 'big' cities suffering heavy population losses to their surrounding districts.

The map of life expectancy (Figure 5.9), likewise does not reflect a very clearly-defined north-south divide. However, a few characteristics do point in this direction. There exists a quite considerable range of regional differences (maximum difference of six years), and the spatial pattern, although complex, is far from being accidental. Long life expectancies can be found, both in economically-prosperous regions, and in those parts of the country which have high recreational value and charming landscapes, such as the Lake Constance area, the southern Black Forest and the Bavarian Alps. It is regions like these which are characterised today by the in-migration of persons with high incomes and high social status. Explanation of spatial differences in life expectancy is made very difficult, because of the complexity and interdependence of various influencing factors. It is true to say, however, that, rather more so than regional differences in diet, degree of environmental pollution and quantity and quality of medical care (which can all be important factors themselves), variations in regional economic health have a paramount effect. Indeed, the economic dimension also influences regional trends, and levels of migration and life expectancy. Physical health is not least a consequence of the economic well-being of a person and of the region in which he or she lives. The correlation coefficient of -0.68 between life expectancy and unemployment rate (computed for 156 *Kreise* in southern Germany), supports this contention (Thieme, 1988).

This chapter does not propose specific measures of regional intervention. However, if the basic aim of West German regional policy is still to reduce regional disparities throughout the country, it will have to bear in mind that new types of inequalities, primarily those that are developing between the north and the south, are now superseding the traditional differences.

References

Böltken, F. et al., 'Laufende Raumbeobachtung. Aktuelle Daten zur Entwicklung der Städte, Kreise und Gemeinden 1986', in: *Bundesforschungsanstalt für Landeskunde und Raumordnung Seminare-Symposien-Arbeitspapier*, Heft. 28, 1987.

Champion, A.G. et al., *Changing places. Britain's demographic, economic and social complexion*, Edward Arnold, London, 1987.

Fischer, K. et al., 'Die reale Kaufkraft in Bayern', in: *Jahrbuch der Absatz- und Verbrauchsforschung*, Heft. 29, pp. 89-200, 1983.

Friedrichs, J., Häussermann, H. and Siebel, W. (eds.), *Süd-Nord-Gefälle in der Bundesrepublik? Sozialwissenschaftliche Analysen*, Westdeutsche Verlag, Opladen, 1986.

Gatzweiler, H.P., 'Der ländliche Raum - benachteiligt für alle Zeiten?', in: *Geographische Rundschau*, Heft. 31, pp. 10-16, 1979.

Green, A.E., 'The north-south divide in Great Britain: an examination of the evidence', in: *Transactions Institute of British Geographers, New Series*, Vol. 13, pp. 179-98, 1988.

Howe, M., 'Does it matter where I live?', in: *Transactions Institute of British Geographers, New Series*, Vol. 11, pp. 387-414, 1986.

Kiesewetter, H., 'Das wirtschaftliche Gefälle zwischen Nord- und Süddeutschland in historischer Perspektive', in: *Neues Archiv für Niedersachsen*, Heft. 35, pp. 327-47, 1986.

Körber-Weik, M. and Wied-Nebbeling, S., 'Ein wirtschaftliches Süd-Nord-Gefälle in der Bundesrepublik Deutschland? Wirtschaftskraft und Wirtschaftsentwicklung der Bundesländer im Vergleich', in: *Der Burger im Staat,* Heft. 36, pp. 275-82, 1986.

Lewis, J. and Townsend, A. (eds.), *The north-south divide. Regional change in Britain in the 1980s,* Paul Chapman, London, 1988.

Martin, R., 'The political economy of Britain's north-south divide', in: *Transactions Institute of British Geographers, New Series,* Vol. 13, pp. 389-418, 1988.

Nuhn, H., and Sinz, M., 'Industriestruktureller Wandel und Beschäftigungsentwicklung in der Bundesrepublik Deutschland', in: *Geographische Rundschau,* Heft. 40:1, pp. 42-52, 1988.

Pacione, M., 'The use of objective and subjective measures of life quality in human geography', in: *Progress in Human Geography,* Vol. 6, pp. 495-514, 1982.

Sinz, M. and Strubelt, W., 'Zur Diskussion über das wirtschaftliche Süd-Nord-Gefälle unter Berücksichtigung entwicklungsgeschichtlicher Aspekte', in: Friedrichs, J., Häussermann, H. and Siebel, W. (eds.), *Süd-Nord-Gefälle in der Bundesrepublik? Sozialwissenschaftliche Analysen,* Westdeutscher Verlag, Opladen, pp. 12-50, 1986.

Statistisches Bundesamt (ed.). 'Datenreport 1987. Zahlen und Fakten über die Bundesrepublik Deutschland', in: *Schriftenreihe der Bundeszentrale für Politische Bildung,* p. 257, 1987.

Strubelt, W., 'Die Raumstruktur in der Bundesrepublik Deutschland zwischen Hoffnung und Resignation. Ein 'räumlicher' Essay', in: *Informationen zur Raumentwicklung,* Heft. 11 and 12, pp. 821-28, 1986.

Taubmann, W., 'Räumliche Disparitäten. Das Beispiel der Bundesrepublik', in: *Geographie heute,* Heft. 1, pp. 2-11, 1980.

Thieme, G., 'Sozialindikatoren in der Geographie. Möglichkeiten und Probleme der Analyse regionaler Disparitäten', in: *Colloquium Geographicum,* Heft. 18, pp. 213-4, 1985.

Thieme, G., *Disparitäten der Lebensbedingungen im raumzeitlichen Vergleich. Theoretische Grundlagen und empirische Untersuchungen am Beispiel Süddeutschlands 1895 und 1980,* Habilitationsschrift, Universität Bonn, in preparation.

Veblen, T., *Imperial Germany and the industrial revolution,* New York, 1915.

Chapter VI

Derek Spooner (University of Hull)

Across the great divide: restructuring at the local scale in eastern England

Introduction: regional and local scales of uneven development

'The pattern of uneven development is now one of increasing spatial division at a variety of geographical scales.' (Martin, 1989)

The symposium which initiated this volume was based in Hull and Cambridge, two cities which are strategically positioned for first-hand examination of the reality of the north-south divide in the United Kingdom, and the fortunes of individual localities on either side of this line, which is usually suggested to run from Severnside to Lincolnshire. 'Location' visits were made to a selection of local economies as representative examples of 'winners' and 'losers' in contemporary Britain. With the exception of the inner-city area of London Docklands, these were all medium-sized towns; two of them (Cambridge and Scunthorpe) 'free-standing', and the three others (Castleford, Wakefield and Halifax) set within the former metropolitan county of West Yorkshire. The problems of industrial decline featured strongly in all these cases except Cambridge, as did the need for the restructuring of the local economy to adapt it to new regimes of capital accumulation and changing positions in the international division of labour. In simplistic terms, such places illustrate the dichotomies of 'sunrise' and 'smokestack' landscapes in the Britain of the late 1980s. This chapter reports on this experience. No attempt is made to provide a rigorous statistical comparison of the performance of the various towns under scrutiny. Rather than this, it is the intention to provide a set of cameos of the variety of circumstances and conditions that create uneven development at the local, as well as at the regional scale, and the role of different actors and agencies in the pursuit of local restructuring.

Analysis of uneven development in the United Kingdom has proceeded most frequently via broad regional categories such as 'north' and 'south', or 'centre' and 'periphery', often utilising data for the set of 11 Standard Regions. Analysis of regional trends at this macroscale reveals patterns, such as the north-divide, which are hardly in serious dispute (Green, 1988). The broad pattern of regional fortunes is also relatively persistent, although it may be temporarily disrupted (as, for example, with the fall in standing of the manufacturing-based economy of the West Midlands in the early 1980s), and suggests a rippling out of growth impulses from a dynamic metropolitan core in the south-east, as well as the 'two nations' syndrome of rich south/centre and poor north/periphery.

However, geographers and other writers have increasingly drawn attention to the pattern of *subregional* variation - the varied mosaic of regional fortunes within the acknowledged broad regional divisions (Regional Studies Association, 1983); in the words of Martin,

'like regional differentials, interlocality inequalities have widened dramatically as a result of the contemporary restructuring process'.

Within each of the 11 Standard Regions there are patterns of polarisation and disjunction (and major variations in performance and prosperity) between urban and rural, between inner city and suburb, and between large, medium and small urban centres. However, as this chapter will illustrate, intraregional differences also exist, even between similar-sized industrial towns, reflecting their specific problems, inherited characteristics and different potentialities. New growth sectors and occupations respond in varied ways to perceived local conditions in different 'crisis' localities.

This chapter attempts to illustrate how the impact of dramatic and rapid industrial change has fallen upon different localities across the 'great divide', and how these localities are now restructuring at the end of the 1980s. That restructuring, of course, is not taking place entirely unaided. Regional and local restructuring can be a policy objective, pursued by actors and agencies from many different institutions and scales of operation. Various strategies of intervention may be pursued by these agents. Martin (1989) suggests six such strategies for regional or local restructuring:

- reindustrialisation (most often through the development of high-tech industry);
- modernisation of existing industry;
- tertiarisation;
- reskilling and 'flexibilisation' of the labour force;
- infrastructure renewal;
- the creation of regionally- and locally-based financial markets.

In practice, it is likely that policies will contain a mixture of these elements, with the nature of the mix reflecting, and responding to, local circumstances. In Britain, central government regional policy has been in eclipse during the Thatcher years, placing more onus on local and regional actors and agencies, while at the same time leading to quite sharp differentiation between the few residual favoured areas and the many non-favoured. Moreover, the establishment of more localised initiatives, like Enterprise Zones and Urban Development Corporations, has intensified the pattern of differentiation between localities within regions. In the late 1980s, the greater parsimony of central government aid has increased the importance of designation of favoured status from Brussels: many northern localities (including some which will be described in this chapter) campaigned desperately for inclusion in the listing of areas eligible for aid from the restructured EC regional funds.

There has been considerable attention paid, in recent years, to the relative merits of 'top-down' and 'bottom-up' approaches to regional and local regeneration. 'Bottom-up' policies strike a convenient chord with a national government which is wedded to a belief in the enterprise culture and self-help philosophy. In practice, within the 'north' there seems to be a growing gap between, on the one hand, the favoured few localities which still benefit from the largesse of government 'top-down' policies (assisted areas and Enterprise Zones capital subsidy) and, on the other hand, the non-favoured localities, where experimentation with bottom-up initiatives is not only desirable, but is very much a necessity in the absence of external aid. The case studies which will be described in this chapter illustrate quite strikingly the variety of subregional experiences in policy terms, and the impact which this is having on the form, direction and pace of the restructuring process.

The purpose of this chapter, therefore, is to emphasise the variety of local experience, and in the next two sections this will be illustrated with respect to four northern communities (all in the Yorkshire and Humberside Region) which might be characterised as 'losers'. They represent highly-specialised industrial areas of the old order - dependent on coal, textiles or steel. Champion and Green (1988), using 10 variables, constructed an 'amalgamated index' to rank the recent performances of Britain's 280 Labour Market Areas. Each of our example northern towns, Castleford, Wakefield, Halifax and Scunthorpe, lies in the bottom half of the rankings (Table 6.1, column 1). However, it is interesting to note that, of these four, Scunthorpe, with its Development Area and Enterprise Zones, is the only one which can be said to have been *strongly* favoured by government aid during the 1980s. Scunthorpe is also the only one to appear in the top half of Champion and Green's 'index of change' rankings (Table 6.1, column 2). There appears, therefore, to be a new growth dynamic in Scunthorpe, which is certainly not mirrored in Wakefield, Halifax or Castleford. The differential impact of policy on local restructuring is strongly suggested by this observation.

Table 6.1: 'Winners' and 'losers' in eastern England in the 1980s

LLMA	column 1	2	3	4	5	6	7
Castleford	250	269	13.6	4.4	37,791	-0.1	-9.2
Halifax	161	218	10.4	8.1	23,173	-1.5	-2.3
Scunthorpe	188	109	14.3	5.0	27,123	-1.7	+3.7
Wakefield	230	245	12.7	4.4	27,021	+0.6	-1.1
Cambridge	6	8	4.9	19.7	53,152	-0.9	+12.4

Key to columns:
1. 'Amalgamated index' (ranking out of 280 LLMAs).
2. 'Index of change', 1984-7.
3. Unemployment rate, July 1987 (as %).
4. % employed in producer services and high-tech industries, 1984.
5. Mean house price, 1986 (in £).
6. Change (percentage points) in unemployment rate, July 1984-July 1987.
7. Employment change (%), 1981-4.

Source: Champion and Green, 1988.

Cambridge, ranking sixth on the 'amalgamated index', contrasts clearly with all the other centres under study. Even at the beginning of the 1980s, it was already identified as 'one of the really booming places of contemporary Britain', and could be seen as part of a growth diagonal extending across southern England from Exeter to Norwich (Hall, 1981). More recently, Cooke (1986) saw it as one of a string of towns and cities in this belt, with a disproportionately large share of firms producing goods and services based on microprocessor technology, aerospace, computers, research, and business services. He describes these places as:

'the locations where housing demand is buoyant ... where land shortages caused by planning controls still exist, and where life-

styles, leisure patterns and political attitudes reflect the heightened market capacity which comes with high incomes ...'

The final section of this chapter will examine briefly the phenomenon of London Docklands; a locality which is embedded within the
inner city, and whose recent spectacular transformation has come to
symbolise many of the features of the Thatcherite enterprise culture.
This formerly decaying, redundant space showed clearly that local
conditions could be poor, even on the prosperous side of the north-
south divide; its revival illustrates dramatically the potential of a particular style of intervention, given a right combination of
circumstances and, in particular, a highly-favourable location
(though not without some negative consequences for the existing
Docklands residents).

Problems of restructuring in Yorkshire and Humberside: coal and textiles towns along the M62 Corridor

The Yorkshire and Humberside region is an artificial entity, and might
be seen as a 'greater Yorkshire'; it is intermediate in location and
economic performance between the prosperous and dynamic south,
and an 'outer', or peripheral, Britain. In the late 1960s, the region
was described by the Hunt Committee (Department of Economic
Affairs, 1969) as being 'economically vulnerable' and characterised
by slow growth. Its economic structure has traditionally been
weighted towards a relatively narrow group of manufacturing industries, and energy production. These features of a 'basic industrial
region' are particularly evident in the old metropolitan counties of
West and South Yorkshire, and have made the region especially liable
to the ravages of de-industrialisation during the 1970s and early
1980s, when its position on the 'wrong' side of the 'great divide' was
confirmed. In the late 1980s, some parts of Yorkshire and Humberside
have begun to recover, with new dynamism and growth impulses

126

emanating from major cities such as Leeds (with its relatively strong service economy), but these are in marked contrast to the situation within the coalfield, where the renewed problems of the mining industry since the 1984-5 National Union of Mineworkers' strike have led to a deterioration of local economic conditions. Overall, Yorkshire and Humberside face a continuing need for restructuring, and in some localities this need is urgent.

The Hunt Committee considered that a major transformation of the region's road system would enhance the growth potential of the problem areas. The M62 transpennine motorway, and links with the main north-south arteries of the M1 and A1, were completed in the mid-1970s. Accessibility to these transport corridors has become a highly significant strategic advantage for the location of certain types of economic activity, especially distribution. Other key problems identified by Hunt, and re-emphasised by the Flowers Commission in 1981, include the massive scale of physical dereliction, especially in the coalfield. The phase of reconstruction which followed the 1974 'Plan for Coal' heightened many of the difficulties in what, by then, had become Britain's leading coal-producing region and the focus of the National Coal Board's investment strategy (North and Spooner, 1982).

The M62 corridor between Goole and Calderdale illustrates several phases in the development of the economy of West Yorkshire, and some strikingly different local economic problems, profiles and potential. This section of the chapter focuses on that part of the corridor in *Wakefield* District known as the 'Five Towns', a coalmining area, and also on the textiles District of *Calderdale*, in which Halifax is the principal urban centre (see Figure 6.1 for location). What the M62 Corridor as a whole has shared, has been a minimalist approach by national government to regional aid. After 1972, all of this area formed part of the Yorkshire and Humberside Intermediate Area, but (except for Bradford, to the north) this status was eventually lost in the 1979 and 1982 redrawing of 'assisted areas'.

Figure 6.1: The M62 axis in West Yorkshire in the 1980s

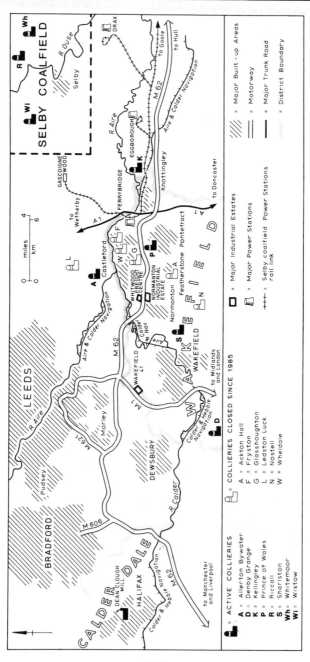

In the most recent redefinition of Britain's assisted areas in 1984, the three travel-to-work areas of Wakefield-Dewsbury, Castleford-Pontefract, and Calderdale (including Halifax), were all again left unaided. Arguably, this placed them at a considerable disadvantage within the region, especially compared with the Development Areas (Rotherham and Scunthorpe) to the south and east. Nor did these small- and medium-sized towns benefit from the government's Urban Programme. It is true that Wakefield District was successful in obtaining an Enterprise Zone during the first round of such designations in 1981, but this is located in the south-eastern part of a very large district, and is a long way from the M62 Corridor. Its impact in the northern part of Wakefield District, now ravaged by recent colliery closures, was minimal. Moreover, the absence of assisted-area status has denied Districts like Wakefield the benefits of eligibility for European funding.

Along the coalfield part of the M62 Corridor, energy landscapes of varying ages are manifest. That of the easternmost zone, around Selby and Drax in North Yorkshire, is a creation of the 1970s and 1980s, and illustrates on a massive scale the symbiotic development of coalmining and electricity generation in this period. The Selby 'coalfield' is a major 'greenfield' complex, developed under the expansionist 1974 plan. With its huge driftmine at Gascoigne Wood (and five satellites), it is targeted to produce 10 million tons of coal per annum for transfer by 'merry-go-round' rail operations to Drax, the most recent and largest (4,000 megowatts per annum) coal-fired power station complex to be built in Britain, and now the site of the electricity industry's first major investment in flue gas desulphurisation facilities. Drax is arguably the last of the 'dinosaurs', as the newly-privatised industry seems likely to eschew massive capital investments of this nature and is currently showing a strong preference for small combined-cycle, gas-fired plants. To the west of Drax lie the creations of an earlier postwar phase of investment; notably the Kellingley mine (developed in the 1960s and for many years Britain's largest individual pit), the Eggborough and Ferrybridge C power stations, and the man-made plateau of fly ash and colliery spoil at Gale Common (Figure 6.1 for location).

In the north of Wakefield District, straddling the M62, lie the 'Five Towns' of Castleford, Featherstone, Normanton, Pontefract and Knottingley, each with a population between 10,000 and 40,000. Apart from Knottingley, these communities had experienced the development of coalmining mainly between 1870 and 1900, though many of the mines here, notably the 'Prince of Wales' at Pontefract, subsequently became foci of heavy investment (and virtual complete revamping) during the expansionist 1970s. Some of the Five Towns exhibit the classic coalfield community syndrome described vividly by Dennis, Henriques and Slaughter (1956) in their *Coal is our life*. The syndrome includes dependence upon a narrow range of industries (including glassmaking, as well as coal and electricity), a sporadic shortage of female jobs, a tawdry environment, poor housing, a lack of higher-ordered services - and yet, paradoxically, a strength of local loyalty and community spirit that is exemplified by the fanatical support given to the local rugby league clubs of Castleford and Featherstone Rovers.

Some of the coalfield towns suffered from the decline of manufacturing, especially glassmaking, in the recession of the early 1980s, but their problems have been compounded since then by the change in fortunes of coal. Overproduction in a stagnant and declining market has produced enormous stresses in this industry. Paradoxically, the overproduction was linked to the rise in productivity in the wake of the 'Plan for Coal' of 1974 and the coming on stream of production from new pits, especially in the Selby coalfield (now virtually complete). As Winterton (1987) has explained:

'with falling demand for coal, introduction of new capacity causes the elimination of corresponding capacity, not through exhaustion, but because it is closure of surplus capacity'.

The 1984-5 National Union of Mineworkers' strike was essentially about the defence of jobs and resistance to the National Coal Board's accelerated programme of mine closures; it was led from Yorkshire. The ultimate collapse of the strike left the workforce impotent in preventing a drastic restructuring by a (renamed) British Coal Corporation, operating with much stricter financial parameters. In the post-strike era, cost parameters are ruthlessly applied to the performance of individual mines, which have been found wanting in many of the pits in the Five Towns. In 1984, 17% of the workforce here was engaged in mining. Since then, Ackton Hall (Featherstone) and Fryston, Glasshoughton and Wheldale (all Castleford) have closed: today only two mines still remain open. Within just three years, 1984-7, Wakefield District as a whole lost 9,000 mining jobs. In 1984 the unemployment rate in Castleford and Pontefract journey-to-work area was almost exactly the same as that in Great Britain as a whole; thereafter it increased while Great Britain's declined. The localisation of mining within the Wakefield District, in towns like Featherstone, produced pockets of high unemployment, large derelict sites and an unattractive landscape and townscape, while the collapse of mining has produced some knock-on effects in other industries. Nor are there grounds for optimism for the coal industry: the privatisation of electricity is opening the door to cheap imports (possibly through new jetties on the Humber), while the growing disquiet about the environmental consequence of coal-burn (the 'greenhouse effect') is reducing the ability to profit from the recent discomforts of the nuclear power industry.

To combat the deteriorating position of these coal towns, little government help has been forthcoming (quite apart from the fact that it is government policy towards energy that is a root cause of the problem). The Five Towns - and Wakefield District - do not have assisted-area status, although some belated recognition of the severity of their problems has arrived in the designation from Brussels as an Objective 2 (declining industrial) region under the reformed Structural Funds. The outcome of this mismatch between central government and EC policy remains to be seen. Aid to local authorities for derelict land reclamation is available from central government, but there is a huge backlog; funding (about £600,000 per annum) is inadequate to keep pace with the growing stock of derelict sites. A variety of small-scale programmes exist to aid small businesses, but the tradition of entrepreneurship tends to be weak in coalfield regions (Spooner, 1981).

Among the agents for this type of assistance are Wakefield District Council, the West Yorkshire Small Firms Fund and British Coal Enterprises Ltd (with a development in Featherstone), while larger indigenous firms may obtain venture capital from Yorkshire Enterprises Ltd. The local authorities are making spirited attempts to foster new economic development of the 'bottom-up' variety, but themselves concede that 'without the added impetus of new industry coming into the area its efforts will be marginal' (Wakefield MDC, 1986). Attempts to lure manufacturing industry are handicapped by the lack, since 1982, of assisted-area status, and the 'shadow' effect from neighbouring assisted areas.

Along the motorway corridors (M62 and M1) towards Leeds, there are signs of an increased tempo of activity, especially on the three industrial estates of Normanton, Whitwood Freight Centre and 'Wakefield 41' (which have a combined area of 236 hectares). The growth here, however, is largely in the service sector, rather than in manufacturing, and has a special emphasis on warehousing and distribution, which is possibly spurred on by the shortage of industrial land in Leeds and a consequent rippling-out effect. The reclamation of Glasshoughton colliery site may further add to this complex of motorway-based distribution centres, which already accommodates major companies like ASDA and Morrisons. Inevitably, the job density on these estates is low. A major exception to the warehousing emphasis is the selection by Coca Cola of 'Wakefield 41' for the site of a major soft drinks bottling factory and associated canning plant, which will eventually create nearly 700 jobs. This choice, however, was apparently influenced by the potential for distribution via the motorway system. 'Wakefield 41' also has a small version of the newly-fashionable 'business park'. But a final point to note about

Wakefield District as a whole is that only 1% of its jobs are in high-tech industry.

Further west the District of Calderdale exemplifies a different set of problems. A high proportion of Britain's wool textiles and clothing industries have been located in West Yorkshire, in which Calderdale has been one of the leading locations, especially for worsteds and carpets. These manufactures, however, continue to decline in the face of low-cost imports and changes in fashion, and are greatly hampered by obsolete industrial premises, outdated infrastructures and an old-fashioned economic structure with few large firms. Carpet production, for example, suffered in the early 1980s from competition from Belgian imports, stimulated by the appreciation of sterling. Textiles manufacture is no longer the leading employment branch in Calderdale; it has fallen behind both engineering and food and drink (which themselves have also suffered recently from the closure of major local employers, such as United Biscuits and Blakeborough Valves). Between 1978 and 1984, manufacturing employment in Calderdale fell by 30%; a further 28% decline has been forecast for the three main branches by 1995. In 1984 as much as 45% of employment was still in manufacturing, and the area remains highly vulnerable to further de-industrialisation - the more so because, although Calderdale has a predominantly small-firms economy, it also has a few large factories owned by multinationals. The dangers of external control are apparent:

'... the closures and takeovers of the past year provided evidence that decisions affecting employment and investment within firms locating in the District is increasingly being made as a result of factors external to Calderdale' (Calderdale Metropolitan District, 1988).

There are few modern, high value added or high-tech industries. In the steep Pennine valleys, around the principal town of Halifax, there is a dearth of industrial sites for modern factory development. There is a tendency for employment to expand via part-time jobs (in

1981 these accounted for 21% of Calderdale employment), and the area is heavily represented in industries which contain a high percentage of low-paid workers. A major exception to this gloomy picture is obviously the Halifax Building Society, which still has its headquarters in Halifax and, with more than 1,500 workers, is one of the town's three chief employers. Halifax, however, has a relatively low rate of unemployment (marginally below the EC average for 1985-7), partly because of the considerable population out-movement, and partly because of the large amount of part-time employment. Consequently, despite its unfavourable industrial structure, it has received scant help from regional policy in the process of restructuring. Indeed, as in the Five Towns, it can be argued that regional policy has had a negative effect, diverting potential inward investment to neighbouring favoured areas. For example, one fast-growing local company, Ram Hi (bathroom furniture), expanded its activities by establishing a branch factory at Scunthorpe in the Enterprise Zone.

Yet the problems of Calderdale were recognised in the European Community with its inclusion, between 1984-9, in the European Regional Development Fund's Non-Quota West Yorkshire Textiles Area. From 1985-8 about £3.5 million was obtained from the ERDF, mainly for small industrial units and industrial improvement areas. Non-Quota status also gave a qualification of regional priority to the area under the European Social Fund, leading to a similar level of funding for valued projects. There have been few other significant sources of outside finance, and this one is set to disappear with Calderdale's failure to gain inclusion in the Objective 2 set of regions (under the recent reform of the EC Structural Funds).

Halifax, therefore, has been forced to rely considerably on self-help, while Calderdale District's economic strategy has emphasised aid for small businesses, the formation of co-operatives, retraining, innovation, and an 'inheritance initiative' for Halifax's mainly Victorian town centre. Clearly the limitations of capital resources are acute, and private money is potentially of great importance.

One emblem of hope is Halifax's Dean Clough Mills complex. Crossleys Carpets once employed 5,000 workers in this physically-dominant symbol of the old industrial order, though this workforce had dwindled to just 600 by the time Crossleys closed in 1982. The derelict multistoreyed mills were bought by Ernest Hall, an unconventional entrepreneur and property developer. Hall set out to create an environment to stimulate and encourage enterprise, while at the same time seeking a marriage between enterprise and art. In this he claims to have copied many of the ideas of the Dartington Trust, but translating them from a rural to an urban context. Without government aid, Hall has succeeded in developing Dean Clough into the home of about 180 small businesses (mainly in the service sector), employing at least 1,800 workers - 'a wholly integrated industrial, educational and cultural community', which portrays itself as a 'practical Utopia'. Within Dean Clough are provided a range of support services (offices, design facilities and training) for small businesses and, since 1988, an Enterprise Campus has been established in partnership with Calderdale District Council, to address the training needs of 14-16-year-olds. There is little doubt that Dean Clough Mills is a significant success story, but how much does it owe to the imagination and commitment of an unusual and outstanding individual? Is this evidence that bottom-up strategies are a truly valid alternative, or is it just a unique experiment which is unrepeatable elsewhere?

The steel town of Scunthorpe

The defection of Ram Hi from Halifax to Scunthorpe is but one example of a considerable stream of inward investment that has made the south Humberside steel town one of the success stories of the Yorkshire and Humberside region in the late 1980s, following a calamitous industrial setback (North and Spooner, 1987). But, whereas in Calderdale and in the coalfield, government aid has been tardy and parsimonious, in this instance national government support was relatively swift, substantial and multifaceted (Spooner, 1987).

De-industrialisation in the late 1970s and early 1980s produced dramatic changes of fortunes for many British towns and cities: there are few better examples, however, than Scunthorpe, as a result of the savage pruning of its steel industry. Within less than a decade, Scunthorpe's economy passed from boom to crisis. It was the classic specialised industrial town: in 1967 as much as 92% of its manufacturing employment was in steel and associated industries. Scunthorpe was an 'island' of development which owed its origin to the discovery, in 1859, of a low-grade workable ironstone in the Liassic limestone beds at Frodingham; this was once described as 'the worst ironfield in the world' (Pocock, 1963). Five rural settlements, with a combined population of only 1,400 in 1861, became a thriving iron and steel town of 20,000 people by 1914 (and 77,000 today). Early rail links to the Yorkshire coalfield to the west, and to Immingham Dock (now the main source of imported iron ore) to the east, have been reinforced in the modern period by the construction of the M180 motorway (Figure 6.2).

Before nationalisation of the British steel industry in 1967, Scunthorpe boasted three integrated iron and steel plants under different ownerships: Normanby Park (Guest Keen and Nettlefolds), Redbourn (Richard Thomas and Baldwin) and Appleby-Frodingham (United Steel). In 1972 the Redbourn plant was merged with the Appleby-Frodingham complex with which it shared a boundary. Appleby-Frodingham received a massive £223 million investment in modernisation in the British Steel Corporation's Anchor project (begun in 1970). This was not a greenfield project, but a huge reconstruction, with open-hearth furnaces being replaced by three basic oxygen converters. New mills and a continuous caster were built. Although some job losses did arise, the future, as one of a small number of major BSC complexes, looked bright.

Figure 6.2: Scunthorpe area; industrial land and industrial estates

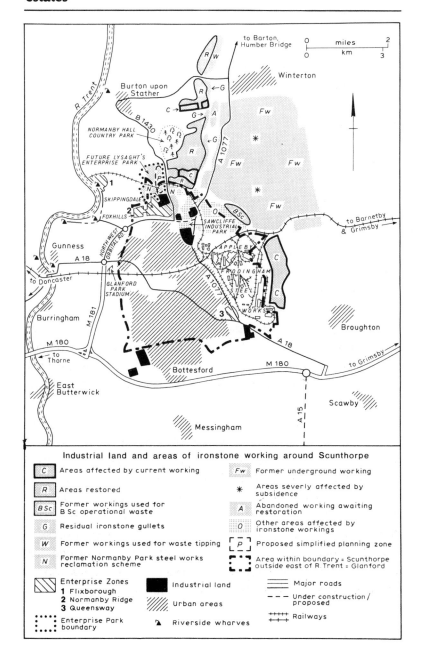

Industrial land and areas of ironstone working around Scunthorpe

C	Areas affected by current working
R	Areas restored
BSc	Former workings used for B Sc operational waste
G	Residual ironstone gullets
W	Former workings used for waste tipping
N	Former Normanby Park steel works reclamation scheme

Fw	Former underground working
*	Areas severly affected by subsidence
A	Abandoned working awaiting restoration
O	Other areas affected by ironstone workings
[P]	Proposed simplified planning zone
[- -]	Area within boundary = Scunthorpe outside east of R. Trent = Glanford

Enterprise Zones
1 Flixborough
2 Normanby Ridge
3 Queensway

Enterprise Park boundary

Industrial land

Urban areas

Riverside wharves

Major roads

Under construction / proposed

Railways

However, worsening problems of overcapacity in Europe in the late 1970s led to the drastic McGregor 'survival plan', in which the complete closure of the Normanby Park Works in 1981 was a major element. Scunthorpe lost more jobs than any other British steel town: the steelmaking workforce dropped from 20,000 to 9,000 within just four years and, by 1989, had been slimmed down further to approximately 7,000.

One effect of closure was a sharp rise in unemployment, affecting not only Scunthorpe, but also a penumbra of smaller settlements like Winterton. By late 1984, the unemployment rate (18.5%) in the Scunthorpe travel-to-work area was the worst on Humberside. A dearth of jobs for women was a long-standing problem. Even before the closure, the local authority had embarked on an economic development strategy targeted at producing more female employment.

Both national and local government agencies responded vigorously to the crisis. From 1972, Scunthorpe had qualified for moderate levels of regional policy aid as part of a broad Intermediate Area covering the Yorkshire and Humberside region. However, in 1980 it was 'upgraded' to Development Area status, while its Humberside neighbours, Hull and Grimsby (DAs since 1977), were downgraded to Intermediate status. This gave Scunthorpe a substantial advantage in industrial promotion. Indeed, apart from Corby (another steel closure town) and parts of south Wales, Scunthorpe was the nearest Development Area to London.

Scunthorpe gained an important additional weapon in its fight for new economic development, with the designation of its Enterprise Zone in 1984. The EZ experiment had been initiated by the Conservatives in an attempt to rehabilitate older urban areas of economic and physical decay by a mixture of subsidies (including 100% derating of property) and deregulation. The 104 hectares of the Scunthorpe EZ are divided into two separate sites - Queensway (close to Appleby-Frodingham) and Normanby Ridge. The latter includes part of the former Normanby Park steel works site at Foxhills, but also has an almost separate development (the Skippingdale Industrial Park) on a greenfield site at the foot of the Jurassic escarpment. Reclamation of derelict land has been required on an enormous scale on Normanby Park's 180 hectares. The local authorities are reclaiming the northern end of the site for the Lysaght's Enterprise Park, which will comprise 65 ha^2 of industrial land.

In 1984 Scunthorpe's encircling neighbour, the borough of Glanford, was rewarded for persistent campaigning by the designation of a second Enterprise Zone (52 ha^2) at Flixborough, close to the river Trent. This was the site of the former Nypro chemicals plant, devastated in 1974 by the worst industrial disaster in modern British history, and subsequently rebuilt with government regional aid, but eventually closed in 1981.

The development of the EZs has been the prime focus for the industrial promotion drive by Scunthorpe and Glanford Borough Councils, although a few important developments have occurred elsewhere (like the Citizen Watch factory). This drive has been most successful, with the rapid expansion at Foxhills of several major manufacturing plants, including the huge Unigate (chickens) and Ram Hi developments. Industrial expansion, however, has not been without controversy, notably at Skippingdale, where alongside the one major factory (Hygena furniture), development has taken the form of an out-of-town, one-stop, shopping centre, to the chagrin of some town-centre retailers. By 1988, the job totals on the EZs were: 1,157 for Normanby Ridge, 303 for Queensway, and 194 for Flixborough. Scunthorpe and Glanford have taken a broadly non-selective approach to inward investment. Occasionally this has had its drawbacks, as with the environmental problems encountered in respect of the Unigate intensive chicken rearing units which supply the Foxhills factory.

Most recently, a further boost to the campaign for new development has come with the granting of European Integrated Operations status to the Yorkshire and Humberside steel area (YHSA) in late 1988. This followed the 1986 adoption by the European Commission of an Action Programme for stronger structural measures to assist steel-restructuring areas. The YHSA includes the former county of South Yorkshire and the Scunthorpe travel-to-work area. An earlier proposal from Humberside for an integrated development operations programme was superseded.

By 1988, reindustrialisation had made substantial progress in Scunthorpe, to the extent that a shortage of land in the EZs has been reported, and unemployment had fallen to 14.2%. It is clear that, unlike the coal and textiles areas, Scunthorpe's main source of reindustrialisation has been inward investment, including several overseas companies like 'Devalit' (West German plastic automobile components) and 'Citizen Watch' (Japanese electronics). Scunthorpe has been able to pursue restructuring successfully in this way, through its strong support from central government aid to industry, together with the town's excellent location with respect to both British and European markets (via the motorway network and the Humber ports). In the future, the benefits from Development Area status and the Enterprise Zones may be seen as dwindling advantages, particularly since the EZ benefits are scheduled to last only 10 years. Substantial problems in the Scunthorpe area remain in the residual core of long-term unemployed; also the mismatch between job opportunities and the skills of the unemployed, as well as the physical dereliction arising from both the ironstone mining (underground mines have now been closed), and the Normanby Park closure. Some 142 hectares of derelict ironstone land (out of a total 285 hectares) are to be reclaimed under the Integrated Operations in a multiagency programme starting in 1989.

Boom town locality in the south: high-tech industry and the Cambridge Phenomenon

Only 110 miles to the south of Scunthorpe, but quite clearly well across the 'great divide', a vastly different type of restructuring has been proceeding in and around the university city of Cambridge, and without any assistance from regional policy. Since the mid-1970s,

Cambridge city and its surrounding region have experienced a remarkable growth of high-technology industry; a growth described by Segal (1985) as the 'Cambridge Phenomenon'. Indeed, between 1981-4, Cambridgeshire recorded a larger volume of high-technology employment growth (+5,000 jobs; a gain of 38%) than any other county in the United Kingdom (Keeble, 1988). High technology is defined in terms of sectors characterised by high levels of research and development, technologically-advanced products or services, and employment of highly-qualified graduate staff. Much of this growth has occurred in small new companies set up as independent organisations by one or more entrepreneurs. In addition, however, large firms from outside the region, and from abroad, have increasingly also been establishing research-focused units in the area. By 1986, more than 300 high-technology companies, employing 13,000 workers or 12% of the local labour force, were operating within a 12-mile radius of the city; three-quarters of these companies were new since 1975.

In employment terms, high-technology industry is spread widely across several sectors, the largest of which are chemicals/pharmaceuticals/biotechnology (29%), electronics (27%), scientific instruments and systems (21%), and computer hardware and software (11%). Most Cambridge high-technology firms are, however, research-focused, and employ exceptional proportions of highly-paid scientific, research and technical staff (47% on average, compared with only 12% for 'conventional' local manufacturing industry). The local income multiplier of Cambridge's high technology development is, therefore, very considerable, generating substantial growth in consumer services (especially retailing, leisure activities and restaurants).

The reasons for the rapid recent development of Cambridge's 'technology-orientated complex' are rooted in advantages which the city affords high-technology firms during a period of exceptional national and global technological change, focused on microelectronics, computers and biotechnology. Two fundamental advantages are the presence and role of Cambridge University, and the attractiveness of Cambridge's residential and cultural environment to researchers and entrepreneurs. Close proximity to London, Britain's dominant focus of international communications, financial capital and decision-making organisations of all kinds, is another important advantage.

Cambridge University is internationally famous for its scientific research, and has provided entrepreneurs, graduate staff and research and technological innovations for local high-technology development. The directly entrepreneurial role of Trinity and St John's Colleges is noted below. At the same time, the competitive success of most local firm's is fundamentally dependent on successful research by highly-qualified scientists and engineers. The exceptionally-attractive residential environment provided by Cambridge is a powerful influence on the recruitment and retention of such staff, as well as on the presence in the area of entrepreneurs and new-firm founders themselves. This also helps explain the marked geographical clustering of high technology firms within the city, rather than a scattered distribution amongst outlying settlements.

Perhaps the most visible and well-known symbol of the Cambridge Phenomenon is the Cambridge Science Park (CSP), established by Trinity College in 1973 on poor agricultural land between the city's northern boundary and the A45 bypass (Figure 6.3). The CSP, which has been subsequently expanded to occupy 53 hectares, was a direct outcome of a recommendation to the university and city by the Mott Committee that encouragement should be given to high-technology enterprises arising from university research.

Figure 6.3: Cambridge area; science parks, research institutes and laboratories

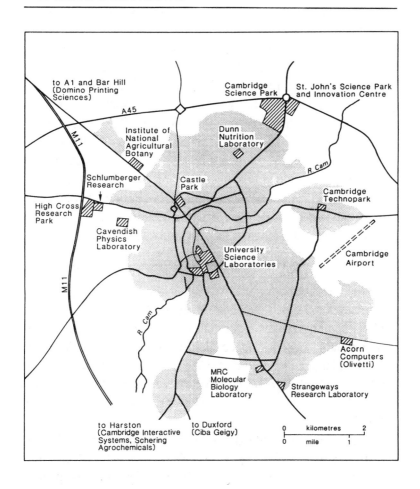

The Cambridge and Heriot-Watt (Edinburgh) Science Parks were the first to be set up anywhere in Britain. After a slow start, development in the 1980s has been rapid, and the Cambridge Park now (January 1989) houses 68 firms employing 2,730 workers. The largest tenant is Napp: a pharmaceutical company specialising in controlled-release drugs, and employing 350 staff. Expansion is continuing, with the most recent building - a 38,000 square feet development by Dencora - being designed to house former start-up companies needing extra space. The smaller St John's Science Park (8 hectares) across the A10, is more recent and contains an Innovation Centre, specifically designed to meet the needs of new start-up high-technology businesses. Other significant sites housing high-technology companies around Cambridge include the Castle Park 'technology village', promoted by the Cambridgeshire County Council, and the High Cross and Schlumberger sites on land owned by the university in west Cambridge.

A recent survey of 38 operational science parks in Britain indicated that the Cambridge Science Park is still, by some way, the largest (none of the others exceeds 30 hectares). Indeed, when all the current building schemes are completed, the CSP will have over one million square feet of floorspace; almost double that of Herriot-Watt, the second largest. Definitions of science parks vary: not all of the 38 would meet Cambridge's own standards, which include landscaped surroundings and also research institutes situated close to a major university.

There is some argument about the relationship between the CSP and the broader 'Cambridge Phenomenon' - which is cause and which is effect? Certainly the CSP contains a mixture of companies: some are small firms established by business-minded scientists, others are branches of multinationals which perceive that the scientific excellence of Cambridge provides a favourable environment to develop a particular sector of their activities (for example, GEC's Marconi Maritime Applied Research Laboratory), or an essential location for 'a listening post' (as in the case of IBM Academic Systems Mar-

keting). Commercial activities are restricted to applied scientific research - light industrial production which is dependent upon regular
consultations with Cambridge scientists, and ancillary activities appropriate to a science park. In the words of the Senior Bursar of Trinity
College, John Bradfield:

> 'the majority of CSP companies benefit greatly from personal,
> technical, financial or less tangible kinds of liaison with Univer-
> sity laboratories' (The Financial Times, 1989).

The links, however, tend to be informal.

As was the case with Ernest Hall and Dean Clough Mills at Halifax,
the role of key individuals like Bradfield, or William Bolton, the
'mover' behind the St John's Innovation Centre, is intriguing. Dynamic and far-sighted individuals have often played a crucial part in
the initiation of ventures of this kind. How else does one explain the
absence of a science park at Oxford University, where presumably
the critical mass of entrepreneurial scientists also exists but, at the
same time, there is apparently no person with sufficient vision and
drive to overcome the obstacles?

Restructuring the inner city: the case of London Docklands

The final cameo presented in this chapter takes us once more into
different territory - the inner city of London's East End. The current
redevelopment of the London Docklands alongside the river Thames
to the east of Tower Bridge (Figure 6.4) is arguably the largest and
most dramatic inner-city regeneration project in Europe in the 1980s
(Church and Hall, 1986). By 1981, closure of all of the Port of London's extensive range of up-river docks (Figure 6.4) had left 800
hectares of PLA land derelict, within a wider 2,000 hectare zone of
economic and population decline.

Figure 6.4: London Docklands

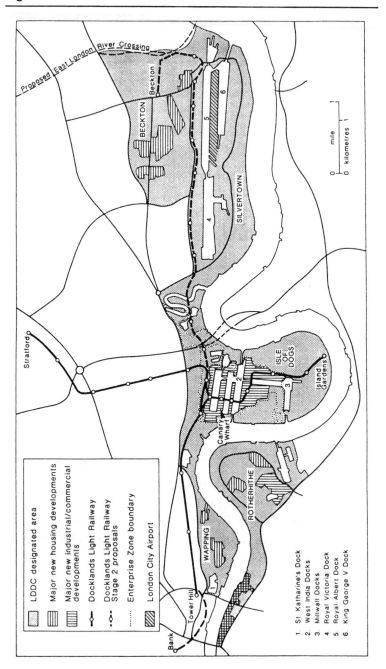

Legend:
- LDDC designated area
- Major new housing developments
- Major new industrial/commercial developments
- Docklands Light Railway
- Docklands Light Railway Stage 2 proposals
- Enterprise Zone boundary
- London City Airport

1. St. Katharine's Dock
2. West India Docks
3. Millwall Docks
4. Royal Victoria Dock
5. Royal Albert Dock
6. King George V Dock

Proposed East London River Crossing

BECKTON
Beckton
SILVERTOWN
Stratford
ISLE OF DOGS
Island Gardens
Canary Wharf
ROTHERHITHE
WAPPING
Tower Hill
Bank

146

Massive job losses in Docklands port and manufacturing industries (a decline of 10,000, or 27%, in 1978-81 alone), had resulted in severe local unemployment, which for males reached a huge 32% in Docklands in 1985.

The approach of the post-1979 Conservative government to this problem involved the establishment in 1981 of the London Docklands Development Corporation, a central government-appointed agency, modelled on New Town Development Corporation lines. This is charged with the economic, social and physical regeneration of the Docklands areas of three east London boroughs - Tower Hamlets, Newham and Southwark. The Corporation is responsible for investment of £60-80 million of Treasury grants per year for infrastructural development, industrial support and environmental improvements. It wields full planning powers, taken over from the local authorities. The latter's initial fierce opposition has given way more recently to greater co-operation, as with the 1987 Newham/LDCC agreement over low-cost housing and infrastructural development in the Royal Docks. Development in the Isle of Dogs was greatly helped by its designation in 1981 as an Enterprise Zone, in which, for the period to 1991, firms can benefit from 100% capital allowances and freedom from local property taxes (rates).

The pace of economic development in Docklands since 1981 has been remarkable. The LDDC claim that between 1983 and 1988 the number of jobs has risen by 46% to 36,400, while expenditure of £456 million of government infrastructure and other grants has attracted no less than £4.4 billion (i.e. a 10:1 private/public ratio) of completed or committed private-sector investment. Since 1981, 5.2 million square feet of commercial and industrial floorspace has been completed (to March 1988), with a further 5.9 million under construction. Some 8,780 new dwellings have been built, with work now begun on a further 6,220.

The nature and rate of economic development reflects the unique proximity of Docklands to central London, together with the initial relative cheapness of land in the area. Land values in Docklands have, however, rocketed in recent years (1983-7), from £120,000 per acre to £4 million for housing land in Wapping, and from £50,000 per acre to £2 million for commercial land in the Isle of Dogs. Commercial development has focused on:

- firstly, offices for financial, business and legal services associated with the City of London, one of the world's three largest financial centres;

- secondly, newspaper printing and publishing (virtually all Britain's national newspapers are now produced in Docklands);

- thirdly, on media, entertainment and leisure functions.

Major communication improvements include the £160 million Docklands Light Railway, (currently being extended underground to Bank, with plans for an eastern extension to Beckton), the new London City Airport with services to European and United Kingdom destinations, and the planned East London River Crossing and M11 road link. Massive future schemes now under way include the £3 billion, 12.2 million square feet, Canary Wharf financial and banking centre in the Isle of Dogs, and Rosehaugh Stanhope's £500 million business, shopping and housing scheme for the northern Royal Albert Docks. Redevelopment of the huge Royal Docks area as a whole is planned to include 7,000 new houses, 1.6 million square feet of office space, and major new shopping and leisure facilities (*Estates Gazette*, 1988).

Docklands, however, is not uncontroversial. The social and political context of the London Docklands redevelopment has included vocal ideological and political opposition to LDDC aims and impacts from local groups (Docklands Consultative Committee, 1988), and frequent criticisms over the lack of benefit and increasing costs for the traditional local Docklands population (Kane, 1987). The local social impacts of successful economic revitalisation thus raise important questions for government policy and academic evaluation. What seems clear, is that Docklands development, like that in Cambridge, has been 'pulling with the tide': its central London location has provided a suitable geographical context to exploit the opportunities for a restructuring in tune with the direction of national economic and political change.

Acknowledgements

This chapter is based partly on the Symposium Excursions Guide, parts of which (on Cambridge and London Docklands) were written by David Keeble. Sections of his account have been included without major amendment, and I am grateful to David Keeble for his permission to use this material. I am also indebted to my colleague John North for his help in preparation of the excursions and the maps, and to officers of Wakefield, Scunthorpe, Glanford and Calderdale District Councils for their advice and information.

References

Calderdale Metropolitan Borough Council, *Annual review 1987/8: strategic policy, economic development and research*, Halifax, 1988.

Champion, A.G. and Green, A.E., *Local prosperity and the north-south divide: a report on winners and losers in 1980s Britain*, Institute for Employment Research, University of Warwick, 1988.

Church, A. and Hall, J., 'Discovery of Docklands', *Geographical Magazine*, December, pp. 632-39, 1986.

Commission (Flowers) on Energy and the Environment, *Coal and the environment*, HMSO, London, 1981.

Cooke, P., 'The changing urban and regional system in the United Kingdom', *Regional Studies*, Vol. 20, pp. 243-52, 1986.

Dennis, N., Henriques, F. and Slaughter, C., *Coal is our life*, Eyre and Spottiswoode, London, 1956.

Department of Economic Affairs, *The intermediate areas: report of a committee under the chairmanship of Sir Joseph Hunt*, HMSO, London, 1969.

Docklands Consultative Committee, *Urban Development Corporations: six years in London's Docklands*, London, 1988.

Estates Gazette, 'Focus on London Docklands', *Estates Gazette*, pp. 73-107, 1988.

Financial Times, Science and Business Park supplement, 7 July 1989.

Green, A.E., 'The north-south divide in Great Britain: an examination of the evidence', *Transactions, Institute of British Geographers New Series*, Vol. 13, pp. 179-98, 1988.

Hall, P., 'Issues for the Eighties', *The Planner*, Vol. 67, pp. 4-5, 1981.

Humberside County Council, *Humberside Enterprise Zones, Progress Report 1988*, Humberside County Council, 1988.

Kane, F., 'Local people 'left out' by Docklands boom', *Independent*, 7 December 1987.

Keeble, D.E., 'High-technology industry and local environments in the UK', in Aydalot, P. and Keeble, D.E. (eds.), *High-technology industry and innovative environments: the European experience*, Routledge, London, pp. 65-98, 1988.

Keeble, D.E., 'High-technology industry and regional development in Britain: the case of the Cambridge Phenomenon', *Environment and Planning C, Government and Policy*, Vol. 7, pp. 153-172, 1989.

Martin, R., 'The new economics and politics of regional restructuring: the British experience', in Albrechts, L. et al., *Regional policy at the crossroads: European perspectives*, J. Kingsley, London, pp. 27-51, 1989.

North, J. and Spooner, D.J., 'The Yorkshire, Nottinghamshire and Derbyshire coalfield: the focus of the Coal Board's investment strategy', *Geographical Journal*, Vol. 148, pp. 22-37, 1982.

North, J. and Spooner, D.J., 'Land for industry', in Symes, D.G. (ed.), *Humberside in the Eighties,* Department of Geography, University of Hull Miscellaneous Series, Vol. 34, pp. 67-78, 1987.

Pocock, D.C.D., 'Iron and steel at Scunthorpe', *East Midlands Geographer,* Vol. 3, p. 19, 1963.

Regional Studies Association, *Report of an inquiry into regional development problems in the UK,* Geobooks, Norwich, 1983.

Segal, Quince and Partners, *The Cambridge Phenomenon: the growth of high-technology industry in a university town,* Segal, Quince and Partners, Cambridge, 1985.

Spooner, D.J., *Mining and regional development,* Oxford University Press, Oxford, 1981.

Spooner, D.J., 'Regional policy and Humberside', in Symes, D.G. (ed.), *Humberside in the Eighties,* Department of Geography, University of Hull, Miscellaneous Series, Vol. 34, pp. 133-148, 1987.

Wakefield Metropolitan District Council, *Castleford and Pontefract travel-to-work area; a submission to the Minister of State for Industry,* Wakefield, 1986.

Winterton, J., 'The source of the crisis', in: *Coalfields Communities Campaign, Making the Case,* Barnsley, 1985.

Chapter VII

Stephen Fothergill (University of Reading) and Nigel Guy (Northern Ireland Economic Research Centre)

Branch factory closures and the north-south divide in the United Kingdom

This chapter summarises the results of a two-year research project investigating the closures of branch factories in various parts of the United Kingdom during the 1980s. The first section describes the aims of, and background to, the research, and this is followed by a brief description of the methodology employed. The main results of the survey are summarised in the third section, followed by a conclusion which also looks at some of the policy implications of the results.

Why study closures?

The recession of the early-1980s was the worst for 50 years in the United Kingdom: around one in four of all manufacturing jobs were lost between 1979 and 1983. The impact of the slump was, however, spatially uneven, with the peripheral regions and those most dependent on manufacturing being the hardest hit. The higher rate of closure of branch plants in the assisted areas was responsible for much of this differential employment performance, so the study of these closures is vital to our understanding of one of the most turbulent periods in British economic history. In addition, the research is relevant for current and future economic policy, because the recent recovery of the UK economy has itself been uneven. The north-south divide has widened considerably since the early 1980s, with southern England showing many signs of economic overheating, while many parts of the north have yet to benefit noticeably from the recovery. However, if the high rate of closures in peripheral regions during the early 1980s was not due to the inherent unsuitability of these areas as locations for manufacturing, then there remains a prima facie case for a stronger regional policy which tackles the north-south divide, without reducing the overall level of economic efficiency.

In fact, the whole field of branch closures has been considerably underresearched. Previous work falls into two main types:

- large-scale statistical investigations into the plant characteristics which are associated with closure (O'Farrell and Crouchley, 1983);

- detailed studies of rationalisation within individual corporations (Townsend and Peck, 1984; 1987).

Our approach lies between the two, in adopting a large-scale, case study methodology. This allows us both to examine the reasoning within individual firms which led to the closure of a plant in one location rather than another, and to identify any general factors which influenced closures in the 1980s. In a sense this approach replicates the methodology of the classic research into branch plant openings which established the conventional wisdom in that field. Most notable amongst these studies were those of Luttrell (1962), Townroe (1971) and the Department of Trade and Industry (1973). We believe that the closure decision is usually a two-stage process, analogous to that which occurs when firms decide to open a new branch plant. First, firms identify a problem and decide that they need to reduce capacity in some fashion; then they decide in which location the closure will occur.

Because of this lack of previous research, there is no theoretical framework which is yet established as the best explanation for the location of branch closures. In our conclusion, we assess the validity of three such frameworks:

- firstly, neo-classical economic theory, which suggests that the company will close the plant with the highest costs within the group;

- secondly, the product life-cycle theory, which suggest that branches set up away from the company headquarters, as mass-production units at times of expansion, will become vulnerable when the product nears the end of its life cycle;

- thirdly, organisational theory which argues that firms will tend to close plants without senior management functions, regardless of their efficiency, since these functions are not easily transferable between locations.

Research method

Four areas of the United Kingdom, with contrasting experiences of industrial change during the 1980s, were studied: two peripheral assisted areas (Northern Ireland and Tyneside) and two parts of southern England which have never received regional aid (Leicestershire and south Hampshire). For each area we identified all the plants which were closed between 1980 and 1986 and had been externally owned, that is, with their ultimate head office located outside the area. Some closures were excluded because it was felt they would not greatly add to our knowledge of the processes involved; most notably plants employing less than 50 persons and short-lived projects such as the De Lorean car plant in Northern Ireland. The total 'population' of closures, which met our criteria for inclusion, was studied in three of the areas: 49 closures in Northern Ireland, 28 in south Hampshire and 17 in Leicestershire. There were 42 eligible closures in Tyneside, but 18 of these were excluded in order to make the sample more manageable. The study, therefore, covers 118 factory closures, of plants which employed almost 40,000 people in 1980.

Table 7.1: The extent of external ownership and closure in the study areas

	Northern Ireland	Tyneside	South Hampshire	Leicestershire
(i)	136,500	137,400	111,900	143,500
(ii)	48.6	45.8	71.4	39.9
(iii)	49	42	28	17
(iv)	20,138	13,499	5,588	4,045
(v)	30.4	21.5	7.0	7.1

Key and notes:

(i) Manufacturing employment in 1980.

(ii) Externally-owned employment as a % of the total: the Northern Ireland percentage excludes employment in Harland and Wolff, and also in Short Brothers; the Tyneside percentage excludes employment in shipbuilding.

(iii) Number of closures in scope.

(iv) 1980 employment in closures: the 24 plants in the Tyneside survey employed 10,066 in 1980.

(v) Closures as a % of total employment.

(vi) Closures as a % of externally-owned employment.

Sources: Regional industrial databanks; survey data.

Table 7.1 shows the level of external ownership in each area in 1980. Perhaps somewhat surprisingly, the highest proportion was found in south Hampshire, but external ownership was widespread in all areas. The bottom half of the Table shows that there is indeed a problem worthy of investigation. The rate of job losses among externally-owned plants in Tyneside was three times higher than the rate in the non-assisted areas: job losses in Northern Ireland were four times higher.

The main part of the project comprised contacting and interviewing, wherever possible, managerial personnel who had been directly involved in taking the closure decision. Tracing the most appropriate person in each case was difficult and painstaking work, and great persistence was required to obtain a good response rate. Wherever necessary, initial interviews were supplemented by further conversations with other people involved in the closure, such as former plant managers, trade unionists and Industrial Development Agency officials. These interviews, together with information gathered from an extensive trawl of contemporary press reports, allowed us to make an informed assessment of the reasons for closure in 115 out of the 118 cases. The information gathered in the course of this study is, we believe, of the highest quality, and represents an invaluable body of knowledge about one of the most important periods in recent economic history.

The results

Plant characteristics
Before looking at the reasons for closure in detail, it is useful to examine the characteristics of the closures in each of the four areas, since (as Table 7.2 shows) there were important differences. In brief, the closures in the northern areas conformed much more closely to the classic definition of the 'branch plant' than those in the non-assisted areas. They were considerably larger, more likely to be foreign owned, and much more likely to have been opened as a branch by their parent during the boom years of the 1950s and 1960s. By contrast, external ownership in the southern areas developed more via the acquisition of existing locally-controlled companies, many of which, in fact, had been in operation since before the World War II. However, as Table 7.3 indicates, plants across all areas were similar, in that they mostly lacked senior white-collar functions, such as marketing and research and development on site. Very few were head-office plants for a division or group within a company. In all categories, the Leicestershire plants had a greater degree of autonomy than those elsewhere, because so many of them were acquired plants that had retained some of their independence after the takeover.

Table 7.2: The characteristics of branches by area; plant size and ownership

	Northern Ireland	Tyneside	South Hampshire	Leicestershire
average 1980 employment	410	419	200	238
% of employment in foreign ownership	60	39	28	30
% of employment in plants opened since 1950	71	82	52	26
% of employment in acquired plants	30	27	51	95

Sources: Survey data.

Table 7.3: The characteristics of branches by area; the presence of senior white-collar functions

	Northern Ireland	Tyneside	South Hampshire	Leicestershire
headquarters	12	17	11	29
research & dev.	10	13	18	10
marketing	20	8	32	59

Source: Survey data.

Table 7.4: Reasons why a closure was necessary; the most important factors

| | % of 1980 employment in closures | |
	major or minor factor	major factor
Structural shift in demand	54	50
Recession	45	11
Profitability crisis	28	21
Import penetration	27	11
Exchange rate	21	7
Change in product	17	16
Loss of market share	15	5
Change in production process	12	10
Pulling out of the market	10	4
Takeover/merger	7	5
Local environment	6	3
International cost differences	5	5

Note: since more than one factor can influence each closure decision, the two columns do not sum to 100%.

Source: Survey data.

Why was a closure necessary?

The first part of the assessment of the reasons for closure of each plant was to ask, why had the company decided that it needed to close one of its plants at all? In making the assessments we distinguished between 'major' and 'minor' factors. Major factors are those which were primary causes of closure. Minor factors are influences that affect only the timing of the closure, or those that act as an irritant to the parent company, but are not sufficient to lead to closure by themselves. Table 7.4 shows the proportion of 1980 employment affected by the 12 most important factors, both major and minor. All subsequent Tables in this chapter also show the proportion of 1980 employment in plants influenced by each factor, rather than the number of plants affected.

One factor stands out as the most significant major cause of closure: this is the structural shift in demand. By this, we mean the cases in which the demand for a particular product manufactured by the company is on a long-term downward path, to the extent that the firm eventually has to consider reducing capacity. These are changes which are the results of shifts in taste, social habits or fashion: the tobacco industry is a prime example. Half the job losses (over 20,000 people) in the sample, were in cases in which such a shift was a major factor in the closure decision. Technical change can also have a fundamental long-term effect on production, and works in two different ways. One is technical change in the production process; for example, the speeding up of production lines as a result of automation. The other is the more fundamental type of change in the product itself, whereby one good is superseded by a newer and more efficient one, as for example, in the replacement of electromechanical telecommunications equipment by electronic exchanges.

The recession was the second most important factor, when major and minor factors were taken together, but was a major one in only about 10% of all job losses. The principal impact of the early-1980s recession in the United Kingdom was to bring forward closures which would have been necessary at some point anyway, rather than to eliminate plants which would have survived otherwise. The severity of the recession was itself quite closely related to the high level of the exchange rate and the growth of import penetration. Both of these factors also had their biggest impact on the timing of closures.

It is worth noting three other points in brief:

- first, the direct impact of takeovers and mergers on closure was small;

- second, there is also very little evidence to support the argument that large numbers of jobs are being relocated out of the United Kingdom because of international differences in the cost of production;

• third, the importance of closures due to company profitability crises may have been inflated in this survey by the problems facing the Courtaulds textiles giant; 10 of its plants are covered by this survey, and all of these closures were related to the company's financial difficulties in the late 1970s and early 1980s.

Table: 7.5: Reasons why a closure was necessary, by area

	Northern Ireland	Tyneside	South Hampshire	Leicestershire
recession-related factors	23	31	19	34
long-term shifts	78	86	32	48
firm-specific reasons	26	21	47	66
plant-specific reasons	12	10	5	0

Note: since more than one factor can influence each closure decision, columns do not add up to 100 %.

Source: Survey data.

In Table 7.5 the individual factors have been grouped into categories of related influences; regional differences in reasons for closure are also shown. A very significant north-south divide emerges from this analysis. In the assisted areas, the group of factors representing long-term shifts in demand was a major influence on as many as 80% of the job losses. This category includes structural shifts in demand, technical change and international cost differences. By contrast, in the non-assisted areas, it is the firm-specific reasons which comprise the most significant category; notably factors such as corporate profitability, loss of market share and the pulling out of certain markets. This reinforces the impression that the nature of closures in the assisted areas was somewhat different from those in the southern areas.

Why was this particular factory closed?

The analysis so far does not necessarily say anything about the locational component of the closure decision: why the management chose to close a plant in one area, rather than in another. Table 7.6 details the 12 most important factors which influenced plant selection.

Two factors stand out as being the most significant in determining the choice of which of its plants a company would choose to close. These are plant size and product, each of which was an influence in the loss of around 40% of the jobs in the sample. It is vital to understand the way in which plant size affects the chances of closure. It is not simply that large absolute size confers some advantage to a plant, rather, it is the relative size of the plant, compared to others within the same company, that counts. The production-driven logic of the closure decision must be stressed. A company wishing to consolidate production into fewer plants, will usually close the smaller of two factories, since its output can be fitted into the larger plant whereas this can rarely be done the other way round. Expressed simply, a quart can not be squeezed into a pint pot. Thus, some of the largest closures in the sample (plants which employed 2,000-3,000 people) were selected because they were part of very large enterprises which possessed bigger factories elsewhere. Size is also significant, because the more important a plant is, within the group as a whole, the more likely it is that operational problems will be tackled before they get out of hand. In a smaller plant, difficulties such as managerial failings, or ageing equipment, may not be dealt with immediately and may eventually become serious problems which endanger the survival of the plant.

162

The product made by the particular plant was the other most significant selecting factor. The way in which this worked was usually straightforward: if there was only one plant in the firm engaged in the line of production for which demand was declining, then clearly that was the candidate for closure. In the majority of cases there was more than one factor which influenced the selection of the plant to be closed, but it was clear that the plant which was eventually shut down would not have been selected if it had not been manufacturing a particular product.

Table 7.6: Reasons why a particular factory was closed; the most important factors

	% of 1980 employment in closures	
	major or minor factor	major factor
Plant size	44	39
Product	42	31
Remoteness/hassle	24	11
Building design	22	6
Absence of HQ functions	22	13
Limited capacity	20	12
Labour productivity or attitudes	19	13
Site constraints	14	8
Peripheral to main business	13	7
Transport costs	11	4
Poor management	10	3
Ageing plant and machinery	10	3

Note: since more than one factor can influence each closure decision, columns do not sum to 100%.

Source: Survey data.

Two factors in Table 7.6 refer to the problems of remoteness. The more obvious disadvantages of higher transport costs was, in fact, much less significant in selecting plants for closure than the 'hassle' which arises from peripherality. The time and energy required from senior management to keep an eye on the distant plant, and to deal with any problems that arise there, were often seen as being disproportionate to the importance of the factory within the company as a whole. Northern Ireland plants, in particular, have suffered from this attitude. In general, however, problems of remoteness were minor influences in the closure decision.

Table 7.7: Major reasons why a particular factory was closed, by area

	% of employment in closures			
	Northern Ireland	Tyneside	South Hampshire	Leicestershire
what the factory makes	32	49	32	50
how well it does it	27	9	14	0
place in company structure	43	86	29	60
location/environment	17	22	32	19
site/buildings	2	0	56	36

Note: since more than one factor can influence each closure decision, columns do not sum to 100%.

Source: Survey data.

In Table 7.7, the individual factors that affected the selection of plants for closure, have been placed into five grouped categories. The north-south divide is not so clearly evident in this Table as in

Table 7.5, except in the impact of property-related factors. The most frequently-mentioned property-related problem was the inefficiency of older, multistorey factories, which are increasingly unsuitable for modern manufacturing processes. A number of plants were also selected for closure because they occupied a very cramped site and had little development potential. These difficulties are clearly related to the way external ownership developed in each area. A far higher proportion of the establishments in the non-assisted areas dated back to before 1945, whereas the bulk of the closures in the north were of plants opened as branches since the 1950s, and which had often been purpose-built by the local industrial development authorities.

The most important category overall is the plant's place in the company structure, which includes factors such as plant size and the absence of headquarters functions (that is, the role played by the plant within the company's overall operations, rather than its location). 'What the factory makes', which includes the plant's product line and production capability, is also significant across all four areas. Operational problems at plant level are covered in the 'how well it makes it' category. Northern Ireland is the only region in which this category assumes major significance, and this is due to problems with labour force attitudes at a small number of large plants. The circumstances of these closures are such that it would be quite wrong to generalise and to assert that there is a substantial industrial relations problem in Northern Ireland. The characteristics of the location in which the factory is situated were something of an influence on selection, but the northern areas do not appear to be at a disadvantage in this respect. This category also incorporates our assessment of the impact of the 'troubles' on closures in Northern Ireland: we concluded that the political situation had very little influence on a decision to shut a plant in Northern Ireland rather than anywhere else.

Conclusions and policy implications

In brief, it can be concluded that there is a difference in the nature of the closures in the assisted and non-assisted areas. Table 7.1 showed that there was a far higher closure rate in the assisted areas during the 1980s. However, this did not occur because the north is an unsuitable place in which to produce. The higher rate of closure here was largely due to the fact that the externally-owned plants in the assisted areas possessed characteristics that made them more prone to closure. They were more often small, in relation to other plants within the company, or were producing mature goods at the end of their life cycle, or lacked senior management functions. They were the factories which were opened in the peripheral regions as a result of regional policy, and were the first ones to close when the good times disappeared. The closures in the south were more often part of companies which found themselves in particular difficulties, rather than those which were affected by long-term shifts in the economy. Property-related difficulties were as significant in selecting plants for closure as problems with size or product.

The diversity of types of closure was such that none of the three theoretical frameworks outlined in the introduction was universally applicable. The neo-classical framework does not appear to have been relevant in very many cases. There was very little indication that the relative costs of the various plants within the group were a significant factor in the decision-making process. The other two theories did receive a good deal of support. The product life cycle theory, in particular, is able to explain a substantial number of closures. Many of the closures had been set up as mass-production plants, 20 or 30 years previously, but were the first ones to be closed when the cycle was coming to an end towards the beginning of the 1980s.

Organisational factors were also at work in a considerable number of cases. There were relatively few factories in the sample which possessed substantial managerial autonomy, or had senior white-collar functions actually on site. However, relative size was more important than the absence of headquarters functions in selecting plants for closure.

Policy implications

The main conclusion of this study - that the higher rate of closures in the assisted areas was largely due to the nature of the plants themselves, rather than the characteristics of the regions - is highly important for policy. One of the major economic problems in the United Kingdom in the 1990s will be regional imbalances in economic prosperity which have widened during the 1980s. This research suggests that the relocation of industry and services from the south-east to other parts of the country would not conflict with the wider goal of overall economic efficiency. This does not mean, however, that the regional policy instruments of the 1960s and 1970s can simply be 'dusted off the shelf' and reused in the same fashion as before. The very reason for the higher closure rate in the assisted areas during the past decade has been the nature of the plants attracted to those locations by the old policies. However, the principle of strong regional policy should certainly be placed back at the top of the policy agenda for the next decade.

References

Department of Trade and Industry, *Evidence to the Expenditure Committee (Trade and Industry Sub-Committee)*, Wednesday 4 July, HMSO, London, 1973.

Luttrell, W.F., *Factory location and industrial movement*, National Institute of Economic and Social Research, London, 1962.

O'Farrell, P.N., 'An analysis of industrial closures: Irish experience 1960-1973', *Regional Studies*, Vol. 10, pp. 433-48, 1976.

O'Farrell, P.N. and Crouchley, R., 'Industrial closures in Ireland 1973-1981: analysis and implications', *Regional Studies*, Vol. 17, pp. 411-27, 1983.

Townroe, P.M., *Industrial location decisions*, Centre for Urban and Regional Studies, Occasional Paper 15, University of Birmingham, 1971.

Townsend, A. and Peck, F., 'Contrasting experience of recession and spatial restructuring: British Shipbuilders, Plessey and Metal Box', *Regional Studies*, Vol. 18, pp. 319-38, 1984.

Townsend, A. and Peck, F., 'The impact of technological change upon the spatial pattern of UK employment within major corporations', *Regional Studies*, Vol. 21, pp. 225-39, 1987.

Chapter VIII

Helmut Nuhn (Universität Hamburg)

De-industrialisation and problems of revitalisation in the Hamburg port area

Seaports are attractive locations for firms dealing with the construction and maintenance of transport and transshipment equipment, as well as for firms involved in the processing of incoming and outgoing goods. These locations are particularly suitable for industries which rely heavily on raw materials and for those which deal with goods that lose high proportions of weight during processing. These include the typical merchandise industries which concentrate on the processing and packaging of high-grade imports.

The Hanseatic city of Hamburg is a typical example of this form of industrialisation, which developed strongly here during the second half of the nineteenth century, following some earlier expansion in luxury products, such as spices, coffee, cocoa, tea and tobacco. Figure 8.1, showing land use in the port area in 1988, indicates that the largest sites today are not used for cargo handling and temporary storage, but for manufacturing industries, such as oil refining and steel and non-ferrous metal production. Initially, a heavy emphasis was placed on milling and food industries based upon imports of bulk grains, such as cereals and oil seeds. This was followed by a shift to the use of heavy bulk goods, such as coal and ores, for the development of energy plants and metal industries. At the same time, prior to the building of extensive pipelines in West Germany in the 1960s, there was considerable investment in the petrochemical industry alongside the lower Elbe river.

Figure 8.1: Port of Hamburg; land use, 1988

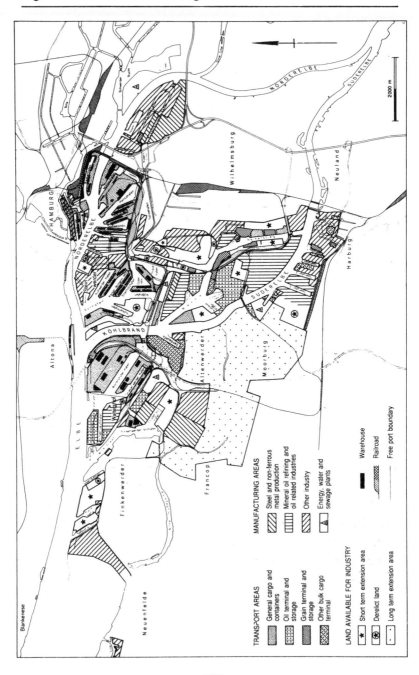

Figure 8.2: Employment and value-added change in Hamburg; share of principal economic sectors, 1970-87

This chapter aims to provide a short description of the decline of Hamburg's port industries, with a closer examination of the fate of the shipbuilding industry. It will conclude by demonstrating how business initiative in Hamburg has tried to overcome the structural crisis, and also the part played by government institutions in this context. The growth and decline of port-linked industries does not merely underlie changes in the city's employment and the city's budget; it also affects land use and creates environmental problems, especially in connection with soil contamination.

The structure and decline of port industries

As shown in Figure 8.2, there has been an appreciable decline in the importance of the manufacturing sector in Hamburg. In 1970 it occupied 35% of the city's active workforce; by 1987, however, this proportion had fallen to 27%. A similar decline is represented in the manufacturing component of the city's total economic output (value added). This decline in manufacturing involved losses in most industrial branches and also reflected the effects of structural changes in Hamburg's important food-processing and consumer-goods manufacturing activities.

Any precise quantitative recording of industrial trends meets with the problem of insufficient availability of data, especially on specific branches of port industries. In many cases, definitions of these do not just come between port-orientated activities and non-port activities, but often cut through the operations of a single company. For this reason, in compiling Table 8.1, only clearly identifiable 'key' activities, such as shipbuilding and petroleum refining, are included. This Table, however, does provide us with some insight into the general structure of Hamburg's shrinking manufacturing base, and indicates the continuing importance here of port industries, despite their decline.

Table 8.1: Employment in port-linked manufacturing industries in Hamburg, 1960, 1970 and 1985

industrial branch	employment (industrial plants with over 10 employees)			employment mfrg firms with over 20 employees)		
	1960	1970	1960-70 (% change)	1970	1985	1970-85 (% change)
Petroleum refining	8,672	10,025	+15.6	10,055	7,779	-22.6
Chemical products	17,471	18,741	+7.3	18,444	14,004	-24.1
Timber products	1,392	694	-50.1	642	375	-41.6
Rubber products	13,883	11,449	-17.5	10,538	5,429	-48.5
Nonferrous metals	3,084	3,018	-2.1	2,999	3,968	+32.3
SHIPBUILDING	31,818	17,077	-46.3	17,448	7,459	-57.3
Oil mills	2,790	1,710	-38.7	1,710	1,330	-22.2
Fish products	3,159	1,749	-44.6	1,781	750	-57.9
Coffee, tea etc.	3,171	3,242	+2.2	3,180	1,379	-56.6
Tobacco products	3,503	2,770	-20.9	2,770	1,989	-28.2
PORT-LINKED IND.	88,943	70,475	-20.8	69,567	44,462	-36.1
OTHER MFRG. IND.	143,488	140,919	-1.2	144,681	87,689	-39.4
ALL MFRG.	232,431	211,394	-9.1	214,248	132,151	-38.3

[handwritten margin note: Comment — less decline]

Note: the 1985 employment column includes 1983 figures for the non-ferrous metal and coffee, tea etc. branches.

Source: Industrieverband Hamburg, *Struktur und Entwicklung der Hamburger Industriezweige*, Hamburg, 1986.

In 1960, as many as 38.3% of Hamburg's 232,000 industrial employees were engaged in the port-linked sector. With its 31,818 workers, representing 13.7% of the city's total workforce, shipbuilding at that time was easily the most important single branch of manufacturing. Since 1960, however, shipbuilding, along with timber processing and the making of fish products, has endured the highest rate of job losses. Altogether, while other branches of industry were not yet affected, about one-fifth of the workforce in port-linked manufacturing lost their jobs. From 1970-85, however, contraction of employment spread into all the activities represented in Table 8.1; but even so, the steepening decline in shipbuilding, in which the numbers of workers fell by a huge 57.3%, was particularly acute.

The shipbuilding industry as an example of port-linked manufacturing

As early as the mid-1950s, Hamburg's shipbuilding industry had regained its prewar level. At that time it was experiencing a phase of prosperity which involved about 50 plants of various sizes and types. By the beginning of the 1960s, however, the situation had deteriorated very abruptly into a prolonged structural crisis which, as time progressed, was interrupted only by a few short spells of recovery.

The location of the shipyards during the height of the 1950s' boom can be seen in Figure 8.3. Also marked (in open circles) are those plants which closed between 1955 and 1987, and those major abandoned sites which have yet to attract any new lasting usage.

The main shipyard area is situated in the free port. This is the location of the last big shipbuilding enterprise, Blohm and Voss, still in business in Hamburg. The vacant industrial site to the east, which Blohm and Voss had obtained from Stülcken in 1966, has remained unused for more than 20 years, and today is in government ownership. The site adjoining Ross on the southern side, was developed originally by the Vulcan shipyard in 1905, before forming the main plant of Howaldt AG. This, in turn, became the headquarters of Howaldtwerke-Deutsche Werft AG (HDW) which was taken over by Blohm and Voss in 1985. This site was abandoned during 1987 and 1988, and is now available for alternative usage. Hamburg's many small shipbuilding firms tended to concentrate outside the free port area. The large majority have been closed down or, at best, have retained just a shadowy existence. Also outside the free port are the shipyards of Finkenwerder, where the Deutsche Werft (DW) operated from 1918 to 1973. It still ranked seventh in the list of world shipbuilding companies in 1959.

Figure 8.3: Port of Hamburg; shipyards, 1955 and 1988

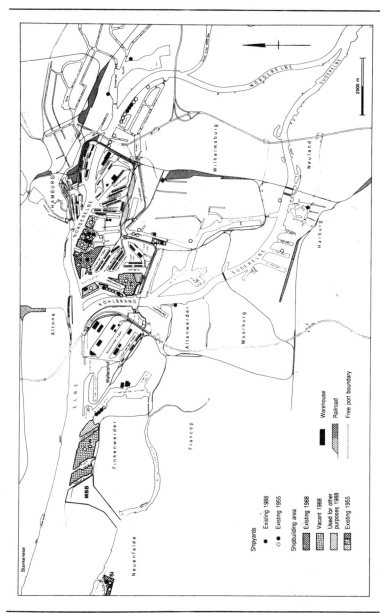

: shipyards closed during the period 1955-88 are shown by open circles.

Figure 8.4: Concentration process in Hamburg shipbuilding since 1896

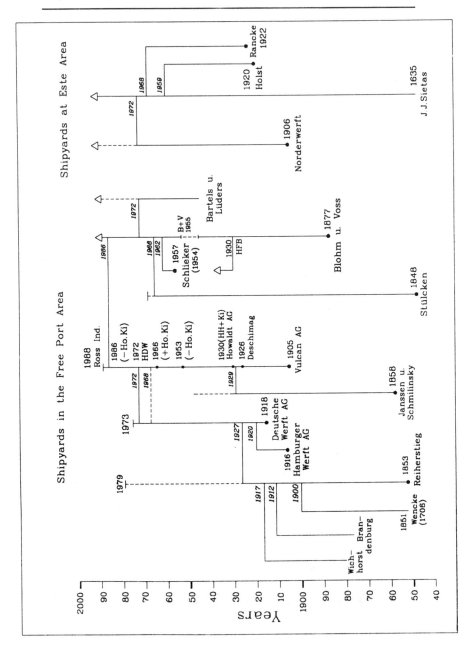

Figure 8.5: Development of Hamburg shipbuilding, 1835-1985

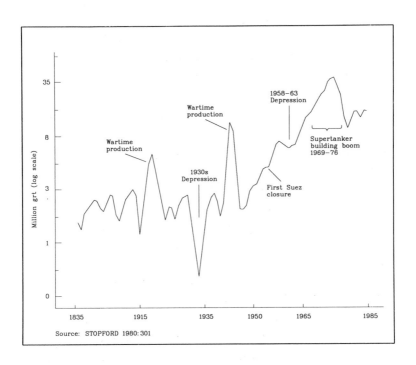

Source: STOPFORD 1980:301

: *based on Stopford, 1988.*

Figure 8.4 illustrates the historical process of concentration amongst the traditional Hamburg shipbuilding firms; and Figure 8.5 shows the cyclical development of world shipbuilding over the long period since 1896. The industry received major impulses in the middle of the nineteenth century, in connection with the transition from wooden to steel construction, and also with the increasing demands for commercial and naval vessels. A diversified growth took place, which involved a number of middle-sized shipyards forming limited companies (GmbH), and then larger stock companies (AG). The foundation of the Vulcan shipyard in 1905 as a branch plant of the Deutsche Werft AG (with capital support from the big stock companies of GHH at Oberhausen, AEG at Berlin and HAPAG at Hamburg), reflects the growing national importance of the Hamburg shipbuilding industry. It also indicates the special interest of large steel and mechanical engineering companies which, at the time, viewed the expansion of shipbuilding as a major outlet for their products.

After Germany's period of very rapid industrial expansion, which ended with the World War I, an economic crisis set in and with it came a wave of shipyard failures. In 1930 a group of insolvent firms joined together and, with government support, organised themselves into the Howaldt AG concern. The four big Hanseatic shipyards of the 1930s were eventually able to extend their activities through the expansionist policies of the Third Reich, especially where naval orders were concerned. After further bankruptcies and also destruction during the World War II, another boom followed during the years of the 'economic miracle' and postwar reconstruction. This boom ended in 1961 with the revaluation of the German Deutschmark and the growing competition from Japanese shipbuilders.

In 1962 the Schlieker shipyard went bankrupt after only five years of existence, and 5,000 workers lost their jobs. The two Howaldt shipyards in Hamburg and Kiel agreed to co-operate, and Blohm and Voss took over Stülcken in 1966. Six years later, the Howaldt group was extended by incorporating the Deutsche Werft AG. In spite of closing down the plants at Finkenwerder in 1973 and Reiherstieg in 1978, and concentrating its ship-repairing activities in Hamburg and Kiel, the Howaldt co-operation was unsuccessful and was eventually terminated in 1985. Blohm and Voss took over the Hamburg branch of HDW (now named Ross Industrie) and closed the plant in 1988. Thus, the concentration of major shipbuilding industries in Hamburg had come to an end. Only the big diversified company of Blohm and Voss, the middle-sized firm of J. Sietas and about 15 small shipyards have survived.

The shipbuilding crisis and government intervention

There are various reasons for the long-term crisis in the Hamburg shipbuilding industry. They relate not so much to problems on a local and regional level, but more to those on an international scale. There is, first of all, the changing economic situation in world maritime traffic which reflects, particularly in oil transport services, the shift of many traditional economic activities from developed industrialised countries to the Third World. There is also the tendency for the political decisions of underdeveloped countries to gain in importance, thereby lessening the regulative mechanisms of the market and encouraging considerable overcapacities in world shipping tonnage and ship production. These have had negative effects on price structures and sales potentials.

Under these global economic conditions, only limited alternative actions are possible on a national level. Most major shipbuilding countries have responded by bringing in schemes of government subsidies for preservation, and even some expansion, of capacity. Japan, and later Korea as well, encouraged exports by directly and indirectly subsidising their own shipbuilding companies. Sweden and Britain reacted by nationalising much of their industry, whilst in West Germany, since the 1960s, shipbuilding-aid programmes have been extended by both the Federal government and the coastal *Länder*.

Public subsidies are against the principles of a non-interventionist, free market economy. However, arguments in favour of subsidies in

West Germany arise from the fact that the shipbuilding industry is located in the country's structurally-weak coastal areas. Moreover, in several urban communities here, it is still the backbone of the local economy. For maintaining the necessary infrastructure in the larger harbours and ports, repair facilities must be provided, whilst in some centres strategic considerations make it necessary to keep sufficient new construction capacities for the navy and the domestic merchant fleet. A last point is that new technological development in maritime activities and related economic fields is very worth sustaining, on account of their links with several other industries. With considerations like these in mind, the West German government introduced aid programmes for the shipbuilding industry, based on subsidising ship construction and making it easier for owners to obtain loans for meeting new orders. At first the priority was given to the financing of exports; later, however, encouragement was extended to domestic requirements, especially the needs of the navy. In addition to this Federal government aid (which, in fact, has not been very helpful for the long-term reconstruction of the industry and saving of jobs), the coastal *Länder* have initiated their own programmes of intervention. These were focused upon diversifying the shipbuilding industry and, through retraining, making the workforce better equipped for alternative occupations. In Hamburg, during the years 1986-8, a total of DM 22.5 million was given to five shipbuilding firms which invested in new forms of production. Blohm and Voss received the largest share of this money but, because they have already started their own diversification programme, the full impact of the public subsidies here cannot be accurately assessed.

Reactions of the shipbuilding companies

Shipbuilding companies have been very much aware of these Federal and *Land* government aid programmes, and they have used these welcome resources almost as soon as they were made available. A subsidy-orientated mentality dominated the rather unprogressive managements of several of Hamburg's firms, with the result that opportunities for reforming company structures were not properly taken. Another problem arose from the common tendency for the principal shareholders of shipbuilding companies to be connected with the depressed West German steel industry, which itself was also having to grapple with severe structural difficulties.

In the mid-1970s, when the end of the tanker boom was marked by an abrupt decline in orders for new ships, fierce competition on international, national and regional scales intensified to such an extent that individual companies were increasingly being forced to adopt measures at plant level. Here construction capacities were tightened and repair businesses were extended, whilst functions not directly linked with shipbuilding were developed to diversify and supplement the activities of the concern. In the shipbuilding sector itself, specialisation on high-quality vessels offered the best chances, but, to do this, it was essential for firms to rationalise their production programme and to gain orders for 'series' outputs. Since all enterprises were hoping to overcome the mid-1970s crisis by applying similar concepts (but at the same time lacking co-ordination), the big shipbuilding companies increasingly penetrated fields of production which had formerly been the preserve of specialised medium and small firms. Not surprisingly, ruinous competition followed. Fluctuations in exchange rates, which for West German producers had the effect of increasing the costs and prices of exports, added to the problem. Furthermore, the partial ownership of shipping companies by shipbuilding firms led to higher awards of orders, but also thinned their capital resources and ultimately brought about excessive debts.

New investments in establishing and extending production of propelling engines and loading gear have been important elements in the expansion of shipbuilding 'subproduction', and have met with some success. However, attempts to develop a 'non-shipbuilding' sector of production have made less progress. The high expectations in markets for offshore and maritime oil-extracting technology have not been fulfilled, mainly due to the protectionism of Britain and Scandinavian countries.

181

Attempts to gain footholds in the steel and machine manufacturing industries, and to push through innovations in the sectors of energy and environment, have nearly all failed; firstly, because the respective markets were already firmly in the hands of competitors, and secondly, on account of a general lack of capital for necessary investments in the fields of research development and the training of skilled workers.

Blohm and Voss has been the most successful Hamburg shipbuilding company to develop a strategy of diversification by changing its inner structures, and also by acquisitions of other enterprises. The construction of ships and equipment for the navy has also been important. By taking over Schlieker in 1962 and Stülcken in 1966, extensive and only partly-used sites were neutralised, as far as competitors were concerned. Moreover, the acquisition of smaller firms enabled Blohm and Voss to obtain new patents and plants for the construction of machines, engines and boilers. At the same time, through redundancy programmes and retraining schemes, it was possible to adapt skilled workers to new methods of production.

From shipbuilding to chip production

Port-related industries still represent about 30% of Hamburg's manufacturing. The technologies used are mainly of a quite low standard; this is why they can be applied easily in underdeveloped countries where raw materials are also available. A further decline of these activities in Hamburg, therefore, is to be expected. To a large extent, port-linked industries are dependent on the cyclical variations of the world market and accordingly, risks can hardly be controlled at a local, or even national, level. Firms, therefore, require more diversification and regional integration of production, including new high-tech industries.

Regional development policy in the Hamburg region, which until the 1970s was based on growth-pole theory and traditional maritime concepts (Kern, 1970), was replaced by innovation-orientated strategies and the promotion of the region's endogenous potential by fiscal, infrastructural and educational measures (Lange, 1985/86). In addition, emphasis is now placed upon research and development in the manufacturing sector, including the foundation of a new technical university at Hamburg-Harburg, technology transfer agencies of the Chamber of Industry and Commerce, government-backed organisations to benefit small- and medium-sized firms and lastly, 'venture centres' in empty factory buildings to facilitate the setting up of new innovative enterprises. At the same time, larger established companies are encouraged to invest in new technologies and markets: in doing this they are able to gain large amounts of public subsidies. In the Hamburg area the pacesetters in this process of reconstruction are:

- electrical engineering, with the giant plants of Philips (9,000 workers), AEG (4,000), Siemens (3,000) and a total of 119 firms and 19,000 employees;

- aircraft industries, with MBB and Lufthansa (15,000);

- mechanical engineering, with 153 firms and 17,300 employees;

- the chemical industry, with 56 firms and 13,600 workers.

In 1988 these four manufacturing branches together accounted for 41% of industrial employment, 30% of turnover and 40% of the total export value of Hamburg's industrial production.

References

Behörde für Wirtschaft, Verkehr und Landwirtschaft, *Hafen Hamburg. Entwicklungsplan. Konzepte für Morgen*, Hamburg, 1976.

Bürgerschaft der freien und Hansestadt Hamburg (ed.), *Hamburger Aktionsprogramm Wirtschaft. Mitteilung des Senats an die Bürgerschaft*, Vol. 12/137, Hamburg, 1986.

Fante, W., 'Die Hintergründe der Schiffbaukrise', *Hansa*, Vol. 7/8, pp. 353-56, 1987.

Hajen, L., 'Krise des Schiffbaus - Krise der Schiffbauförderung?', *Jahrbuch für Sozialökonomie und Gesellschaftstheorie*, Opladen, pp.132-50, 1983.

Hamburgische Landesbank, *Wirtschaftsanalysen*, Hamburg, 1980ff.

Handelskammer Hamburg, *Ideen machen Märkte. Innovative Unternehmen in Hamburg*, Hamburg, 1987.

Handelskammer Hamburg, *Vom Schiff zum Chip. Industrieplatz Hamburg im Wandel*, Hamburg, 1989.

Husain, M.S., 'Influences on development policy in the port of Hamburg', in Hoyle, B.S. and Pinder, D.A. (eds), *Cityport industrialization and regional development*, Oxford, pp. 223-42, 1981.

Industrieverband Hamburg (ed.), *Struktur und Entwicklung der Hamburger Industriezweige*, Hamburg, 1986.

Kappel, R. and Rother, D., *Wandlungsprozesse in der Schiffahrt und im Schiffbau Westeuropas - Möglichkeiten einer Beeinflussung*, Bremen, 1982.

Kern, H., *Ein Modell für die wirtschaftliche Entwicklung der Region Unterelbe*, Hamburg, 1970.

Kramm, K., *Die Seeschiffswerften und ihre Standorte in der Bundesrepublik Deutschland unter Berücksichtigung der Zulieferindustrie und der internationalen Wettbewerbslage*, Essen, 1980.

Lange, V., 'Wirtschaftspolitik für Hamburg. Impulse für den Wirtschaftsstandort Hamburg 1985/86', *Schriftenreihe der Behörde für Wirtschaft, Verkehr und Landwirtschaft der FHH*, Vol. 16, 1986.

Nuhn, H., 'Industriestruktureller Wandel und Regionalpolitik dargestellt am Beispiel der Hansestadt Hamburg', *Geographische Rundschau*, Vol. 37, pp. 592-600, 1985.

Nuhn, H., Oßenbrügge, J. and Söker, E. (eds.), *Expansion des Hamburger Hafens und Konsequenzen für den Süderelberaum. Durchführung der Umsiedlung Altenwerders und Reaktion der Betroffenen*, Hamburg, 1983.

Rother, D., *The restructured west European shipbuilding industry*, Bremen, 1985.

Stopford, M., *Maritime economics*, London, 1988.

Verband der deutschen Schiffbau-Industrie, *100 Jahre Verbandsgeschehen*, Hamburg, 1984.

Verband für Schiffbau und Meerestechnik. *Jahresbericht 1987*, Hamburg, 1988.

Chapter IX

Bernhard Butzin (Universität Münster)

Regional life cycles and problems of revitalisation in the Ruhr

Regional development cycles and the Ruhr

The course of growth and decline of the Ruhr region during its 150 years of eventful industrial history, contains a series of regional development cycles very typical of old industrial core areas. The cycles themselves are responses to a succession of long 'technological waves', each of which has regional and local effects in terms of economic, political and sociocultural changes.

The driving force behind a regional development cycle is the so-called 'Kondratieff wave' (Figure 9.1), the principal assumptions of which are well known. The major economic, social and spatial reorganisation of societies does not occur evenly in time, but periodically, in cycles of about 40-60 years' duration. The beginnings of these cycles are each characterised by a cluster of technical innovations, caused by a fundamentally new generation of technology.

Generally speaking, the economic history of advanced industrial societies is based on a regular pattern of changes, with successive alternations of stable periods of growth on the one hand, and unstable periods of creativity, trial and error, restructuring and innovation, on the other. Each cluster of basic innovations creates a unique pattern of spatial organisation, social values and strategies of local and regional structuring (Butzin, 1987).

Figure 9.1: The last three Kondratieff long waves in terms of annual trend of industrial production (by volume)

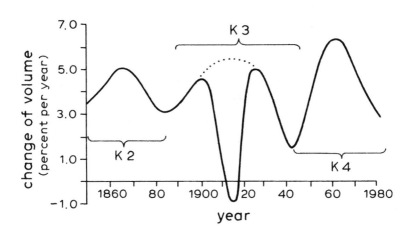

: based on Andersson et al., 1984.

The past industrial era left the Ruhr region's central parts (the Emscher zone) with overgrown industrial complexes and underdeveloped cities. The efficiency level of its human capital, especially its skills, management and organisational networks, had become outdated, while local political claims were still based largely on past successes. The determining factor leading to economic downturn and industrial stagnation or decline, is endogenous loss of creativity and development potential. The disappearance of the Schumpeterian entrepreneur in big companies and their subcontractors, is only one side of this loss. The self-sustaining coalition of management, labour and regional and local policy-makers is another aspect. The influences of this coalition become progressively stronger as the needs of, and experience in, crisis management increase.

The modernisation of the late-1960s, in the form of investment in the Ruhr's housing, transport and education infrastructures, follows separate life cycles. Only a few (and the most recent) elements of this modernisation are flexible enough for proper adaptation into 'post-Fordist' locational requirements. The new University of Dortmund is an interesting case in point: here some recreational and cultural facilities have been established, but it still has bad links to the nearest international airport at Düsseldorf, and its environs still have a negative image.

The concept of cycles of regional development provides an initial theoretical basis for assessing the risks and possibilities of structural changes and planning requirements. Yet old industrial regions in West Germany are facing additional problems which interfere with the 'regular' revitalisation pattern of undisturbed wave dynamics which, for example, do occur in the monocentric countries of northern Europe. The so-called 'upas tree effect', or 'shifting industrialisation', provides an additional theoretical concept for understanding the decline of the Ruhr: according to Checkland (1981) the upas tree of Java was believed to have the power to destroy other growth within a radius of 15 miles.

New technological waves tend to be excluded from, and to avoid, old industrial regions, which have been structured by preceding generations of technology. There are numerous examples of chemical, electrotechnical and vehicle manufacturing firms which have tried and failed to locate in the Ruhr area. Established companies blocked the attempts of prospective newcomers to come into the region. Some Ruhr firms refused to sell parts of their accumulated industrial land. Firms looking for new locations, and also young local entrepreneurs who were dealing in branches other than heavy industry, were unable to find a positive business climate and basis for growth. Such new enterprises prefer the attractive regions of the south, which are now booming in accordance with the implementation there of the most recent generation of high technology. Significantly, the highly-qualified 'human capital', trained in the Ruhr's universities and other seats of scientific and technological training, is now following this southwards drift (Butzin, 1987).

With its very considerable physical, social and image problems (notably soil contamination, high unemployment and poor creativity), the Ruhr region was considered to be very much a 'dying giant' at the beginning of the 1980s. Any attempts to apply the planning and development strategies of other regions appeared to be doomed because of the Ruhr's clear lack of endogenous development potential.

Figure 9.2: Model of regional development cycle and reality in the Ruhr

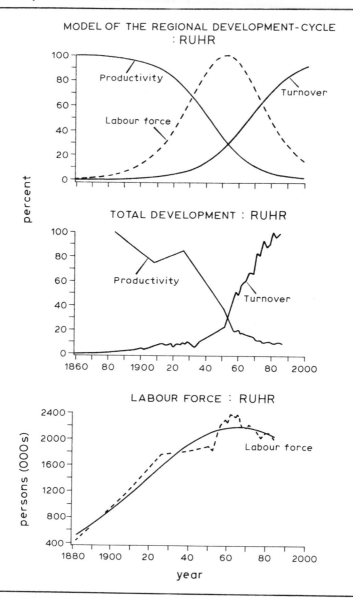

MODEL OF THE REGIONAL DEVELOPMENT-CYCLE : RUHR

TOTAL DEVELOPMENT : RUHR

LABOUR FORCE : RUHR

Source: Noll, 1987.

Economic change and regional subdivision in the Ruhr

The general economic situation of the Ruhr will now be discussed. When one considers the relationships between the labour force, turn-over and productivity of old industrial regions (Figure 9.2), an 'S'-shaped decline of labour input per unit of production is to be expected: in theory, the lower the ratio, the higher the rate of productivity. A corresponding shape should also occur for turnover. The empirical facts for the Ruhr are in accordance with this; therefore, the crucial question that must arise is, why is the region's total turn-over now showing decreasing rates of growth? The answer lies in the Ruhr's very limited development of the five general attributes of new technology. These are listed by Nijkamp (1987) as:

- the use of highly-skilled employees, many of whom are scientists and engineers;

- a high proportion of research and development in business activities;

- a nationwide, or worldwide, market for products;

- a high growth rate;

- lastly, a high degree of labour intensity in the production stage.

Professional and production-orientated services, research and development functions, and the ability to keep highly-trained human capital, especially skilled young workers, are now considered to be the most important dynamic forces behind regional development. In each of these, however, the Ruhr has severe deficiences. As shown in Table 9.1, the growth of professional services in the region (only 3.3% during the period 1978-85) is very slow, and lags well behind the 8.9% increase in *Land* North Rhine-Westphalia.

Table 9.1: Employment changes in professional services in the Ruhr region and North Rhine-Westphalia

	persons employed					
	Ruhr region			NRW (excluding Ruhr)		
	1978	1985	% change	1978	1985	% change
Engineers, professionals	31,313	31,659	+1.1	55,405	61,477	+10.9
Chemists, physicists, mathematicians	2,558	2,889	+12.9	7,488	8,439	+12.7
Entrepreneurs, senior accountants, organisers	30,728	30,508	-0.7	76,613	80,688	+5.3
Members of councils, executive administrators	2,858	3,197	+11.9	9,361	9,687	+3.5
Computer experts	35,656	30,833	-13.5	87,893	84,119	-4.3
Legal profession	849	943	+11.1	2,801	2,569	-8.3
Librarians, translators, publishers	3,244	3,737	+15.2	10,197	11,939	+17.1
Professional artists	7,442	6,735	-9.5	18,130	18,350	+1.2
Physicians, pharmacists	6,592	8,675	+31.6	13,891	18,613	+34.0
Social services	19,559	25,935	+32.6	46,834	63,325	+35.2
Teachers	12,906	12,387	-4.0	31,837	31,934	+0.3
TOTAL	156,076	161,293	+3.3	366,986	399,774	+8.9
Graduates	62,000	73,000	+17.7	137,300	176,500	+28.5
Technical experts	96,081	92,296	-3.9	177,557	182,951	+3.0

Note: the Ruhr region is defined here as the *Kommunalverband Ruhrgebiet.*

Source: Noll, p.14, 1987.

For several service activities, especially those that are closely linked with industrial production, the gap is even wider. For example, the Ruhr lost 0.7% of its entrepreneurs, organisers and senior accountants (compared with a gain of 5.3% in North Rhine-Westphalia). The Ruhr also lost 13.5% of its trained computer experts (4.3% loss in NRW) and gained only 1.1% in professional engineers (10.9% increase in NRW).

The Ruhr region, moreover, has major deficiencies in terms of qualified and skilled workforce. The proportion of employees here who have graduated from a university or from a *Fachhochschule* (broadly equivalent to a polytechnic), grew by 17.7% during 1978-85, but this was much slower than the 28.5% increase in North Rhine-Westphalia. Technical specialists are another important example: they decreased in numbers in the Ruhr by 3.9%, compared with a gain of 3% in NRW. Even more striking is the fact that legal, consulting and real estate services, together with advertising agencies and trade fairs in North Rhine-Westphalia, exceeded those in the Ruhr by as much as two and a half times. On the other hand, the Ruhr is producing large numbers of human capital - the most valuable source of endogenous growth potential. Yet, through heavy population out-migration, this vital resource is leaving in quantities considerable enough to constitute a substantial 'brain drain'.

What is to be done, in a situation where endogenous development potential, at least as far as the local training of qualified human capital is concerned, is certainly being generated but is only being used in part within the Ruhr region itself? First of all, it should be stressed that the consequences of these problems have never been close to anything like a full regional collapse; nor are they likely to be so in the future. The region's southern areas, namely the Ruhr valley and the 'Hellweg axis', did, in fact, manage to adopt some of the growth dynamics of tertiary and quaternary activities, and saw the establishment of centres of technology and innovation. The closures of the steel mills in the Ruhrtal at Hattingen (Henrichshütte) and very recently, on the left bank of the Rhine at Rheinhausen (Krupp), were successfully isolated as local problems. Regional protests did occur, but generally they took the form of open air 'happenings' and festivals which, if anything, operated as 'safety valves'.

The Emscher zone; problems of revitalisation

However, the revitalisation of the region's southern parts is very much in contrast to what has been happening in the Emscher zone further north. This part of the Ruhr has traditionally had a much more vulnerable local economy. It is here where huge complexes of power plants and chemicals combines are surrounded by waste tips, waste-recycling plants and sewage works. The cities and districts of the Emscher zone are experiencing population losses at considerably higher rates than the regional average. For example, during the period 1970-87, the Emscher cities of Gelsenkirchen and Herne suffered population declines of 17.4% and 14.3% respectively; the trend for the whole of the Ruhr (defined as the area of the *Kommunalverband Ruhrgebiet*) was a loss of 11.6% (KVR, 1988).

In the Emscher zone, the notion of subregional differentiation of development cycles provides a distinct conceptual framework for the design and application of new social-economic policy instruments (Knaap, 1988). The Ruhr region as a whole, is developing a subregional division of labour, in which the southern areas, particularly the Hellweg zone, prepare for a technological 'take-off', but the Emscher zone has still to deal with problems and burdens inherited from the past.

This phenomenon, however, is not entirely a problem of the labour market and the subregional division of labour. The willingness and ability of Emscher zone firms to invest must not be ignored. To use a catch phrase: we are facing a polarisation of regional 'entrepreneurial culture'. The large steel companies in the area are engaged in a process of restructuring and diversification: they are taking over, or merging with, companies in growth branches of manufacturing, but in doing so they are very often placing investments outside the Ruhr region. Modernisation strategies, which are concentrated actually within the traditional locations, are exceptions. Many Emscher firms, in fact, are quantitatively and qualitatively disinvesting in local human capital, and are leaving it to government bodies to subsidise and control the contraction process. The search for endogenous development potential for the Emscher zone cannot be seen to lie with the large companies.

In an analysis of predominantly small- and medium-sized firms in the cities of Gelsenkirchen, Herne and Castrop-Rauxel, in the core of the Emscher zone, a recent study (Aring et al., 1989), reveals a remarkable polarisation here in local entrepreneurial strategies and attitudes. In many cases firms declared no experience at all in innovating products and creating new markets. Yet an extremely high degree of inflexibility in product innovation was matched by strong levels of acceptance and adoption of high-tech production processes. However, too much capital in the area is being invested in types of machinery which only process a very small range of specialised products. Moreover, all too often a rather pessimistic expectation of the Emscher zone's future was declared. This was combined with the obvious image problems of weak location and poor environment.

Instruments of economic restructuring, such as technology transfer and co-operation with research institutions and universities, can work quite well when there is sufficient demand from small- and medium-sized companies. But these 'top-down' offerings do not fit in easily with managerial attitudes. Some entrepreneurs are openly not in favour of innovations. Those who are, generally tend to favour innovations in processing facilities, rather than the development of new products and markets. What the Emscher zone most urgently needs for developing its endogenous potential, are 'bottom-up' mechanisms which facilitate entrepreneurial creativity in the spheres of organisation, co-operation and development of appropriate products and markets.

A further problem in developing the endogenous potential of the Emscher zone, is the size of the unemployed labour force and its attitudes, especially the youthful segment. In spite of rapidly growing social problems, which tend to be encapsulated and hidden from observers, many people in the disadvantaged labour force manage to develop strategies for muddling through. It is not the quantity and variety of 'top-down' initiatives, job-qualification courses and re-training schemes that are in short supply; it is the small numbers of people who are willing to join them, which is the problem.

When dealing with endogenous development potential at the local authority level, there are repeated complaints from officials that rules regulating planning and administration are too tight and involve too much red tape. Designed to meet the problems of the past, the network of rules and regulations is considered to inhibit creativity, co-operation and the introduction of new projects severely, each of which is crucial if local and regional authorities are, in fact, going to be able to adapt to their changing future functions.

Conclusion

This chapter makes the point that instruments like technological transfer, financial aid, and training required sections of the labour force for higher job qualification, are one-sided and, in some repects, overrated. Modern regional development mechanisms of this type can work effectively but, on their own, cannot change the entrenched attitudes of management, officials and workers. For the proper open-ing up of the endogenous potential of heavily-industrialised areas like the Emscher zone, new forms of creativity and a more co-operative form of organisation are essential. Such initiative should take the form of personal networks, rooted in *local* competence and abilities, which bring together key local persons, public authorities and exter-nal professionals.

References

Andersson, A.G. et al., *Regional mangfald till rikets gagn. En idebok fran ERU,* Liber, Stockholm, 1984.

Aring, J. et al., *Erscheinungsformen des 'räumlichen Bewußtseins' im Ruhrgebiet und seine Bedeutung für die Regionalentwicklung,* forthcoming publication, 1990.

Butzin, B., 'Strukturwandel im Ruhrgebiet? Zum Entstehungs- und Wirkungszusammenhang der Krise', in Köhler, E. and Wein, N. (eds.), *Natur- und Kulturräume, Ludwig Hempel zum 65 Geburtstag,* Münstersche Geographische Arbeiten, Vol. 27, Paderborn, pp. 301-14, 1987a.

Butzin, B., 'Zur These eines regionalen Lebenszyklus im Ruhrgebiet', in Mayr, A. and Weber, P. (eds.), *100 Jahre Geographie an der Westfälischen-Wilhelms Universität Münster,* Münstersche Geographische Arbeiten, Vol. 26, Paderborn, pp. 191-210, 1987b.

Checkland, S.G., *The upas tree. Glasgow 1875-1975 and after,* University of Glasgow Press, Glasgow, second edition, 1981.

Knaap, van der, G.A., *Development cycles and spatial management,* paper presented to the IGU Commission on Industrial Change, *Rutherglen, Tasmania, 14-21 August 1981.*

Kommunalverband Ruhrgebiet, *Kurzinformation zur Wohnbevölkerung im Ruhrgebiet, Erste VZ-Ergebnisse,* KVR, Essen, 1988.

Der Minister für Stadtentwicklung, Wohnen und Verkehr des Landes Nordrhein-Westfalen (ed.), *Internationale Bauausstellung Emscher-Park. Werkstatt für die Zukunft alter Industriegebiete. Memorandum zu Inhalt und Organisation,* Düsseldorf, 1988.

Nijkamp, P., 'New technology and regional development', in Vasko, T. (ed.), pp. 274-84, 1987.

Noll, W. (1987), *Die Entwicklung der produktionsorientierten Dienste im Ruhrgebiet 1978-1985*, KVR, Essen.

Stadt Essen, *Bevölkerungs-und Arbeitsmarktentwicklung. Auswirkungen im sozialen Bereich*, Amt für Entwicklungsplanung, Essen, 1988.

Vasko, T. (ed.), *The long-wave debate. Selected papers*, International Institute for Applied Systems Analysis, Weimar, East Germany, 10-14 June 1987.

Chapter X

Thomas Hauff (Universität Münster)

De-industrialisation, socioeconomic change and revitalisation in the west Münsterland textile area: the case of Gronau

Introduction

Industrial change in Britain since 1960 has been marked by heavy employment losses in the manufacturing sector. This phenomenon, which has also been clearly represented in the United States since the end of the 1970s, can be described in national economic terms as 'de-industrialisation' (Blackaby, 1978; Bluestone and Harrison, 1982). In West Germany, however, the experience has been rather different. As in other major advanced industrialised countries, the numbers of workers in manufacturing have decreased generally since 1970, but there have also been, during this period, some brief phases of employment upturn in this economic sector; notably 1977-80, and 1985-6 (Figure 10.1). This is why there has yet to be a real debate on the de-industrialisation phenomenon and its implications in West Germany.

In certain branches of West German industry, however, de-industrialisation is all too evident, especially in mining, steel production and shipbuilding. The West German textile industry is also a clear case in point. Here, during the period 1962-84, the numbers of workers dwindled by as much as 60%. The North Rhine-Westphalian textile industry was hit particularly severely, with a huge 84% decline in its workforce. Of course, the employment trend on its own cannot serve as a complete indicator of the de-industrialisation trend (Watts, 1987). Production and turnover in the textile industry are also lagging behind and have, in fact, shown periodic losses.

Figure 10.1: West Germany; sectoral trends in employment, 1962-87

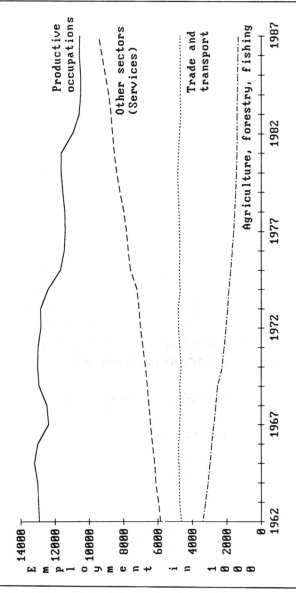

Source: Statistisches Jahrbuch für die Bundesrepublik Deutschland.

Declining industries cause fundamental changes in the regional economy, and social difficulties cannot be avoided, especially in a monostructured industrial concentration like that of the west Münsterland textile area. Here, the city of Gronau, with its extension into the district of Epe in 1975, is highly representative of vigorous de-industrialisation and intensive economic change, and accordingly merits investigation in some detail.

This chapter will turn, first of all, to Gronau's regional setting and the characterisation of the local textile industry. Government and local intervention in the process of de-industrialisation here will then be considered, followed by an examination of its socioeconomic effects. Lastly, the possibilities of economic revitalisation of Gronau through government aid will be discussed.

Characterisation of the west Münsterland textile region

In considering de-industrialisation in the west Münsterland textile region, existing regional structures and aspects of historical growth should be taken into account. The region itself stretches along the German-Dutch border, from Bocholt in the south-west, to Gronau and Rheine in the north-west (Figure 10.2). In the north it extends beyond North Rhine-Westphalia into a small part of the *Land* Lower Saxony, where it includes the town of Nordhorn. We are dealing with an industrial belt which is situated very close to the national frontier, cuts across a *Land* boundary, and has a loose, dispersed pattern of industrial and urban development, with a plurality of small towns. The main urban centres in west Münsterland are Rheine (69,307 inhabitants) and Bocholt (67,441). Gronau, with a population of 39,412, is located in the far north-western corner of North Rhine-Westphalia, very close to Lower Saxony and the Dutch frontier (Table 10.1).

Figure 10.2: Location of Gronau and other west Münsterland urban centres

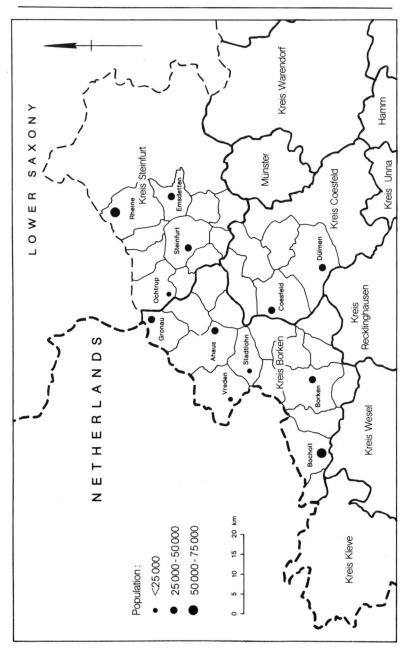

Table 10.1: Population of main urban settlements in the west Münsterland in 1988

number of inhabitants					
<25,000		25,000-50,000		50,000-75,000	
Ochtrup	16,943	Steinfurt	30,140	Bocholt	67,441
Stadtlohn	17,150	Ahaus	30,140	Rheine	69,307
Vreden	18,767	Emsdetten	31,075		
		Coesfeld	31,843		
		Dülmen	39,206		
		GRONAU	39,412		

Source: Mitteilung des Landesamtes für Datenverarbeitung und Statistik Nordrhein-Westfalen, 1988.

The region's textile industry originated in cottage and farmhouse linen-weaving, based initially on locally-grown flax and hemp. The adoption of spinning machinery and, later, power-loom weaving, led to factory production from the 1840s onwards. By the end of the nineteenth century, numerous mechanised textile factories had been founded in Rheine, Bocholt and Gronau, and also in the many country towns and villages that were situated in-between. The dominant type of firm was the small, family-owned company. Subsequently, the development of the west Münsterland textile industry became more complex. The northern part of the region became dominated by the spinning process, whereas in southern west Münsterland there emerged a greater diversity of production (Kersting, 1958).

Helped by its lower wage levels (compared with those on the other side of the adjoining German-Dutch frontier), factory production of textiles developed rapidly in Gronau during and after the mid-nineteenth century, with a wave of mainly Dutch-financed mill constructions (Döhrmann, 1925). Of particular importance were the Dutch firms of Mathieu van Delden and Gerrit Van Delden, who opened their large mills in Gronau in 1854 and 1875 respectively. These two firms later merged into the 'Van Delden Konzern' which, at the time, was the largest textile trust in Western Germany. With the opening of more spinning mills in 1888, 1890 and 1896, Gronau emerged as one of Europe's most important linen-spinning centres (Kötter, 1952). Its position was further strengthened by the opening of another group of mills in the growing village of Epe which, as has already been mentioned, is now part of the administrative area of the city.

Decline of the Gronau textile industry: a case study of local de-industrialisation

Gronau was not very badly damaged during World War II, and textile production was resumed quickly, despite the general difficulties of the early postwar years. By 1951, employment in textiles in Gronau and Epe had reached its maximum prewar level. In that year there were 8,467 textile workers, representing an overwhelming 90% of the local industrial labour force. During the first 15 or so years of the postwar period, the development of the textile industry here, and elsewhere in west Münsterland, was marked by brief cyclical crises of production, accompanied by short-time work and redundancies. Nevertheless, the industry continued to dominate the local economy.

Due to the automation and rationalisation of the production process, the number of textile workers in Gronau began to fall during the 1960s (a decline of about 25% from 1959-69), but there were still no real signs of lasting de-industrialisation: turnover and production, helped by the introduction of new products, were still expanding. The Van Delden group played a major part in this growth, mainly through its involvement in partnerships and takeovers of other textile firms. By the end of the 1960s, it had advanced to fifth position among European textile companies.

Figure 10.3: Textiles employment in Gronau, 1959-87

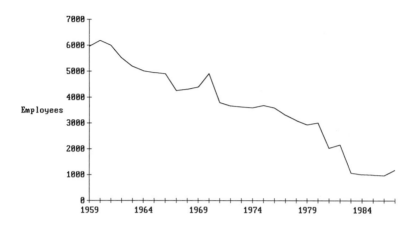

Source: Statistisches Landesamt für Datenverarbeitung und Statistik Nordrhein-Westfalen.

While the number of textile workers in Gronau and Epe fell by a further 25% during the 1970s (Figure 10.3), the Van Delden Konzern started to transfer its production to overseas countries; initially the United States and Brazil. The reasons for this were not only its desire to take advantage of growing international wage differentials, but also considerations such as protective duties, freight costs, risk calculation and intensified usage of skills (Fröbel et al.). Van Delden could not remain untouched by the growing structural problems of the West German textile industry. In 1979 the authorities of North Rhine-Westphalia and of Lower Saxony stepped in to provide securities for this firm's factories, as an attempt to save 2,500 jobs. At the time, this intervention by the two *Länder* provoked much argument in both public and private circles. In spite of this financial assistance, by 1980 Van Delden had mounting debts. The final collapse came two years later when the firm's last 1,250 workers were made redundant. Some of the factors leading to the Van Delden breakdown are still undefined. General issues, such as cheap imports, the economic downswing of the early 1980s, and high wage costs, certainly all played significant roles. However, factors specific to the firm itself, such as poor financial resources, miscalculations of markets and wrong product orientations, must not be overlooked. Today, only three large spinning mills are still active in Gronau, once one of Europe's leading spinning centres. In 1987 these mills, together with some minor firms, provided work for just 1,185 employees. Thus, as many as 7,282 jobs have been lost since 1951; a decline of 86%. More than one-half of these job losses have come since the end of the 1970s when, with production figures also sinking, the term 'de-industrialisation' became fully appropriate here.

Local consequences of de-industrialisation

The Van Delden shutdown in 1982 resulted in the creation of extensive industrial wastelands in the northern parts of inner Gronau. The civic planners had to face a new situation, since the vacant sites now offered some potential for reinvigoration of the inner quarters of the city, and through this the creation of new jobs. In 1985, *Land* North Rhine-Westphalia and a private investor acquired large sections of the Van Delden land and properties. The original intentions of the new owners here were to redevelop the sites and buildings into large-scale retail premises. So far, however, there have been no real positive changes. The mills, some of which have been classified as historical monuments, have been lying vacant for several years, and are in a very poor condition. Dilapidation proceeds rapidly, as evidenced by the increasing numbers of broken roofs, smashed windows, missing gutters and the all too obvious manifestations of vandalism. If these historical factories are to be used properly in urban renewal and in improving the image of the city, the original plans of 1985 must be implemented straightaway, before there is further decay.

Plans drawn up by the city council to concentrate civic resources and investment in the inner city, place a high priority on converting the former Van Delden 'Eilermark' mill to new uses. However, this scheme is endangered by the intentions of a private company to de-velop the premises into a new superstore, which, bearing in mind the generally cheaper West German prices and the proximity of the Dutch frontier, would be particularly well located.

Social and demographic consequences

The unemployment rate in Gronau climbed steeply to 15% in 1982 and reached around 20% in 1983. This dramatically high level, which was maintained for the next four years (Figure 10.3), created very severe social hardships. In the wake of the Van Delden collapse, Gronau's unemployment rate was, in fact, higher than that of any other urban community in North Rhine-Westphalia. It is, indeed, sur-prising that, despite the tenseness of the job situation in and around Gronau, there were neither protest movements, nor occupations of factories like those which had accompanied pit and steel closures in the more militant Ruhr. A plausible historical reason for this lack of organised opposition in Gronau is that, for generations, textile workers in west Münsterland have always been loyal to their companies and have been accustomed to periodic unemployment and short-time work (Balsen, et al., 1983). In addition, workers and their shop stewards hoped that, by being passive, they could positively influence takeover negotiations with other firms.

Unemployment on this scale, with its accompanying cuts in household incomes, loss of self-confidence and family conflicts, has drastic social consequences. The sharp reduction in the spending power of jobless workers and their families has damaging effects on local commerce, particularly the retail trade. The high unemployment rate is causing heavy population migration from Gronau, especially among young workers and *Gastarbeiter*. Textile firms based in southern Germany, which are still seeking skilled operatives, are encouraging this movement by placing job advertisements in the local newspapers.

The 'exodus' of textile workers has left its mark on the townscape of Gronau, where several deserted blocks of streets are awaiting restoration or renewal. The condition of a large proportion of the city's former company-owned dwellings, which were sold off to tenants during the last textile crisis, is deteriorating rapidly. Many of the owner-occupiers are unemployed, or have suffered substantial reductions in income and, therefore, lack the financial means to keep the houses in good repair.

Also very serious, is the way in which the high unemployment rate is leading to a running down of the urban image of Gronau. It is being labelled as a 'dying' town, and this negative perception of the community will most likely inhibit future attempts at local economic revitalisation (Hartleb, 1983).

De-industrialisation and Gronau's financial situation

The Van Delden breakdown cost Gronau as much as one-third of its trade-tax revenues, and meant that the community was encumbered with large financial deficits. Indeed, by 1985, the debts of the city had risen to nearly DM 2,500 per person: two years later the per capita figure had risen to DM 2,750 (Kreis Borken, 1988). But whilst Gronau was suffering this sharp decline in its tax income, it was also faced with a marked rise in its obligations for expenditure on social needs. The resulting dilemma did not leave the city council much scope for providing money for unemployment relief and financial support for restructuring the local economy.

De-industrialisation and revitalisation: reactions by public authorities

Although there were redundancies in the local textile industry as early as 1955, it took a further decade before the city council first made a serious attempt to achieve some diversification of Gronau's economic structure. A policy of accumulating land for the development of new industrial sites and estates was initiated in the mid-1960s, with the intention of providing basic requirements for the settling of new firms. Until then, the overwhelming influence of the staple textile industry had mitigated against any significant changes.

By 1988, Gronau had spent DM 120 million in developing three industrial zones within the administrative limits of the city. More than 100 new firms, providing 3,000 jobs, were attracted (Stadtdirektor der Stadt Gronau, 1986). But there was some controversy concerning the type of some of the new plants: a large proportion was externally controlled and several could be criticised on environmental grounds. Not surprisingly, the opening of a uranium processing plant by the firm Uranit aroused the greatest amount of public concern. Due to nuclear safety precautions, only certain parts of the plant have been put into operation so far and, apart from the construction work, it has created few jobs.

Although there is now a trend towards greater employment diversification, Gronau is still dominated by the manufacturing sector, which accounts for 45% of local jobs (Statistisches Landesamt, 1988). The textile industry is still important in this, but has recently lost its leading position to plastics manufacturing. Other new branches of industry in the city include food processing, electrical engineering and the production of machine tools and vehicle components. Job creation in these activities, however, continues to lag well behind the employment losses in textiles.

In 1968 Gronau was designated as a Federal Development Area (*Bundesausbauort*) and, with this, plans to attract new manufacturing firms into the city were integrated into the Federal Regional Development Programme. From 1970-5, Gronau retained this status of Development Area, but within a new and more intensive programme of regional assistance. This, the 1969 'Joint Task: Improvement of Regional Economic Structures' and its 21 'Regional Action Programmes' (of which the *Aktionsprogramm Nord Ruhr-Westmünsterland* involved Gronau), offered a financial support within a 10-15% range for investment plans, such as foundations of new firms, extensions of factories, rationalisation of production methods and technical improvements.

In 1987 the 'Improvement of Regional Economic Structures' programme was modified, and as a result, Gronau qualified for grants of up to 20% for new operational investments. In addition, the city could now receive subventions from the European Community's special programme of aid for designated 'textiles closures areas'.

Although the problems inherent in overdependence on one single branch of an old manufacturing industry were recognised quite early in west Münsterland and Gronau, the huge scale of de-industrialisation here was certainly unforeseen. Accordingly, measures to compensate for this trend and to develop new economic activities came too late and fell well short of what was really required. The various subvention programmes did help to offset some of the worst consequences of de-industrialisation in the city, but regional policy in general failed to draw up a clear enough strategy. Apart from the recent European Community intervention, there has been no special programme for declining textile areas similar to those implemented in West Germany for localities engaged in steel, shipbuilding and even shoe manufacturing.

Conclusion

As well as facing general structural problems, Gronau's recent economic history has been dominated by very rapid de-industrialisation, which within the timespan of just three years, 1980-3, resulted in a 65% decline in jobs in the city's staple textile industry. The violence and speed of de-industrialisation were caused by the collapse of one single giant Fordist firm, the Van Delden Konzern.

Intervention by public bodies, with their large subsidies, has so far not really succeeded in regenerating Gronau's economy and bringing unemployment down to an acceptable level. The negative image of the city, and also its peripheral geographical location within the West German national space, continue to serve as major obstacles to progress. The latter problem will most likely be eased with the introduction of frontier-free trade in the European Community after 1992, but realistically no ending of the decline of the west Münsterland and Gronau textile industry can be expected. A radical turnaround in the fortunes of Gronau can only be achieved if local decision-makers become properly aware of its resources, and if they use this potential in the appropriate direction. More new firms must be attracted into the city, which is difficult in present economic conditions and these firms should be ones which are environmentally sound and not likely to lead the community into a new state of dependence.

References

Balsen, W. et al., *Ohne Arbeit geh'ste kaputt. Reportagen aus dem Innerleben der Krise,* Pahl-Rugenstein, Cologne, 1983.

Blackaby, F., *De-industrialisation,* Heinemann, London, 1978.

Bluestone, B. and Harrison, B., *The de-industrialisation of America. Plant closings, community abandonment and the dismantling of basic industry,* Basic Books, New York, 1982.

Döhrmann, K., *Die Entstehung der Gronauer Textilindustrie und ihre Entwicklung,* Cologne, 1925.

Fröbel, F., Heinrichs, J. and Kreye, O., *Die neue internationale Arbeitsteilung. Strukturelle Arbeitslosigkeit in den Industrieländern und die Industrialisierung in den Industrieländern,* Rowohlt, Hamburg-Reinbeck, 1977.

Hartleb, D., 'Eine Stadt gibt sich nicht auf. Gronau im Westmünsterland hat eine Arbeitslosenquote von 21,3 Prozent', *Kommunalpolitische Blätter,* Vol. 35, pp.281-85, 1983.

Kersting, A., 'Das Textilindustriegebiet des westfälisch-niederländischen Grenzbezirks. Entwicklung und Probleme des 'Baumwollgebietes Rhein-Ems'', *Westfälische Forschungen,* Vol. 11, pp.86-105, 1958.

Kötter, H., *Die Textilindustrie des deutsch-niederländischen Grenzgebietes in ihrer wirtschaftsgeographischen Verflechtung,* Geographisches Institut der Universität Bonn, 1952.

Kreis Borken, *Szenario Kreis Borken 2000,* Borken, 1988.

Nuhn, H. and Sinz, M., 'Industriestruktureller Wandel und Beschäftigtenstruktur in der Bundesrepublik Deutschland', *Geographische Rundschau*, Vol. 40, pp. 42-52, 1988.

Stadtdirektor der Stadt Gronau (ed.,) *Gronau. Statistisches Jahrbuch, Ausgabe 1986 Stadt Gronau*, Gronau, 1986.

Stadtplanungsamt Gronau (ed.), *Städtebauliche Neordnung der Innenstadt des Stadtteils Gronau*, Stadtplanungsamt Gronau, annual.

Statistisches Landesamt für Datenverarbeitung und Statistik Nordrhein-Westfalen, *Mitteilung des Statistischen Landesamt für Datenverarbeitung und Statistik Nordrhein-Westfalen*, SLDS NRW, Düsseldorf, 1988.

Temlitz, K., 'Siedlung und Struktur des Grenzraumes', in: Geographische Kommission für Westfalen, *Westmünsterland-Ostniederlande. Entwicklung und Stellung eines Grenzraumes*, Vol. 30, pp. 25-38, 1984.

Watts, H.D., *Industrial geography*, Longman, Harlow, 1987.

Chapter XI

Wolf Gaebe (Universität Mannheim)

De-industrialisation and industrial restructuring in the Rhine-Neckar area

This chapter first outlines the general development tendencies of West German industry, using the Rhine-Neckar area as an example, and then proceeds to demonstrate the problems of old-industrialised areas from the West German viewpoint. The limited dynamic qualities of this particular part of south-west Germany can be attributed to the combined effects of three issues:

- firstly, unfavourable branch, firm-size and product structures;

- secondly, inadequate environmental protection measures;

- thirdly, the political and economic dependence (and lack of opportunities for appropriate action) of local authorities on external decision-makers.

The chapter will conclude by indicating those measures which are now being taken to stimulate structural change and economic improvement in the region.

General trends in West German industry

Structural shift towards the tertiary sector
In West Germany, as in other western industrialised countries including Britain and the United States, activity in industry, especially in production, transportation, storage and administration, is becoming less important, both in absolute and in relative terms. On the other hand, service functions, and research and development in particular,

are becoming more and more important in both the secondary and the tertiary sectors of the economy (Table 11.1).

Table 11.1: Changes in the spatial distribution of industrial (secondary sector) and tertiary employment in West Germany, 1970-85

| locations | % of 1985 labour force in | | % change 1970-85 | |
	secondary sector	tertiary sector	secondary sector	tertiary sector
old-industrialised areas	52	48	-16	+26
major agglomeration areas				
Rhine-Ruhr north	54	46	-16	+27
Saarland	54	46	-12	+20
Rhine-Neckar	53	47	-18	+32
Munich	39	61	-27	+31
regions				
metropolitan regions	47	53	+19	+27
rural regions	53	47	-14	+25
WEST GERMANY	49	51	-18	+26

Source: Sinz, Hillesheim and Runge, p. 956, 1986.

Even if production-related services, such as advertising, marketing, financing and data processing, are included within the broadest connotation of manufacturing activities, the secondary economic sector has been declining ever since the onset of the 1970s (Henckel et al., 1986). The relative and absolute increases of tertiary employment owe themselves to fundamental socioeconomic change, and are associated with a new geographical division of labour. What were once perceived as locational advantages, such as local availability of raw materials, have now become disadvantages. Indeed, quite often today it is the lack of raw materials and energy within a locality which counts as a locational 'attraction'.

Structural change in West German industry has come as a response to alterations in locational factors and world economic conditions: in particular, alterations in international exchange rates, national economic policies, wage costs, taxation systems and, increasingly today, levels of pollution control. At the same time, traditional industrial location factors have been replaced by the so-called 'soft' factors, such as quality of living and leisure opportunities. The weight attached to these, however, does vary according to type of branch, firm-size and product specialisation.

The principal general features of structural change in West German industry are:

- decreases in employment with low skill components; reductions in the length of product life-cycles;

- increases in the functional division of labour within firms;

- the worsening of West Germany's position as a manufacturer of certain ranges of products within both the consumer and the investment fields of industry.

Comparative advantages in production have shifted from mass products, with their economies of scale and their strong degree of competition, to specialised products and price-intensive items, which are made to order. There has also been a shift from wage-intensive products (with their low proportional returns, limited price elasticities and high sensitivity to cyclical changes and exchange-rate influences), to high-technology products, services and problem-solving activities, which can utilise West Germany's prime advantage of highly-educated, skilled and experienced human capital.

It is debatable whether a long-term decline in industrial employment within a region can really be called de-industrialisation when it is accompanied by continually-growing industrial outputs, expanding industrial exports and an increasing share of trade in industrial goods (Cairncross, 1979). Mining and manufacturing was West Germany's most important general economic sector until the 1970s, and had dominated economic and social development for well over a century. It can still be a decisive factor in regional development, but is now becoming less important in terms of its contributions to labour markets and regional product.

Disparities in regional development
Unequal regional development is a characteristic of all societies, irrespective of whether they have a capitalist or a socialist political economy. West Germany is no exception, although in this country traditional patterns of regional imbalances, particularly in industrial employment trends, are now being replaced. The rural regions have been increasing their share of the nation's industrial employment since the mid-1970s; correspondingly, the share of the urban areas has been declining. Until then, the main problem for urban and regional planning in West Germany was the weak development and backward living standards of the rural parts of the country. The extension of industrialisation, and other forms of economic activity, into the rural regions, has greatly eased this problem, but many of these areas are still disadvantaged as far as the actual *quality* of employment is concerned. Generally speaking, jobs in rural areas are still less well paid than those in towns and cities. The centres of gravity for job creation (but not so much for quality of employment) are moving centrifugally from the urban agglomerations to the urban-rural fringes, and beyond into many of the rural regions. This movement is linked to important changes in the functional organisation and division of labour; for example, in manufacturing, the management and administrative functions of major firms are still concentrated within the cities, but the production, storage and distribution activities are increasingly carried out in the surrounding districts.

Over West Germany in general, the contribution of the newly-industrialising areas to job opportunities is increasing, whilst that of the traditional industrial locations is declining. The newly-industrialising areas, particularly those in southern Germany, have distinctly higher overall economic growth rates, much lower unemployment rates and substantial in-migration of population (Sinz, Hillesheim and Runge, 1986). The region in and around Munich, for example, now provides important locations for robotics research, aviation and aerospace industries, laser and medical technologies. The old-industrialised parts of the country have now replaced the rural regions as the major problem areas confronting West Germany's regional policy-makers.

The spatial directions of industrial development are conditioned by economic needs and type and structure of the units of production. Employment is falling markedly in the old industrial locations and in those industrial branches that had developed during earlier forms of industrialisation. In the Ruhr and in the Saarland, two classic old-industrialised regions, the decline of coalmining and steel production has achieved crisis proportions. In the Rhine-Neckar area the chemical industry has taken the lead in de-industrialisation, whilst in the Stuttgart region, the trend (which is less acute here) has been underlain by employment losses in a group of newer, Fordist-type industries, which include mechanical engineering, motor vehicle manufacture and electrical engineering. In each of these situations, large-scale, highly-concentrated firms and branches are becoming less dominant. Regional industrial structures are becoming more diversified and more differentiated, although in the old-industrialised areas these changes are by no means as strong as in the new locations of manufacturing production.

The example of the Rhine-Neckar area

The Rhine-Neckar area is West Germany's sixth-largest urban agglomeration and accommodates 1,750,000 people. It exhibits, particularly in the core of the conurbation, the characteristic structural problems of the heavily-populated, old-industrialised parts of the country; in particular heavy demographic decline in the central cities of Mannheim and Ludwigshafen, large losses of industrial employment and consequent above-average unemployment (Table 11.2), major environmental problems, land use conflicts and increasing municipal debts.

Table 11.2: Changes in total employment and industrial employment in the Rhine-Neckar region, 1961-87

	total employment % change 1961-87	industrial employment % change 1961-87	unemployment rate (%) Dec. 1988
central cities	+5.3	-15.8	9.5
major	+5.6	-13.7	9.5
medium-sized	+4.3	-25.3	9.7
suburban areas	+47.9	-22.0	6.0
RHINE-NECKAR REGION	+18.1	-17.9	7.7

Note: the major cities in the Rhine-Neckar region are Mannheim, Ludwigshafen and Heidelberg; the medium-sized cities are Frankenthal, Neustadt, Speyer and Worms.

Sources: Land Statistical Office; Bundesanstalt für Arbeit.

The weaknesses of the Rhine-Neckar area stem from the combined effects of unfavourable branch, firm-size and product structures, inadequate environmental protection and the shortage of resouces for action by local authorities. These problems tend to be self-reinforcing and collectively contribute greatly to the cumulative contraction of the area's industrial sector.

Unfavourable branch and firm-size structures

Regional imbalances in the labour market are the results of spatially-uneven economic growth. This can come from combinations of comparative locational advantages, especially accessibility, environmental qualities, local skills and local innovation (outstanding inventions in the Rhine-Neckar area have been the bicycle, by Freiherr von Drais, the first petrol-driven automobile, by Carl Benz, and the 'Bulldog' tractor, by Heinrich Lanz). Agglomeration economies serve to reinforce an established growth impetus. However, because the economic advantages of locational agglomeration tend to weaken in the course of time, former growth areas eventually come to face falling rates of industrial expansion and have increasing structural difficulties.

Mannheim, easily the largest of the Rhine-Neckar cities, has an industrial structure which is dominated by large firms and large plants. More than 80% of industrial jobs here are in electrical engineering, motor vehicles assemblage, mechanical engineering and chemicals production. Today, none of these can be regarded as truly 'growth' industries; not even the activities of such well-known local companies as BASF (chemicals), Asea Brown-Boveri (electrical engineering), Daimler-Benz (commercial vehicles and engines) and John Deere (agricultural machinery). In 1987, for example, Asea Brown-Boveri's sales were 21% below those of the preceding year.

As many as 77% of workers in Mannheim in 1987 were engaged by firms with more than 500 employees. For Baden-Württemberg as a whole, the ratio was 49%, and for West Germany it was 53% (Pohl, 1988). In 1987 too, the average number of people employed per industrial firm (excluding those with less than 20 payroll workers) in West Germany was 161; in Mannheim the figure was 328, more than twice as high.

Small- and middle-sized industrial firms have a poor showing in the Rhine-Neckar area, and their contribution to overall regional employment is dwarfed by the giant engineering, chemicals and vehicle assemblage companies. As many as 50,000 workers are employed in BASF's Ludwigshafen complex; 23,000 are employed in the Freudenberg AG plant (plastics and textiles) at Weinheim, and 14,000 and 12,000 respectively at the Daimler-Benz and Asea Brown-Boveri factories. As a general rule today, the larger an industrial firm is, the smaller is the possibility that it will create more jobs than it will lose. In West Germany, during the period 1977-87, large firms (those employing more than 500 people) only managed to increase their total workforce by a modest 34,000, or just 0.6%. On the other hand, very small firms (with less than 20 employees) were responsible for the net addition of 650,000 jobs, a rise of 14.4% from their previous contribution (Statistisches Bundesamt, 1988). It is on this particular category of enterprises that regions now depend for the generation of new job opportunities.

Unfavourable product structure

Regional imbalances in industrial development cannot be explained wholly on the grounds of spatial variations in branch structures. There are some markedly different trends in employment and value added, actually within each major branch of manufacturing. On the one hand, there are expanding product ranges, whilst on the other hand, there are stagnating and declining ones. Trends above or below the averages of particular branches can be explained by the nature of product specialisation.

The bulk of industrial production in the Rhine-Neckar area is currently in either the saturation or, worse still, the declining stages of the product life cycle. Despite their high-quality production, most of the products of this region use the conventional technology of 'old' firms and are subject to strong international competition. They are also severely threatened by their strong sensitivity to cyclical downturns, changes in currency exchange rates, and reductions in profitability. Old-industrialised regions, like the Rhine-Neckar, are generally lacking in the modern high-tech products such as microelectronics, control and measurement engineering, aviation and aerospace. As creations based upon recent innovation 'clusters', these have only just commenced their life cycle and, therefore, can be looked upon as valuable regional assets. Unfortunately, their weak representation in the Rhine-Neckar region and the continued, if declining, strength here of the old industrial giants suggest a not untroubled future for this particular part of southern Germany.

Inadequate environmental protection and high external dependence

Heavy industrialisation, over a long period in the Rhine-Neckar area, has resulted in large tracts of land becoming exhausted and contaminated. Today this land has to be left idle or, at the best, can only be used in a very extensive way. In some cases, the damage caused by past industrialisation has made sites totally unsuitable for reuse. These can only be restored by means of very expensive treatment, requiring massive outlays of financial aid from Federal and *Land* governments.

Very few Federal or *Land* institutions are located in the Rhine-Neckar and, furthermore, few services of national or supraregional importance are provided. There is much political dependence here upon the three *Länder* of Baden-Württemberg, Hesse and Rhineland Palatinate (and their governments, respectively at Stuttgart, Wiesbaden and Mainz); there is also a high economic dependence upon external decision-making. The latter form of dependency is evidenced by the large proportion of plants in the region that are branches or subsidiaries of non-local companies. For example, none of Mannheim's four largest industrial plants, which together account for more than half of the city's total industrial employment, have their head offices there. Daimler-Benz has its headquarters in Stuttgart, Asea Brown-Boveri in Zurich, Böhringer in the Bermudas, and John Deere in Moline in the United States.

Economic and ecological renewal

As in other old-industrialised regions in West Germany, local authorities in the Rhine-Neckar area are carrying out economic and structural policies, supported by financial aid from both Federal and *Land* governments. The aims of such policies are to speed up the processes of adjustment and modernisation, and to actively encourage firms, managerial staff and other highly-qualified personnel to move into the area. High priority is being given to improving the living environment of the Rhine-Neckar area, making it an attractive location for work, residence and leisure. In view of the tendency for today's growth industries to avoid the area, special attention is being given to enhancing the regional image. Environmental protection and recycling of former industrial land, therefore, have assumed major importance in public policy.

The 1979 *Raumordnungsplan Rhein-Neckar* ('Regional Development Plan for the Rhine-Neckar') established a legal framework for planning in the region. However, it is the *Land* governments in Stuttgart, Wiesbaden and Mainz at the higher level, and the local *Gemeinde* authorities at the lower, that actually determine how planning policy is to be carried out here. The following schemes are now being actively pursued:

- development of the region's technical infrastructure, in order to help firms carry out their business, and also to enhance the quality of life of the local population. Of special importance here is the provision of cultural, sport and other recreational facilities, and the modernisation of the local communications infrastructure.

- Renovation of inner-city areas and their residential neighbourhoods. This involves the refurbishing and modernisation of old buildings, redesigning streets and the provision of more open spaces.

- Ensuring an adequate availability of prepared land for industrial and commercial usage, by designating specific areas for these functions, and also by recycling old industrial land for new productive use.

- Encouraging innovation and the setting up of research-intensive enterprises in the region. A major success so far has been the establishment in 1985, of the Mafinex Technology Centre in Mannheim, on the site of a former brewery. This provides facilities and space for up to 15 new enterprises. Another success is the foundation, also in 1985, of a technology park on the campus of Heidelberg University.

- Encouraging service firms, especially those providing advertising and consultancy services, to establish themselves within the Rhine-Neckar agglomeration.

As part of these efforts to stimulate new economic activity within the region, all three *Länder* (Baden-Württemberg, Hesse and Rhineland Palatinate) offer 'foundation' loans to firms at specially-low rates of interest, and provide general support and technical advice for the development and utilisation of new technology. They also try to improve the political climate by providing flexible and unbureaucratic help with locational problems.

References

Bade, F-J., *Regionale Beschäftigungsentwicklung und produktion-sorientierte Dienstleistungen,* Deutsches Institut für Wirtschaftsforschung, Berlin, 1987.

Bundesforschungsanstalt für Landeskunde und Raumordnung, *Aktuelle Daten zur Entwicklung der Städte, Kreise und Gemeinden,* Bad Godesberg, *Symposien Arbeitspapiere,* Vol. 28, 1987.

Cairncross, A., 'What is de-industrialisation?', in Blackaby, F. (ed.), *De-industrialisation,* Gower Press, London, pp. 5-17, 1987.

Gaebe, W., 'Disparities in development between agglomeration areas in the Federal Republic of Germany', *Zeitschrift für Wirtschaftsgeographie,* Vol. 32, pp. 179-91, 1988.

Gaebe, W. and Miodek, W., *Qualität und Entwicklungstendenzen tertiärer Arbeitsplätze im Rhein-Neckar Raum,* Materialien zum Raumordnungsplan Rhein-Neckar, Mannheim, 1986.

Grabherr, G., *De-Industrialisierung oder Neo-Industrialisierung. Innovationsprozesse und Innovationspolitik in traditionellen Industrieregionen,* Edition sigma, Berlin, 1988.

auf der Heide, U., *Strukturwandel im Wirtschaftsraum als Folge industriewirtschaftlicher Wachstums-, Stagnations- und Schrumpfungsprozesse untersucht in ausgewählten Agglomerationen Mittel- und Westeuropas,* Europäische Hochschulschriften, Vol. 913, Frankfurt, 1988.

Henckel, D. et al., *Produktionstechnologien und Raumentwicklung,* Kohlhammer, Stuttgart, 1986.

Pohl, M., 'Wirtschaftsforderung in Großstädten - ein Struktur- und Standortvergleich der 16 größten Städte im Bundesgebiet', *Regionalwirtschaftliche Studien des Bremer Ausschusses für Wirtschaftsforschung*, Vol. 8, 1988.

Raumordnungsverband Rhein-Neckar (ed.), *Raumordnungsplan Rhein-Neckar*, Mannheim, 1979.

Sinz, M., Hillesheim, D. and Runge, L., 'Nord-Süd Kontraste im Spiegel der laufenden Raumbeobachtung', *Informationen zur Raumentwicklung*, pp. 933-1002, 1986.

Statistisches Bundesamt, *Statistisches Bundesamt für die Bundesrepublik Deutschland*, Kohlhammer, Stuttgart, 1988.

Chapter XII

Anne Green (University of Wales College of Cardiff)

High-tech industry, advanced service industries and regional growth in Britain

Introduction

Amongst the most important features of employment change at the national scale in recent years are the shift from manufacturing to service employment and the growing emphasis upon highly-qualified manpower. In this chapter, the focus of attention is placed upon the spatial dynamics of two related groups of industries: high-tech industry and advanced services, which display a greater than average reliance upon professional workers.

The first part of the chapter is concerned with definitions and data sources. Following this, the spatial dynamics of employment in high-tech industry and advanced services are outlined, with particular emphasis on regional variations in the occupational structure of high-tech employment and the electronics sector. In the third part of the chapter, a synthetic index and a classification of Local Labour Market Areas (LLMAs), based on structural and accessibility variables relevant to spatial development prospects, are described.

Definitions and data sources

High-tech industry

Over recent years there has been considerable debate concerning an appropriate definition for high-tech industry (Aydalot and Keeble, 1988; Keeble, 1988; Begg and Cameron, 1988). In this chapter the definition of high-tech industry proposed by Butchart (1987) - based on above-average research and development intensity and the proportions of scientists, professional engineers and technicians in the workforce - is used (Table 12.1).

Table 12.1: Definition of high-tech industries

SIC	industry description
2514	Synthetic resins and plastics materials
2515	Synthetic rubber
2570	Pharmaceutical products
3301	Office machinery
3302	Electronic data processing equipment
3420	Basic electrical equipment
3441	Telegraph and telegraph apparatus/equipment
3442	Electrical instruments and control systems
3443	Radio and electronic capital goods
3444	Components other than active components
3453	Active components and electronic subassemblies
3640	Aerospace equipment manufacturing and repairing
3710	Measuring, checking and precision instruments and apparatus
3720	Medical and surgical equipment, and orthopaedic appliances
3733	Photographic and cinematographic equipment
7902	Telecommunications
8394	Computing services
9400	Research and development

Note: SIC is abbreviation for Standard Industrial Classification.

Source: Butchart, 1987.

Advanced service industries

The heterogeneity of the service sector is now firmly established, as are the different locational logics of producer and consumer services (Marshall, 1988; Green and Howells, 1989). The industries defined here as advanced service industries are listed in Table 12.2. These have witnessed rapid employment growth in recent years, associated with the increased information intensity of production. They are often seen as the 'lead' generators of employment growth and output expansion in the economy.

Table 12.2: Definition of advanced service industries

SIC	industry description
8140	Banking and bill-discounting
8150	Other financial institutions
8200	Insurance, except for compulsory social insurance
8310	Activities auxiliary to banking and finance
8320	Activities auxiliary to insurance
8340	House and estate agents
8350	Legal services
8360	Accountants, auditors and tax experts
8370	Professional and technical services
8380	Advertising
8394	Computer services
8395	Business services
8396	Central offices
8500	Owning and dealing in real estate
9400	Research and development

Occupational classifications

Three different occupational classifications are drawn upon in this study. Firstly, there is the new Standard Occupational Classification (SOC), devised for use in the 1991 Census and in government surveys (Department of Employment, 1988). The nine 'major groups' that are distinguished are presented in Table 12.3. Secondly, a classification differentiating between information occupations and non-information occupations (based on the work of Porat, 1977) is used in the formulation of the index and the cluster analysis in the third part of this chapter. This is in recognition of the shift from a goods-producing to an information-producing economy (Hall, 1987). Thirdly, an eightfold occupational classification used by the Engineering Industry Training Board (EITB) is referred to (Green, 1988; Green and Owen, 1989) in the subsection detailing spatial dimensions of occupational change in the electronics sector.

Table 12.3: Standard Occupational Classification (SOC)

SOC	occupational description
1	Managers and administrators
2	Professional occupations
3	Associate professional and technical occupations
4	Secretarial and clerical occupations
5	Craft and skilled-manual occupations
6	Personal and protective service occupations
7	Selling occupations
8	Plant and machine operators
9	Other occupations

Source: Department of Employment, Standard Occupational Classification, 1988.

Data

A variety of data sources will be used in this study. The spatial dimensions of the occupational structure of high-tech employment are examined using the 1984 and 1987 Labour Force Surveys (LFS). The LFS, which refer to a sample of individuals (approximately 1 in 300 of the British population), provide the most comprehensive and up-to-date data on industrial and occupational structure; but the maximum spatial disaggregation which is available is that of the metropolitan counties and regional remainders. Use is also made of the annual 'occupation by industry' returns from the EITB, disaggregated to the Local Labour Market Area scale, with (at the time of writing), the most recent data available relating to the year 1984.

These latter data sources are used when formulating the index and classification of LLMAs in the final section of this chapter.

Spatial dimensions of high-tech industry and advanced services in Britain

Features of the uneven spatial distribution of employment in high-tech and advanced service industries

Studies using Census of Employment data have revealed that there is an uneven distribution of employment in high-tech and advanced service industries across the British space-economy. Using Butchart's (1987) definition of high-tech industry, Begg and Cameron (1988) showed that almost half of such employment was concentrated in London and the south-east, with the two other regions of southern Britain - East Anglia and the south-west - also displaying shares in excess of the national average.

Begg and Cameron also suggested that the critical elements in the location of such industry were:

- firstly, close access to research and development facilities, universities and higher-learning institutions;

- secondly, a higher-quality environment for living and for production;

- thirdly, a local wide-ranging availability of technical, scientific and technician labour.

Conversely, areas characterised by traditional and declining industries and a poor environment, tended to be rejected by high-tech industry, due to negative images, the inappropriateness of local skills and the difficulties of attracting the necessary professional and technical staff. There are also pronounced urban and regional differentials in the distribution of employment in advanced service industries.

Using Census of Employment data for 1971 and 1981, Gillespie and Green (1987) pointed to a persistence of the spatial concentration of such employment in southern Britain, coupled with a relative deconcentration within metropolitan regions from 'dominant' to associated 'subdominant' centres.

Hence, it is clear that high-tech industry and advanced services tend to favour similar locations. Indeed, as the mutual interaction between high-tech and service industries intensifies, the boundaries of such sectors are becoming increasingly blurred (Rada, 1987).

The occupational structure of employment in high-tech industry

As well as the industrial composition of employment, its occupational profile can have far-reaching consequences for local areas. In terms of the nine major groups of the Standard Occupational Classification, the main features of recent occupational change at the national scale, are the increase in employment in SOC 1 (managers and administrators) and SOC 2 (professional occupations) and SOC 3 (associate professional and technical occupations), and the absolute and relative decline in importance of SOC 7 (craft and skilled-manual occupations) and SOC 8 (plant and machine operatives). Moreover, within the overall increase of 1.7 million people in civilian employment, which is forecast for the period to 1995, the largest increases are projected for the higher groups, SOC 1, SOC 2 and SOC 3 (Wilson, 1988), thus continuing the shift from manual to non-manual occupations and to a more highly-qualified workforce.

Obviously, these changes in aggregate occupational structure arise through a combination of shifting patterns of industrial employment structure and the changing occupational composition of employment within industries. It is the changing occupational structure within industries that is the predominant factor in the growth of professional occupations (SOC 2) and associate professional and technical occupations (SOC 3).

Table 12.4: Changing occupational structure of employment in high-tech industry in the United Kingdom, 1984-7

SOC	employment in 1984		employment in 1987		employment change 1984-7	
	thousands	%	thousands	%	thousands	%
1	104	8.7	131	10.8	+27	+26.0
2	147	12.4	171	14.0	+24	+16.3
3	148	12.5	145	11.9	-3	-2.0
4	230	19.4	229	18.8	-1	-0.4
5	267	22.5	290	23.8	+23	+8.6
6	10	0.8	12	1.0	+2	+20.0
7	33	2.7	27	2.2	-6	-18.2
8	215	18.0	185	15.2	-30	-14.0
9	35	3.0	28	2.3	-7	-20.0
TOTAL	1,189	100.0	1,218	100.0	+29	+2.4

Note: This data refers to a sample of individuals (approximately 1 in 300 of the UK population). Weighting factors are applied in the analysis presented here, but the variance of some of the results will be high.

Source: Department of Employment, Labour Force Surveys (LFS), 1984 and 1987.

Table 12.4, using LFS data, shows the changing occupational structure of high-tech industry in Britain between 1984-7. Over this short period, employment in high-tech industry grew by 29,000, a 2.4% increase. The largest absolute gains (all in excess of 20,000 jobs), were recorded for managers and administrators, professional occupations, and craft and skilled-manual workers. On the other hand, there was a 30,000 decline in employment for plant and machine operatives. Whereas approximately one-fifth of employment in high-tech industry in 1984 was accounted for by managers, administrators and professionals, by 1987 the proportion had increased sharply to one-quarter.

Table 12.5: Proportion of United Kingdom high-tech employment by Standard Occupational Category in major regional divisions, 1984-7

| SOC | year | regional division | | | |
		south %	Midlands %	industrial north %	periphery %
1	1984	63	14	15	9
	1987	62	14	15	9
2	1984	65	13	10	12
	1987	67	12	12	8
3	1984	62	16	9	11
	1987	61	10	12	14
4	1984	60	13	13	14
	1987	59	14	15	14
5	1984	52	15	19	14
	1987	50	15	17	18
8	1984	47	15	15	22
	1987	45	17	13	26
1-9	1984	56	15	14	15
	1987	56	14	15	15

Source: Department of Employment, Labour Force Surveys, 1984 and 1987.

The absolute and relative significance of employment in associate professional and technical occupations remained virtually stable. Relative to other industries, the key differentiating features of the occupational structure of high-tech industry are the greater proportions of employment, not only in professional occupations (SOC 2) and associate professional and technical occupations (SOC 3), but also in craft and skilled-manual occupations (SOC 5) and, despite its losses, plant and machine operatives (SOC 8).

234

Shifting our focus of attention from the national to the regional scale, not only is high-tech industry overrepresented, relative to the national average in southern Britain, but also occupational differentials within the high-tech industry sector tend to favour the south. Table 12.5 shows the proportion of employment in high-tech industry in each of the main occupational categories represented therein in 1984 and 1987 by four macroregional divisions. Over half (56%) of all high-tech employment in the United Kingdom is located in the south (defined as London, the south-east, East Anglia and the south-west), but this same area accounts for approximately two-thirds of those employed in professional occupations and as managers and administrators.

Each of the three remaining regional divisions - the Midlands (West Midlands and East Midlands together), the 'industrial north' (Yorkshire and Humberside, and the north-west) and the 'periphery' (the northern region, Wales, Scotland and Northern Ireland), contain about 15% of British high-tech employment. These regional shares remained roughly stable over the period 1984-7. The Midlands displayed an occupational structure similar to the national average; while in the 'industrial north', professional occupations and associate professional and technical occupations are underrepresented, relative to the national average, but a greater share of employment is accounted for by craft and skilled-manual occupations. Relative to the national average, the elite SOC 1 and SOC 2 occupational groups are underrepresented in the 'periphery', where as much as about one-quarter of the high-tech industry workforce is employed just as plant and machine operatives (SOC 8), compared with 15% in Britain overall. Indeed, in the 'periphery' there is some evidence of an increasing polarisation of the high-tech occupational structure, with professional occupations becoming increasingly underrepresented (relative to the national average), and plant and machine operatives becoming increasingly overrepresented. Nevertheless, in 1987 as many as 45% of all plant and machine operatives in high-tech industry were located in the south.

235

Table 12.6 Change in high-tech employment in selected SOCs by regional division

SOCs	regional division	1984-7 change thousands	%
1	South	+15	+22.7
	Midlands	+3	+20.0
	Industrial north	+4	+20.0
	Periphery	+3	+33.0
	UNITED KINGDOM	+27	+26.0
2	South	+15	+20.0
	Midlands	+2	+10.5
	Industrial north	+7	+50.0
	Periphery	-3	-17.6
	UNITED KINGDOM	+24	+16.3
3	South	-3	-3.3
	Midlands	-8	-34.8
	Industrial north	+4	+28.6
	Periphery	+4	+23.5
	UNITED KINGDOM	-3	-2.0
4	South	-3	-2.2
	Midlands	+1	+3.3
	Industrial north	+3	+9.7
	Periphery	-2.2	-6.1
	UNITED KINGDOM	-1	-0.4
5	South	+6	+4.3
	Midlands	+3	+7.5
	Industrial north	-1	-2.0
	Periphery	+13	+34.2
	UNITED KINGDOM	+23	+8.6
8	South	-19	-18.6
	Midlands	-2	-6.1
	Industrial north	-8	-25.0
	Periphery	+1	+2.1
	UNITED KINGDOM	-30	-20.0
1-9	South	-19	-18.6
	Midlands	-2	-6.1
	Industrial north	+6	+3.5
	Periphery	+11	+6.3
	UNITED KINGDOM	+29	+2.4

Source: Department of Employment, Labour Force Surveys, 1984 and 1987.

Table 12.6 shows the absolute and relative growth of selected occupational groups and all high-tech employment in the four macroregional divisions between 1984-7. Overall, the greatest absolute and relative gains in high-tech employment occurred in the 'periphery', accounting for 11,000 out of the total 29,000 national increase, and representing a relative increase of 6.3%, compared with a national growth rate of 2.4%. This remarkable improvement in the 'periphery', however, is accounted for entirely by the expansion of jobs in high-tech industry in Wales; elsewhere in this regional division there was a slight decline in the northern region (in Tyne and Wear), while employment levels remained virtually stable in Scotland and Northern Ireland. The 3.5% expansion of high-tech employment in the 'industrial north' disguises decline in Yorkshire and Humberside, which is more than compensated for by growth in the north-west (excluding Merseyside). The growth of high-tech employment in the south - albeit at a rate slower than the national average - reflects growth in London and the rest of the south-east; while in the Midlands the 1984 level of high-tech employment was maintained through to 1987, with a slight increase in the East Midlands, and a corresponding small decline in the West Midlands.

There was an increase in managers and administrators in all regional divisions, with Greater London and Scotland displaying amongst the highest absolute and relative increases. Growth in those employed in professional occupations was most apparent in the south, notably in the rest of the south-east, and the 'industrial north', notably in Greater Manchester. By contrast, Yorkshire and Humberside, and also all parts of the 'periphery', were characterised by stability or decline in employment in professional occupations.

Employment in the next occupational group, associate professional and technical occupations, declined in the south, and more notably in the Midlands; whereas in the 'industrial north' and the 'periphery' such employment increased by approximately one-quarter over the three-year period. Within the latter two regional divisions, the rest of the north-west, the rest of the northern region, and

Scotland, displayed the most marked employment increases. The proportion of the workforce in high-tech industry employed in clerical and secretarial occupations (SOC 4), remained virtually the same between 1984-7, with the south and the 'periphery' recording small decreases and the 'industrial north' and the Midlands exhibiting slight increases.

All regional divisions, with the exception of the 'industrial north' (which had the greatest overrepresentation in this group in 1984), shared in the increase in craft and skilled-manual occupations. Increase was most marked in the 'periphery', notably in Wales: it accounted for over one-half of the national growth, with the actual employment level increasing by one-third over the period. Again, the slight increase in the number of plant and machine operatives in the 'periphery' is accounted for by a 50% increase in Wales, which more than made up for declines elsewhere, notably in the northern region. All other regional divisions and their components were characterised by declines, which were most marked in the rest of the south-east and in the south-west.

The electronics industry

A more detailed insight into the spatial dimensions of occupational specialisation and change in one particular high-tech industry - the electronics sector - is provided by analyses of the Engineering Industry Training Board's annual occupation returns over the period 1978-87 at the scale of the 280 LLMAs. The broad isomorphism between the division of strategic, routine administration and production functions within the corporate hierarchy on the one hand, and of urban and regional characteristics on the other, which has been noted in previous studies of the spatial division of labour in Britain (Massey, 1984; Green and Owen, 1985; Hepworth et al., 1987; Johnson, 1988), is well apparent in the electronics industry.

Figure 12.1: Occupational change in electronics in Great Britain, 1978-87

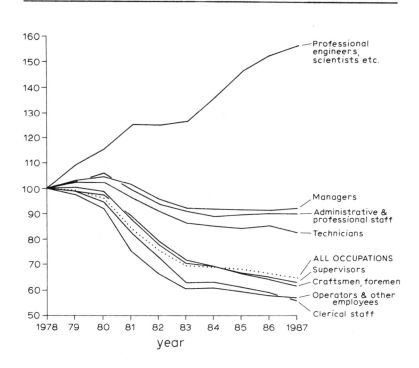

: *the value of 100 on the vertical axis represents the 1978 number of occupied persons for each occupational classification.*

Source: Department of Employment, Labour Force Surveys.

239

Managerial staff, professional engineers, technicians, administrative and professional staff, and supervisory staff are all overrepresented in the south, and most notably in the London Metropolitan Region (Green, 1988). Of the eight occupational groups adopted by the Engineering Industry Training Board, professional engineers show the most uneven spatial division. Indeed, in the 'London subdominant' LLMAs, the proportion of total electronics employment which is accounted for by professional engineers is over twice the national average.

Over the period 1978-87, total employment in the electronics sector at the national scale declined by approximately 20%, but the numbers employed as professional engineers increased by 80% (Figure 12.1). Every one of the 19 classes of LLMA (defined in Champion et al., 1987) shared in the absolute increase of professional engineers. However, despite changes in the spatial distribution of employment in electronics over the decade, and changes in occupational structure, the main dimensions of the spatial division of labour remained unaltered. The initial pattern of overrepresentation of managers, professional engineers, technicians, administrative and professional staff, and clerical staff in the London Metropolitan Region, and underrepresentation there of craftsmen and operators, (mirrored by a converse pattern in the 'conurbation dominants and their subdominants'), was still apparent in 1987, although it was less intense than in 1978.

Comparing the 1978 and 1987 patterns of over- and underrepresentation in professional engineering occupations and of operators (Table 12.7), there is a clear tendency across LLMA classes for a diminution in the degree of initial over- and underrepresentation amongst professional engineers; but at the opposite end of the occupational continuum, such a trend towards convergence was less clear, with the initial overrepresentation of operators in areas described as the 'subregional dominants', 'conurbation subdominant towns', 'smaller northern subdominants', southern and northern 'freestanding cities', and southern and northern 'rural areas' tending to intensify.

Table 12.7: Changing patterns of over/underrepresentation of professional engineers and electronics operators in a 19-fold classification of LLMAs, 1978-87

LLMA classification	professional engineers	electronic operators
London dominant	<0	>x
Conurbation dominants	>x	<0
Provincial dominants	>x	>x
Subregional dominants	>x	>0
London subdominant cities	<0	
London subdominant towns	<0	<x
Conurbation subdominant cities	>x	<0
Conurbation subdominant towns	<x	<0
Smaller northern subdominants	>x	>0
Southern freestanding cities		
Northern freestanding cities	>x	<0
Southern service towns	>x	>0
Southern commercial towns		>0
Southern manufacturing towns		>0
Northern service towns	>x	>0
Northern commercial towns	>x	>0
Northern manufacturing towns	>x	
Southern rural areas	<x	>0
Northern rural areas	>0	

Notes:

> indicates an *increase* in representation, as reflected in a change of location quotient equal or in excess of 0.05.

< indicates a *decrease* in representation, as reflected in a change of location quotient equal or in excess of 0.05.

0 equals LLMA class with overrepresentation in occupational group in 1978.

x indicates LLMA class with underrepresentation in occupational group in 1978.

Hence, it appears that the industrywide requirements for improved human capital are leading to a more even spatial distribution of the qualified personnel at the higher end of the occupational spectrum, but during the same time the retention of an uneven spatial distribution at the lower end (Green and Owen, 1989).

Index and classification of LLMAs: development prospects

From the foregoing analyses it is clear that high-tech and advanced service industries are unevenly distributed across Britain, and moreover that the occupational profiles of these industries also vary across space. These spatial variations may be synthesised by using the techniques of 'index construction', in which LLMAs are ranked on a 'league table' basis by an aggregate score (combining performance across a range of variables) and cluster analysis (used to group LLMAs with similar characteristics). The synthesis can then be used in order to provide an insight into recent, current and future development prospects.

Table 12.8: Variables used in index construction and cluster analysis

variable description
Structural variables
1 % of total employment in high-tech industries and advanced sectors, 1984
2 % of employed residents in information occupations, 1981
3 Likelihood of ceasing to be unemployed, 1988
4 % change in employment, 1981-4
5 % projected change in population, 1986-96
Accessibility variables
6 Road accessibility
7 Airport accessibility
8 Rail accessibility

In this case the five 'structural' variables and three 'accessibility' variables listed in Table 12.8 were used in the synthesising exercise. The proportion of total employment in high-tech and advanced service industries (*variable 1*), along with the proportion of employed residents in information occupations (*variable 2*), were selected to represent 'leading' industries and occupations in the transformation from a 'goods-producing' to an 'information-producing' economy. Table 12.9 shows the top 10 and bottom 10 LLMAs in the ranking of the former variable, and reveals that the proportion of employment accounted for by such industries in 1984 ranged from over one-third in Bracknell, Stevenage and Welwyn to just 3% or less in Peterlee, Llanelli and Barnsley (all areas dominated by traditional industries). From Figure 12.2, showing the share of total employment accounted for by high-tech and advanced services industries across all 280 LLMAs, the M4, M3, M23 and M11 Corridors are all easily identifiable as important concentrations. In contrast, there is a marked paucity of these industries in those parts of the country traditionally dominated by primary production and basic manufacturing.

The other variables (those relating to 'structural' characteristics) used in the analyses are:

- firstly, the likelihood of ceasing to be unemployed, which can be used as a measure of labour market buoyancy;

- secondly, recent employment change;

- thirdly, projected population change.

The last two variables are used as more direct measures of the growth profiles of local economies. In recognition of the fact that accessibility plays an important role in the location and development of high-tech and advanced service industries, variables related to road, rail and airport accessibility were also used in compiling the synthetic index and classifying LLMAs, according to development prospects.

Table 12.9: 'Top 10' and 'bottom 10' LLMAs in their proportions of employment in high-tech and advanced service industries, 1984

	TOP 10			BOTTOM 10	
rank	LLMA	%	rank	LLMA	%
1	Bracknell	36.56	280	Peterlee	2.23
2	Stevenage	35.67	279	Llanelli	3.19
3	Welwyn	33.75	278	Barnsley	3.20
4	Didcot	32.99	277	Alloa	3.28
5	Rugby	28.64	276	Heanor	4.33
6	Yeovil	27.82	275	Wakefield	4.37
7	Harlow	27.79	274	Leigh	4.37
8	Macclesfield	23.77	273	Castleford	4.37
9	Woking/Weybridge	23.07	272	Peterhead	4.43
10	Loughborough	22.79	271	Dewsbury	4.52

Source: Census of employment, 1984.

The spatial distribution of index scores is revealed in Figure 12.3. A clear 'Greater' south-east/'rest of Britain' divide is apparent, with the former part of the country having the most favourable industrial and occupational structure and commanding foremost accessibility in a national context. LLMAs such as Milton Keynes, Newbury, Bracknell and Welwyn appear at the top of the rankings on the synthetic index, while Alloa and Hartlepool are amongst those at the bottom.

Turning to groupings of LLMAs emerging from the cluster analysis, four of the eight clusters identified are particularly worthy of mention. Figure 12.4 shows a group of 'elite' LLMAs, focused on London, and characterised by substantially above-average proportions of employment in high-tech and advanced service industries and also by a much higher likelihood of workers ceasing to be unemployed. Moreover, these 'elite' locations have excellent air accessibility (reflecting proximity to Heathrow and Gatwick), good road and rail connections, and above-average employment and projected population change. However, it is the 'growth centre' LLMAs, in the outer fringe of the south-east and in East Anglia, the south-west and the southern Midlands, that are characterised by greatest population and employment growth. These growth centres share with the elite areas a stronger representation of employment in high-tech and advanced service industries and in information occupations, as well as enjoying relatively buoyant labour market conditions.

By contrast, the 'declining centres' shown in Figure 12.5 (drawn exclusively from northern Britain, and including Glasgow, Liverpool and Newcastle), are characterised by below-average performances on each of the eight variables in Table 12.8. Alongside these, a group of 'poor performance areas' may also be identified, enjoying average or above-average accessibility, but having below-average performance on the structural variables.

The groupings of LLMAs shown in Figure 12.4, compared with those in Figure 12.5, highlight the spatial concentration of advantage in southern Britain. Turning to future prospects, Green and Howells (1989) suggest that this picture is unlikely to change markedly in the medium-term, as the long-term cumulative processes influencing the agglomeration of high-tech and advanced service industries entrench the development of 'advantaged' and 'disadvantaged' regions within Britain.

Figure 12.2: Proportion of employment in high-tech and advanced service industries by Local Labour Market Areas

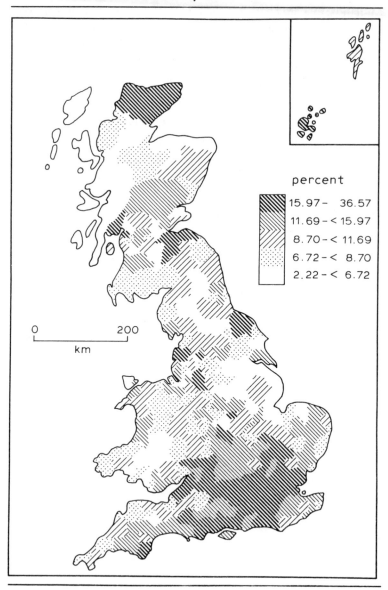

percent

15.97 – 36.57
11.69 – < 15.97
8.70 – < 11.69
6.72 – < 8.70
2.22 – < 6.72

0   200
km

Source: Census of Employment, 1984.

Figure 12.3: Spatial distribution of 'structural' and 'accessibility' index scores

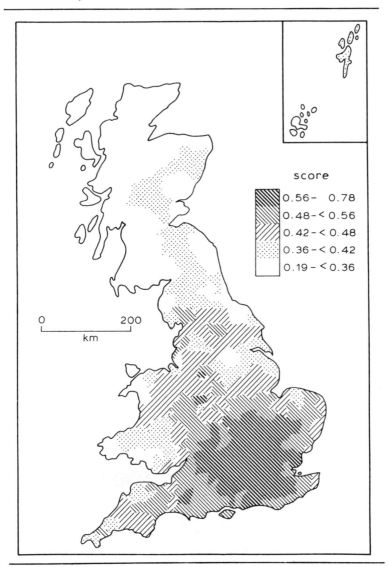

score

	0.56 – 0.78
	0.48 – < 0.56
	0.42 – < 0.48
	0.36 – < 0.42
	0.19 – < 0.36

0   200

km

: the maximum score possible if 1:00; the minimum is 0.00.

Source: based on data from Census of Employment, 1984.

Figure 12.4: 'Elite' LLMAs and 'growth centres'

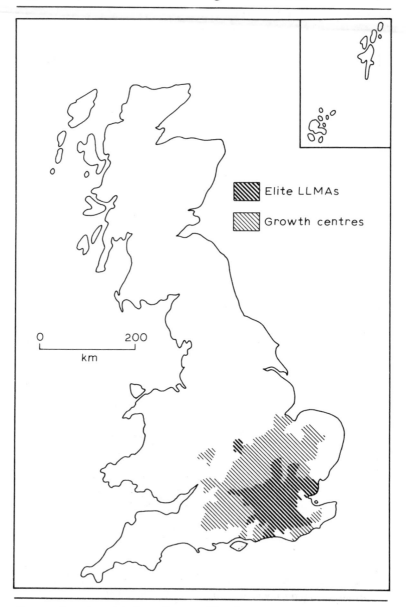

Source: based on data from Census of Employment, 1984.

Figure 12.5: 'Declining centres' and 'poor performance areas'

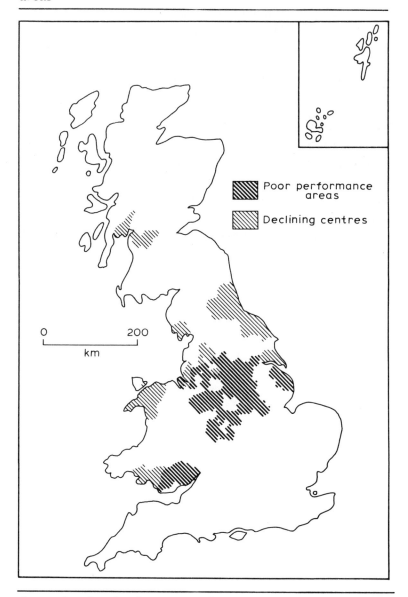

Poor performance areas

Declining centres

0   200
    km

Source: based on data from Census of Employment, 1984.

Conclusion

The analyses presented in this chapter confirm the existence of the spatial division of labour in high-tech and advanced service employment in Britain, and reveal that, although the continuing trend for a shift from manual and low-status, non-manual, occupations is evident in all areas, the south-eastern corner of the United Kingdom remains most favoured. There is some evidence for an increase in high-tech employment in some parts of the 'periphery', notably in Wales, perhaps indicating the importance of factors (such as low wages, the weakening of trade union power, decades of decline in staple industries, and the availability of female labour) which have underpinned some shift of new industry into rural areas. However, despite this 'diffusion' process, the spatial division of labour in Britain has been reinforced, with strategic functions remaining in the south and east.

References

Aydalot, P. and Keeble, D., 'High-technology industry and innovative environments in Europe: an overview', in Aydalot, P. and Keeble, D., *High-technology industry and innovative environments: the European experience*, Routledge, London, pp. 1-21, 1988.

Begg, I.G. and Cameron, G.C., 'High-technology location and the urban areas of Great Britain', *Urban Studies*, Vol. 25, pp. 361-79, 1988.

Butchart, R.L., 'A new definition of the high-technology industries', *Economic Trends*, Vol. 400, pp. 82-88, 1987.

Champion, A.G. and Green, A.E., *Local prosperity in the north-south divide: a report on winners and losers in 1980s Britain*, Institute for Employment Research, University of Warwick, 1988.

Champion, A.G. et al., *Changing places: Britain's demographic, economic and social complexion*, Edward Arnold, London, 1987.

Department of Employment, 'Standard Occupational Classification - a proposed classification for the 1990s', *Employment Gazette*, pp. 214-21, 1988.

Gillespie, A.E. and Green, A.E., 'The changing geography of producer services employment in Britain', *Regional Studies*, Vol. 21, pp. 397-411, 1987.

Green, A.E., *Analyses of EITB occupational and industrial data at the Local Labour Market Area scale*, Institute for Employment Research, University of Warwick, 1988.

Green, A.E. and Howells, J., 'Information services and spatial development in the UK economy', *Tijdschrift voor Economishe en Sociale Geografie*, forthcoming.

Green, A.E. and Owen, D.W., 'The changing spatial division of socioeconomic groups employed in manufacturing in Great Britain', *Geoforum*, Vol. 16, pp. 387-40, 1985.

Green, A.E. and Owen, D.W., 'The changing geography of occupations in engineering in Britain, 1978-1987', *Regional Studies*, Vol. 23, pp. 27-42, 1989.

Hall, P.. 'The anatomy of job creation: nations, regions and cities in the 1960s and 1970s', *Regional Studies*, Vol. 21, pp. 95-106, 1987.

Hepworth, M.E., Green, A.E. and Gillespie, A.E., 'The spatial division of information labour in Great Britain', *Environment and Planning A*, Vol. 19, pp. 793-806, 1987.

Howells, J. and Green, A.E., *Technological innovation, structural change and location in UK services*, Avebury-Gower, Aldershot, 1988.

Johnson, S., 'The changing division of information labour in the UK: some preliminary estimates from the Labour Force Surveys', *Programme on Information and Communications Technology Working Paper MM2*, Centre for Urban and Regional Development Studies, University of Newcastle-upon-Tyne, 1988.

Keeble, D., 'High-technology industry and local environments in the United Kingdom', in Aydalot, P. and Keeble, D., *High-technology industry and innovative environments: the European experience*, Routledge, London, pp. 65-98, 1988.

Marshall, J.N., *Services and uneven development*, Oxford University Press, Oxford, 1988.

Massey, D., *Spatial divisions of labour*, Macmillan, London, 1984.

Ochel, W. and Wegner, M., *Service economies in Europe*, Pinter, London, 1987.

Porat, M., *The information economy: definition and measurement*, United States Department of Commerce, Office of Telecommunications Special Publications, 77-12 (1), Washington DC, 1977.

Rada, J.F., 'Information technology and services', in Giarini, O. (ed.), *The emerging service economy*, Pergamon, Oxford, 1987.

Wilson, R.A., *Occupational assessment*, Institute for Employment Research, University of Warwick, 1988.

Chapter XIII

Peter Wood (University College London)

The single European market and producer service location in the United Kingdom

Introduction

The economic effects of the development of the European Community during the 1990s are essentially unknown. Nevertheless, in the wake of the EC white paper, *Completing the Internal Market* (Commission of the European Communities, 1985) and the subsequent passing of the Single European Act in 1987, most commentators regard the proposed achievement of a 'single European market' by 1993 as a highly significant event. Such a prediction is, of course, based upon estimates of the supposed benefits that may arise from the further integration of 12 national economies (Cecchini, 1988; Emerson, 1988). Its fulfillment depends upon how far the alignment of national regulations and practices to European norms will, in fact, be achieved over the next four or five years. In turn, this will depend upon the political reactions within the EC member states to its various practical implications.

The hoped-for transformation of the corporate structure of European capitalism means that our whole perspective on the economic geography of each EC member state will need to be adjusted as integration proceeds. In the United Kingdom, as elsewhere, this should augment and develop recent geographical debate on the international causes of regional and local economic change, including the corporate basis for such relationships (Massey, 1986; Amin and Goddard, 1986). It should also draw attention to the decision-making mechanisms that might favour different parts of the European 'core', as well as perhaps disadvantaging the 'periphery'.

United Kingdom services functions and the 'single Europe'

The impact of international developments has already become a central theme in explaining regional and local economic change in the United Kingdom, spurred on by Thrift's criticisms (Thrift, 1985). The regional impacts of the long-term failure of British manufacturing industry to compete internationally are not the only reasons for this; the apparent international success of some service industries has also increasingly contributed to regional economic differentiation. In relation to European changes, it can be argued that the consequent restructuring of the service sector in Britain may, in fact, be more radical than that of the manufacturing sector. Put simply, services not only 'probably offer, among all sectors, the greatest scope for economic growth and technical change' (Pelkmans and Winters, 1988, p. 43) but, between the EC countries, this sector also 'appears more barrier-ridden than manufacturing' (p.53). Thus, although the prospects for Europeanwide integration of the service sector are more difficult, they may have greater long-term impacts on service organisation, the restructuring of employment, and locational patterns, than those of parallel changes in manufacturing.

Geographical research into UK services functions has multiplied in recent years, and can now successfully challenge the long-established view that only materials-processing activities sustain patterns of uneven geographical development. Two principal types of service activity also generate unequal regional growth:

- firstly, those services (mainly capital-circulation services, but including tourism) that are largely involved in interregional and, especially, international trade;

- secondly, those services (the 'production-related' services) that provide essential support to traded activities in extractive industries, manufacturing and other service activities.

In practice, many service firms, for example, in banking and in insurance, combine capital circulation and production-related activities, as well as serving consumer needs. The functions of the 'circulation services', however, are quite distinct from production-related activities, even though they are often grouped together under the general heading of 'producer services'. The profits and success of the former depend upon the exchange and manipulation of finance capital (Allen, 1988). Although they are not exclusively international in scope, international market developments have underlain their growth and restructuring in recent decades. Production-related services, on the other hand, are essentially interchangeable with the in-house activities of other economic organisations, both in the private and in the public sector (Wood, 1986). They provide specific expertise, including financial advice, which is required to assist the mainstream activities. Because of their potential export orientation, the two types of services functions are both likely to form as strong a basis of uneven regional development as do materials-processing functions.

Table 13.1: Service employment change by category in Great Britain, 1971-8 and 1978-81

	change 1971-8		change 1978-81	
	% rate per annum	number ('000s)	% rate per annum	number ('000s)
private producer	2.63	292	3.51	192
private consumer	2.15	595	0.57	75
public	2.24	667	-0.89	-123
public distribution	-1.50	-146	0.12	5
private distribution	0.42	33	-0.38	-13
ALL SERVICE SECTOR	1.67	1,451	0.34	135

Source: Howells and Green, 1988.

Table 13.2: Regional distribution of service employment in Great Britain, 1984

employment in thousands

	Greater London	Rest SE	EA	SW	WM	EM	YH	NW	N	Wa	Sc
PRIVATE PRODUCER	633	387	60	149	150	92	116	190	69	55	152
Strategic	34	56	7	12	8	7	5	10	4	2	10
Contract	133	92	11	27	38	19	22	40	11	10	24
Professional	151	88	15	36	36	24	31	46	21	15	43
Property	34	16	2	6	13	6	7	13	6	3	11
Insurance	91	57	13	32	20	10	16	30	10	8	23
Banking/finance	190	78	3	36	35	25	35	51	17	17	41
PRIVATE CONSUMER	791	848	152	384	373	272	392	509	245	193	450
PUBLIC	767	881	141	354	402	290	370	503	248	229	447
PUBLIC DISTRIBUTION	252	135	27	54	55	44	64	85	34	30	71
PRIVATE DISTRIBUTION	276	294	62	109	12	99	128	161	60	51	116

% of national total

	Greater London	Rest SE	EA	SW	WM	EM	YH	NW	N	Wa	Sc
PRIVATE PRODUCER	27	17	3	6	6	4	5	8	3	2	6
Strategic	22	36	4	8	5	4	3	6	3	1	6
Contract	31	22	3	6	9	5	5	9	3	2	6
Professional	30	17	3	7	7	5	6	9	4	3	9
Property	29	14	2	5	11	5	6	11	5	3	9
Insurance	30	19	4	10	7	3	5	10	3	3	8
Banking/finance	36	15	1	7	7	5	7	9	3	3	8
PRIVATE CONSUMER	17	18	3	8	8	6	9	11	5	4	10
PUBLIC	17	19	3	8	9	6	8	11	5	5	10
PUBLIC DISTRIBUTION	30	16	3	6	6	5	8	10	4	4	8
PRIVATE DISTRIBUTION	19	20	4	7	9	7	9	11	4	3	8

Note: the industrial categories are based on the 1980 Standard Industrial Classification.

Source: Employment Gazette, January 1987.

Although official statistics in the United Kingdom do not identify employment in these two critical services categories separately, Table 13.1 adopts a classification employed by Howells and Green to indicate broad service employment trends in Great Britain (Howells and Green, 1988). Table 13.2 illustrates their contribution to regional inequality. The 'private producer' category includes circulation, production-related and consumer functions, but its performance clearly indicates the accelerating rates of growth in business, professional and financial services during the 1970s. In contrast, as well as growing less quickly (and, in the case of public distribution, actually declining), expansion of other services was markedly slower later in the decade. In 1984 Greater London dominated most of the private-producer categories, especially in banking and finance. 'Strategic' central office and research and development activities were, however, most characteristic of the rest of the south-east region. Employment in private and public distribution (or infrastructure) services was also relatively concentrated within London and the south-east.

Because of their external orientation, the capital circulation and production-related service activities that have contributed so significantly in recent decades to unequal regional development in Britain, are the most likely to be affected by a more integrated European market. We need, therefore, to explore in each case how their location patterns are likely to be influenced by European changes, within the wider global pattern of international trends.

Capital circulation services

The evolving international role of the City of London
Although there is growing evidence of a revival of financial services in the major provincial centres (Howells and Green, 1988; Morris, 1988; Leyshon, Thrift, 1989), the part played by London (in competition with New York, Tokyo and such European cities as Frankfurt, Paris, Zurich and Amsterdam) in international developments over the past 20 years dominates the geography of financial services in the

United Kingdom. The activities of the 'City' of London have always been largely divorced from other aspects of the British domestic economy (Allen, 1988; Marshall, 1988). They have also contributed to the long-established economic dichotomy in Britain between the commercial and trading wealth focused on London and the extractive and manufacturing base of the rest of the country (Lee, 1984). Recent events, culminating in the 'financial services revolution', have simply reinforced and transformed this historic situation. The financial services have shown a rapid growth in trade and, unlike tourism and transport, for example, have sustained a substantial surplus in balance of payments since the mid-1970s.

Four types of international market served by the City of London can be defined. These are:

- money and credit;

- securities;

- commodities (including real estate);

- corporate services.

(Marshall, 1988). To some extent, the City plays a 'production-related' role in Britain and abroad. For example, it provides investment funds for manufacturing, insurance cover for transport and buildings, and capital for public investment programmes. Nevertheless, its profits essentially depend upon the manipulation, in current and futures markets, of the large-scale financial assets controlled by its institutions. These markets have very rapidly expanded on a world scale during the turbulent period of economic change of the 1970s and 1980s.

A leading part in these changes has been played by the expanding influence of multinational companies; firstly, in commodity and manufacturing production, but more recently in services and capital circulation. Multinational service conglomerates are now emerging, with interests in banking, insurance, and financial services, as well as in advertising, public relations, the media and telecommunications. Japanese-originated companies are particularly dominant, compared with the significance of American and European multinationals in manufacturing (Marshall, 1988). The future trend seems to be towards even more widely-diversified multinationals, with interests in extractive, manufacturing and service functions.

The growth of the Eurocurrency market, in the aftermath of the oil crises of the 1970s, has provided unprecedented resources to support international credit and exchange. The trade surpluses of both Japan and the oil-rich countries have expanded financial markets, not only quantitatively, but also through wide-ranging innovations in securities trading and other types of financial transaction. Another consequence of this situation in the late 1970s has been the international debt crisis of the 1980s, which has had profound effects on the banking sector.

The ability to exploit these opportunities for profit has been stimulated by developments in communications and information technology. There is now a genuine world market for credit, securities, commodity futures and insurance, which is arising from instantaneous communications and the enormously enhanced capacity to process routine and even non-routine information. Of course, such technical innovations also reduce the employment impacts of business growth, and change the structure of labour demand, increasing the need for skilled technical, as well as financial, expertise (Rajan and Fryatt, 1988).

A further important influence has been the move to liberalise service trade in recent years, through GATT, especially as a result of the current 'Uruguay round' of negotiations. Trade in services has traditionally been small and highly concentrated, especially into European hands (although the USA has become more dominant in the postwar age). International capital transactions and national capital markets have also been deregulated by individual national governments. In the City of London, the 'Big Bang' reforms of October 1986 were intended to encourage further the internationalisation of City institutions and to remove barriers on the development of diversified, integrated financial services corporations (Coggan, 1986). A central aim of the single EC market is to encourage further changes in these directions.

Table 13.3: Selected financial services employment in the City and adjacent boroughs, compared with Great Britain, 1987, and per annum change, 1984-7

	the City and adjacent boroughs		Great Britain		
	employees ('000s)	% change p.a.	employees ('000s)		% change p.a.
banking	114	7.5	407	(28)	1.5
other credit-granting institutions	43	4.5	136	(32)	5.0
securities dealing	28	18.5	46	(61)	17.5
insurance	45	4.0	342	(13)	4.0
accountancy and management consultancy	25	8.5	189	(13)	6.0
software services	18	13.0	109	(17)	11.5

Note: the figures in brackets are of the % of GB employment (in each category) based in the City of London.

Source: Rajan and Fryatt, 1988.

In 1984, the London travel-to-work area contained 560,000 employees in financial and producer services - about 14 times the number in Birmingham TWA which is Britain's next largest financial centre (Leyshon and Thrift, 1989). In the administratively-defined City of London, there were 312,000 jobs, of which 269,000 were in all services. By 1987, after a 25% cumulative increase during the preceding three years, an estimated 195,000 worked in the six financially-related activities outlined in Table 13.3. This Table, which is based on a wider area than the City (it includes several adjacent London boroughs), demonstrates the national dominance of inner London, especially in securities dealing, banking and other credit-granting institutions. Employment growth during 1984-7 was particularly marked in securities dealing (18.5% per annum increase), but a reversal set in after the October 1987 stock market crash. Sustained employment growth is expected in the next few years in accountancy and software services, while banking will expand at a slower rate than in the recent past (Rajan and Fryatt, 1988).

The United Kingdom's international position in City-based service markets varies widely between the various financial service functions, and has recently been subject to intensified competition. It remains strong in insurance: London is still the main world centre for marine and aviation insurance, and Lloyds is the focus of the reinsurance market for large risks. Nevertheless, the major Lloyds' brokers are now controlled by USA conglomerates. British insurance firms operate more widely internationally than those of other countries. To complement this, however, overseas companies had captured about 24% of the UK domestic insurance market by the early 1980s (including equity stakes in British companies). The international market grew more slowly than banking during the 1970s, and the overseas share of British companies' income fell (Howells and Green, 1987). Competition increased, and national protectionism, imposed for prudential and consumer protection reasons, has persisted in domestic life and non-life markets, especially in Europe. One purpose of the Single European Act is the intensification of competition, by reducing as many of these barriers as possible through the establishment of European standards of practice.

London's role in most financial services over the past 20 years has increasingly come to depend upon providing an attractive commercial and regulatory environment for non-British businesses working in international markets. In order to grow, British-based firms also need to expand abroad. In banking, for example, only three British banks are in the world's 'top 20', measured in terms of net assets: the list is dominated by American, Japanese and French-based companies (Howells, 1988). The City's position as the world's leading banking and foreign-exchange market is, therefore, based primarily on the presence there of foreign-owned banks, raising credit through the Eurodollar market (Marshall, 1988). Its position is always under threat, today especially from New York. Nor is the domestic banking sector in Britain, whether wholesale or retail, safe from increased competition. One consequence of London's predominance is that some overseas banks are now introducing innovative sales techniques into the domestic market for personal banking and finance.

Foreign banks have also intervened significantly in the ownership of British stock exchange firms. The UK share of world equities trading is more peripheral than that of other financial services, because of the small size of the UK economy and the ability of large British companies to open accounts in the USA (Marshall, 1988). In the short term, since the October 1987 stock market crash, employment has been falling. This has also increased competition and moves towards mergers, rationalisation and specialisation. Growing shareownership in Britain, and the liberalisation of capital flows in the European Community is, however, expected to favour the long-term growth of the London market (Rajan and Fryatt, 1988).

The impacts of European integration on the City of London

Analysis of the likely effects of European integration on British financial services must take into account the existing international orientation of functions, and the likely influence of competition from continental centres on London's role. The attractions of Europe itself for financial business, in relation to other parts of the world, may increase, due to the growth and economic development arising from further integration. In this context, London might be expected to continue developing as Europe's primary financial centre for the following reasons:

- London's established lead, based upon its diverse pool of skilled labour and specialised information, the agglomeration economies arising from a traditional variety of services on offer, and a sympathetic, but firm, government regulatory environment (under the 1986 Financial Services Act).

- The increasing domination of financial markets by multinational conglomerate corporations, in London's case often based outside Europe. These will primarily wish to develop their European markets in concert with their global operations. The established status of London, in relation to New York and Tokyo, will help it to maintain its position.

- The deregulation of service activities in general, will enable the larger, internationally-orientated, companies to benefit from the economies of scale that they can command throughout Europe. The plethora of protective devices that has sustained smaller, nationally-based, activities in the past, will be removed. Again, this should favour London, although the detailed impact of banking and insurance regulations, for example, is complex, and progress in their reduction is likely to be slow.

Table 13.4: Percentage differences in prices of selected standard financial products, compared with average of the four lowest national prices

'standard service' (ranked by UK price difference)	UK	West Germany	EC countries Highest	EC countries Lowest
Private equity brokerage	123	7	UK	-13 (France)
Consumer credit	121	136	WG	-41 (Belgium)
Home insurance	90	3	UK	-16 (Belgium)
Commercial loans to medium-sized firms	46	6	UK	-7 (France)
Commercial fire & theft insurance	27	43	245 (Italy)	-9 (Belgium)
Company public liability insurance cover	-7	47	117 (France)	-16 (N)
Mortgages	-20	57	118 (Spain)	UK
Life insurance	-30	5	83 (Italy)	UK
Institutional equity transaction	-47	69	153 (Spain)	UK

Source: Cecchini Report, 1988.

On the other hand, the competition between London and other financial capitals in Europe will introduce new conditions which may favour the other centres. These include:

- In some sectors, especially banking, continental companies are more powerful internationally than their British counterparts. Today, intense competition characterises international producer-orientated and risk-based financial activities, and only a few British firms have been successful in developing as fully 'integrated investment banks', which are able to compete with the largest American, Japanese and European companies. London's strength appears more to be in developing customised 'niche' banking in specialised fields and being less dependent upon large capital resources. At the same time, the lucrative domestic market, upon which British banks depend upon for secure profits, will become more vulnerable to competition. Here, as data in the Cecchini Report showed (Table 13.4), the high relative costs in Britain of consumer credit and commercial loans may attract competition, either directly, or through takeover activity from European banks. Domestic and commercial property insurance is another area of financial services where increased competition can be expected.

- Doubts remain over the nature of any agreement, as part of the single European negotiations, about the 'reciprocity' of access by European financial institutions to non-EC service markets. For example, the ability of Japanese, or even USA, firms to operate freely within the European Community may be restricted in response to limitations placed on European firms wishing to operate in Japan or in the USA. Clearly London, as the main base for such non-EC firms, would be most adversely affected.

- Similar uncertainty surrounds the involvement of the United Kingdom in European Monetary Union. London's position is likely to be more isolated, and more dependent upon its global, rather than its European, role if other member states make quicker progress towards co-ordinated monetary and banking policies. On the other hand, a more complex European monetary situation may offer more scope for profit in the circulation services.

- Even if British banking and monetary practices do become more closely aligned with the rest of the European Community, the approach of UK-based companies to developing operations elsewhere in Europe may be affected by their traditional preoccupation with global markets. At present, for example, one leading British bank has 600 employees in the Far East, but only 150 in continental Europe. It may simply appear more profitable to continue giving priority to non-European business. Even with uniform regulations, unfamiliarity with the continuing complexities (including those of language, custom and procedure) of the European financial sector will encourage a cautious approach to the European expansion of London-based financial service firms. It may well develop through takeovers and various forms of co-operative arrangements with continental firms, building upon established local expertise, rather than through expansion of operations in London itself.

- It is likely that European financial centres, such as Frankfurt, Paris and Amsterdam will, in the near future, establish more open and competitive environments for attracting international financial institutions. In the longer term, the scope for doing this will be reduced by any common rules of operation adopted after 1992. Already, the 'capital adequacy rules' (required for the establishment of banks overseas), which were adopted in 1987 by the international supervisory banks, limit the scope for such regulatory undercutting.

- A final, and most important factor affecting London's role in the evolution of European financial services, will be the costs for firms operating there, compared with elsewhere. It is possible that, as London's regulatory environment becomes similar to that of other European centres, and as standards of European telecommunications move into alignment, many British and foreign companies will favour cheap locations of operation for significant elements of their activity. This already seems to be happening within Britain itself, with the high cost of rents and wages pushing office development away from London (Leyshon and Thrift, 1989). The building boom in London Docklands has been stimulated by spiralling costs within the City itself. The future viability of such huge office development schemes essentially depends on the continuing success of London's financial services. If, however, as some writers predict (Rajan and Fryatt, 1988), the City does suffer intense shortages of skilled labour in the 1990s, pushing up wages still further, even the provision of new office space may not prevent many functions from shifting to cheaper centres in continental Europe.

Even if the single European market was not being implemented, the European distribution of financial services, and the role of London within it, would still be affected by these various factors of change. In general terms, any progress in European integration will probably accelerate established trends. The most significant of these will be the continuing corporate restructuring of financial services into international conglomerates, a process in which European, American and Japanese interests will compete. London may expect to attract a major share of the new investment to serve the growing European market, provided that the quality of its infrastructure and costs of operation remain attractive. Some of the employment growth may, nevertheless, continue to spread to other parts of the south-east, and even to provincial England. The changes are also likely, however, to initiate functional shifts between the various European financial centres. London may remain dominant in Europe because of its global role, but its activities may become more specialised, complementing those of continental centres. Meanwhile, it is quite possible that a higher proportion of British domestic banking, insurance and financial consultancy services will be served most competitively from other parts of Europe.

Table 13.5: Regional distribution of business service offices in the United Kingdom, 1980-1

	% of total					
	management consultants	accountancy	market research	marketing	advertising	computer services
Greater London	23.0	14.2	62.7	59.4	44.7	31.9
South-east	25.9	15.7	21.9	25.5	18.9	24.1
East Anglia	1.6	4.0	1.0	0.4	1.6	2.1
South-west	5.9	9.4	2.0	2.2	4.4	5.8
East Midlands	3.2	6.6	0.0	1.1	3.7	3.4
West Midlands	9.4	8.3	3.9	3.6	5.8	8.0
North-west	11.5	12.8	2.0	2.5	8.8	9.3
Yorks & Humberside	4.6	11.1	2.3	1.1	4.4	5.5
North	2.1	3.5	1.3	0.4	1.4	2.4
Scotland	9.1	9.2	1.3	1.1	4.7	4.9
Wales	1.3	3.4	0.7	0.4	0.8	1.8
N. Ireland	2.4	1.7	1.0	2.5	0.8	0.7
Total no. of offices	374	649	306	278	1,402	1,490

Source: Marshall, 1988.

The production-related services

The international context

Even though 'financial services' are sometimes separated from 'business services' in discussions of producer-service activities, the fundamental nature of the distinction between the 'capital circulation' and 'producer-related' activities is often neglected. The essential characteristic of the latter is their actual, or potential, interchangeability with the 'in-house' activities of customers. They include a wide range of 'blue-collar' transport, maintenance, and other support activities, as well as the 'white-collar' (or information-based) services, such as accountancy, legal advice, engineering, technical consultancy, advertising, computer services and personnel services, that have all expanded rapidly in recent years. In Britain, with the notable exception of accountancy (with its dispersed business and consumer markets), these functions have a marked concentration in the southeast (Table 13.5).

In the international arena, business services, including various consultancy, corporate law, computer services, advertising, hotels and travel, market research, newsagency and telecommunications activities, usually contain a few important British companies. The UK share of world activity in these fields, however, is smaller than it is in the capital circulation services. London has a strong position in accountancy and legal services, even though the overseas (especially American) presence is considerable. Moreover, American firms have penetrated European markets most effectively in the newer and more innovative business services, such as on-line information and computer software services. European firms tend to be more dominant in traditional activities such as law, distribution, travel and engineering and business consultancy (Howells, 1988).

The British accountancy profession has long been internationally orientated, and may be expected to be in a strong position within an integrated European Community, in relation to the less well-developed professions of, for example, France, The Netherlands, Italy and Spain. Standards are increasingly being determined by a few large American/British multinational conglomerates (Marshall, 1988). In Britain there are more accountants than in the rest of the EC put together (*Financial Times*, 1988). The core of their work remains the company audit, but diversification of activities has recently characterised the profession. This has involved the rapid growth of consultancy expertise in the fields of taxation, management, insolvency, finance and public sector services - all of which will be in greater demand when the single market develops. Much of the expansion of large companies has occurred through takeovers and mergers (Marshall, 1988; Morris, 1988). These same processes can be expected to continue in Europe as professional qualifications and corporate financial conventions become more closely aligned.

Production-related services and the demand for skilled labour

A few production-related services, such as accountancy, are sufficiently large and professionally autonomous to be viewed as distinct sectors. In more general terms, however, the inherent interdependence of many such services with other activities, means that their growth and locational trends must primarily be understood in relation to the range of expertise required by customers, and how far these needs are satisfied from in-house, rather than from outside service sources.

Much of the relevant expertise is provided in-house, through the internal labour markets of customer firms and based upon their own recruitment, training and promotion policies. In the large companies (especially transnationals), these policies dominate 'primary' labour markets and, therefore, the supply of and demand for key technical and managerial personnel in different companies and regions. The geographical mobility of such personnel, already largely sponsored through career development programmes by large organisations (Salt, 1984; Findlay and Gould, 1989), will be considerably enhanced by the implementation of the Single European Act and the development of 'European' firms. These developments, including their significance for national and regional skilled manpower, have already attracted research interest in Britain (Lindley, 1987).

The changing role of production-related services in each country and region must, therefore, be seen as complementing trends in the development, use, distribution and movement of corporate skills, on an increasingly European scale. The very types of expertise which are likely to be most affected by the liberalisation of the European labour market, and in greatest demand by large companies, have also

271

formed the basis for growth in consultancy and subcontracting arrangements between large organisations and the production-related services. Modern flexibility in the labour market is shifting the boundary between large companies' internal and external markets for expertise, as they divest themselves of their more peripheral or freestanding service activities.

Corporate influences on the location of production-related services

In this context, two general influences on European patterns of demand for production-related services will be significant as the single market emerges. The first, evidently, is the evolution of a European scale of corporate organisation. While increasing the complexity of the commercial environment, and thereby creating new demands for advisory and consultancy services, this will also link many regions more firmly to the centralised, high-level expertise available within large companies elsewhere in the European Community. These changes will, therefore, affect the amount and quality of independent production-related services demanded in each region. Secondly, technological changes, both in particular processes or products and in the general mode of production itself, will also alter and, again, probably increase the demand for high-level skills. Many of these will be supported from in-house expertise, but new international opportunities will also arise for individual production-related service firms and corporations, as barriers to marketing such activities come down.

Current evidence suggests that the demand for production-related support services by manufacturing, whether supplied in-house or independently, appears to depend primarily on the technical sophistication of the product (Marshall, 1983; Howells and Green, 1988; Howells, 1988). Industries with high levels of 'non-production' work within them (over 30% in the United Kingdom), include chemicals production and electrical, instrument and mechanical engineering. These branches seem to draw most upon such outside functions as engineering consultancies, research and development advice and specialised personnel recruitment. Of course, outside the manufacturing sector, many complex information-based service functions also draw upon a wide range of support activities.

At any time, the general climate of business confidence affects the amount of investment in innovative activities, and the employment, for example, of technical consultancies and financial advisers. The business strategies of firms also create distinctive requirements; different ranges of internal and external expertise are required for product innovation, improved production efficiency, and financial restructuring. Similarly, the market position of a firm, in relation to competitors, determines the relative needs for marketing, advertising and sales expertise. These characteristics of production-related service demand suggest that growing European integration will strongly stimulate such activities. The more technically-sophisticated or information-based sectors will respond most actively to the challenges created by the enlarged market, involving enhanced economic growth, widespread corporate restructuring and intensified competition.

Specific use of outside, rather than in-house, expertise, is influenced by the type of task being undertaken and the size of the company (Ochel and Wegner; Howells and Green). New, unpredictable and specialised skills (or those requiring high capital investment) are most commonly bought in. These include legal, financial, advertising and managerial training, and also computer or transportation expertise. Because of the limited range of expertise of their own staff, small- and medium-sized firms tend to be most dependent upon such services. The growing complexity of commercial activity, however, has pushed larger companies into employing them; the development of the European market will most likely accelerate this trend.

When large firms employ their own experts, they very often bring them in from head or divisional office locations. Similarly, if such firms move towards bringing in more outside expertise, organisations from the same headquarter regions tend to be favoured. Thus, growing regional external ownership, of the type likely to be encouraged by the development of 'European' firms, may undermine support for regionally-based production-related services (Marshall, 1979; Smith, 1979). While stimulating demand for production-related services, European integration may, therefore, concentrate this demand into core regions.

At the local level, even where the quality of local services may be high, production-related services may be neglected in the process by which large firms, operating on a European scale, buy in outside expertise (Marshall, 1982). Europeanwide service firms, with headquarters within the same core regions, are also likely to emerge and dominate the European scene. Changes in the regulatory environments, for example, in the fields of transport, distribution and securities dealing, have already stimulated international competition, which is likely to extend to other service activities in the 1990s.

Technological influences on the location of producer-related services

These developments may be further encouraged by technological change in European production. Process innovation, for example, generally reduces employment in routine production, while generating the need for supporting expertise in research and development, installation, monitoring and finance. Similarly, the introduction of new products, while perhaps better sustaining the production workforce, also requires additional supporting functions, including market research and sales. Whichever type of technical innovation is involved, a welter of current evidence in Britain suggests that new technology favours areas of the country which have appropriate established technical infrastructure, whether through the operations of large firms, or through the relative success of innovative small firms (Goddard and Thwaites, 1987).

As well as specific technical innovations, the whole mode of production and its infrastructural context is currently in a state of flux, and some believe that this may create a potential countervailing dispersal to new areas. 'Flexible manufacturing' is supposed to be breaking down traditional horizontal and vertical divisions of labour and, at the same time, exploiting the potential of investment in computerised processing. The full effect of these changes has so far been confined to only a few firms and sectors, although elements of the technology, and the accompanying organisational changes, are being introduced selectively into established mass-production activities (Schoenberger, 1987; Gertler, 1988 and 1989).

The emphases in flexible manufacturing organisation on quality of investment, the close integration of processes, a smooth flow of production, a flexible labour force, a reduced significance of labour costs, and increased skills, favour large-scale, integrated regional investment. This is reinforced by the use of 'just-in-time' delivery of material supplies, which not only reduces inventory costs, but also involves the renegotiation of the terms under which subcontractors and service firms are linked to assembly. Whether such integrated investment needs to take place in core or in peripheral areas seems not to be determined universally. It is possible, for example, that leading investments of this type could draw production-related service support away from established core regions and into low-cost peripheral locations. Such support, however, is likely to be dominated by the materials-handling 'blue-collar' activities, such as transport, distribution, construction and maintenance, rather than by higher-order 'white-collar' functions. It may also be provided mainly by the in-house operations of the dominant firms, or at least by closely-dependent specialist firms, perhaps brought in from outside the local region.

Like the corporate changes already outlined, technological changes will increase demands for inputs of production-related service labour (Ochel and Wegner, 1987). Whether these will be concentrated into existing industrial cores, or whether they will offer new possibilities for geographical dispersal of complexes of interlinked industrial and service development, depends upon wider corporate, competitive, technical and cost factors. The trends described here have little in common with those occurring in the capital circulation services. They are much more intimately related to developments in other sectors of the European economy. When viewed from Britain, the prospects of production-related service growth in competition with continental countries seem poor. The relative weakness of the UK economy, and its peripherality to the European market, do not favour it as a base for European-orientated service firms. The quality, for example, of technical, maintenance, transportation, or personnel training services, is high on the continent; specialist firms already operating there are more likely to penetrate the British market than vice versa. Despite the strength of individual activities in Britain (such as accountancy and commercial law), production-related service activity, under an integrated European regime, is likely to shift across the English Channel.

Further implications for the small-firm sector and for regional development

These complex patterns of internal/external change in provision of business expertise are also important for two other aspects of regional economic change. First, as we have seen, the regional success of the small-firm segment, dominated by service functions, depends to an important extent on the externalisation policies of large local companies. While these policies may be marginally influenced by the variable quality of regional and local service infrastructure, it is more evident that this quality is itself affected by the way large companies patronise local services. This circular relationship means that the quality of services available to independent, regionally-based firms, increasingly depends on the practices of large, externally-owned organisations. Where these favour non-local inputs, arranged through their headquarter locations, the local small-firm segment may be undermined both directly, through lower demand for local services, and indirectly, as a result of the lower quality of local services provided to them. This trend is most marked for the critical information-based services.

276

The externalisation practices of large firms also determine the regional and local employment multiplier impacts of their investment. Those that increasingly use non-local sources of technical, maintenance, transportation, financial, personnel recruitment, and catering expertise, whether from other firms, or from other parts of their own organisation, reduce the regional and local employment impacts of their activities. In this context, the potential of integrated complexes, based upon flexible production methods, becomes of even greater significance.

The increasing role of the production-related service sector in the changing disposition of skilled labour cannot be ignored in any wider appraisal of the effects of the single market in Europe. Equally, changing policies by transnational companies in their acquisition of outside skills, may critically impinge on both the amount of employment they support in different regions, and the quality of service skills available to smaller firms there.

Conclusions

Geographical research on the service sector in the United Kingdom has progressed considerably in recent years, both through the compilation of information and, perhaps more importantly, through an improved understanding of its internal diversity. Its significance for employment, for regional inequality, and even for the international success of the British economy, has given urgency to these tasks. Service sector changes must be viewed not only in the context of wider trends in the international division of labour, but also, in many cases, as a complement to developments in other aspects of production. Corporate priorities and the impacts of technological change also exert profound influences on service trends.

As the single European market develops, its impact will be strongly felt on the operations of most services. In the case of the capital circulation sector, the pattern of European development is likely to remain dominated by London, although not by British firms. Significant modifications are to be expected in international and interregional functional patterns. The disposition and competitiveness of production-related services may be subject to much more radical change, as demand patterns, technology and regulatory barriers to their supply are transformed. These changes may have significant regional impacts on a European scale, and Britain may be less favoured by growth than her continental competitors.

References

Allen, J., 'Service industries: uneven development and uneven knowledge', *Area*, Vol. 20, pp. 15-22, 1988.

Amin, A. and Goddard, J.B., *Technological change, industrial restructuring and regional development*, Allen and Unwin, London, 1986.

Cecchini, P. et al., *The European challenge 1992; the benefits of a single market*, Wildwood House, Aldershot, 1988.

Coggan, P., *The money machine: how the City works*, Penguin, London, 1986.

Commission of the European Communities, *Completing the Internal Market*, Office for Official Publications of the European Communities, Luxembourg, 1985.

Emerson, M. et al., *The economics of 1992*, Oxford University Press, Oxford 1988,

Financial Times, 19 April 1988.

Findlay, A. and Gould, W.T.S., 'Skilled international migration: a research agenda', *Area*, Vol. 21, pp. 3-11, 1989.

Gertler, M., 'The limits to flexibility: comments on the post-Fordist version of production and its geography', *Transactions, Institute of British Geographers New Series*, Vol. 13, pp. 419-32, 1988.

Gertler, M., 'Restructuring flexibility? A reply to Schoenberger', *Transactions, Institute of British Geographers New Series*, Vol. 14, pp. 109-12, 1989.

Goddard, J.B. and Thwaites, A., 'Technological change', in Lever, W.F. (ed.), *Industrial change in the United Kingdom*, Longman, London, pp. 96-107, 1987.

Howells, J., *Economic, technological and locational trends in European services*, Avebury, Aldershot, 1988.

Howells, J. and Green, A., *Technological innovation, structural change and location in UK services*, Avebury, Aldershot, 1988.

Keeble, D., Owens, P.L. and Thompson, C., 'Regional accessibility and economic potential in the European Community', *Regional Studies*, Vol. 16 (2), pp. 419-32, 1982.

Lee, C.H., 'The service sector, regional specialisation and economic growth in the Victorian economy', *Journal of Historical Geography*, Vol. 10, pp. 139-55, 1984.

Leyshon, A. and Thrift, N., 'South goes north? The rise of the British provincial financial centre', in Lewis, J. and Townsend, A. (eds.), *The north-south divide*, Paul Chapman, London, pp. 114-56, 1989.

Lindley, R.M., *Possible employment effects of the creation of the European Internal Market: country report for the United Kingdom*, Commission of the European Communities Study No. 86.686, Brussels, 1987.

Marshall, J.N., 'Ownership, organisation and industrial linkage: a case study in the northern region of England', *Regional Studies*, Vol. 13, pp. 531-58, 1979.

Marshall, J.N., 'Linkages between manufacturing industry and business services', *Environment and Planning A*, Vol. 14, pp. 1523-40, 1982.

Marshall, J.N., *Services and uneven development*, Oxford University Press, Oxford, 1988.

Massey, D., 'The legacy lingers on: the impact of Britain's international role on its internal geography', in Martin, R. and Rowthorn, R., *The geography of de-industrialisation*, Macmillan, London, pp. 31-53, 1986.

Morris, J.L., 'Producer services and the regions: the case of large accountancy firms', *Environment and Planning A*, Vol. 20, pp. 741-60, 1988.

Ochel, W. and Wegner, M., *Service economies in Europe: opportunities for growth*, Pinter/Westview, London, 1987.

Pelkmans, J. and Winters, A., 'Europe's domestic market', *Chatham House Papers, Royal Institute of International Affairs*, Vol. 43, pp. 43 and 53, 1988.

Rajan, A. and Fryatt, J., *Create or abdicate: the City's human choice for the '90s*, Institute of Manpower Studies, University of Sussex, 1988.

Salt, J., 'High-level manpower movements in north-west Europe and the role of careers', *International Migration Review*, Vol. 17, pp. 633-52, 1984.

Schoenberger, E., 'Thinking about flexibility: a response to Gertler', *Transactions, Institute of British Geographers New Series*, Vol. 14, pp. 98-108, 1989.

Smith, I.J., 'The effect of external takeovers on manufacturing employment change in the northern region between 1963 and 1973', *Regional Studies,* Vol. 13, pp. 421-38, 1979.

Thrift, N., 'Taking the rest of the world seriously? The state of British urban and regional research in a time of economic crisis', *Environment and Planning A,* Vol. 17 (1), pp. 7-24, 1985.

Wood, P.A., 'The anatomy of job loss and job creation: some speculations on the role of the 'producer service' sector', *Regional Studies,* Vol. 20, pp. 37-47, 1986.

Chapter XIV

Christof Ellger (Freie Universität Berlin)

The importance of the quaternary (information) sector for spatial development: the case of Baden-Württemberg

The concept of the quaternary (information) sector

Social scientists and economists agree that the classification of economic activities and institutions into general sectors serves a useful purpose. Sectors such as agriculture, manufacturing and services, have different aspatial and spatial characteristics and, therefore, lend themselves to specific investigation. Moreover, a sectoral classification can be used to analyse broad socioeconomic changes by assessing the altering shares of the workforce or, alternatively, the social product in the various sectors.

There is, however, growing dissatisfaction with the commonly-used, conventional, three-sector model, which was developed at a time when most economic functions were directly linked with one or the other of agriculture, mining and manufacturing. Today, however, it is this third, heterogeneous category of services - the so-called 'tertiary sector'- which is the hardest to define. It is composed of an array of very different economic activities, for which general statements concerning their economic performance, spatial requirements and spatial impacts can no longer be made with conviction. To overcome this problem, various attempts have been made to divide the 'service sector' into meaningful subgroups; for example, the simple division of producer services and consumer services, or the more specific differentiation between distributive, producer, social and personal services (Browning and Singelmann, 1978).

The first identification and mention of a 'quaternary' economic sector in the field of human geography dates back as far as 1961 in the publication of Jean Gottmann's, *Megalopolis - the urbanized north-eastern seaboard of the United States* (Gottmann, 1961). In this book Gottmann recognised the growing importance of white-collar employment in the economic and geographical development of his study region, and claimed that, 'services that involve transactions, analysis research or decision-making, and also education and government', should be classified separately as 'a new and distinct *quaternary* family of economic activities'. Whereas he uses the rather vague term 'transactions' as the keyword to pin down his notion of the quaternary sector (thereby arousing misunderstanding, especially in German human geography, and evoking criticism, for instance by Abler, writing in 1975), in his most recent definition, he initiated the notion of information activities which provide 'jobs which revolve around the generation, transmission, processing and utilization of information and knowledge'. On the basis of a similar grouping of economic activities developed by Törnqvist (1973), two British human geographers, Dicken and Lloyd (1981), described a four-sector model of basic economic functions and defined the quaternary sector as that sphere of the economy which deals with information processes. The concept of an 'information sector' has also been developed by American economists, commencing with the pioneering work of Machlup (1962), who analysed what he described as the 'production and distribution of knowledge' and then drew up lists of 'knowledge occupations' and 'knowledge industries'. In the 1970s, Parker (1975) and Porat (1977) followed, with their studies on the information sector in the United States. Their approach was adopted by the Organisation for Economic Co-operation and Development to analyse information sector development in its various member countries. The geographer's notion of a quaternary sector, and the economists' concept of an information sector, have been assessed as being identical by several authors, including Jones (1982) and Kellerman (1985).

If the quaternary, or information, sector is to be defined as the group of economic activities and institutions that are primarily involved in the processing and output of information, we are still left with the question of 'what is information?' Attempts to answer this often return to tautological statements, such as the often-quoted comment, 'information is information, neither matter nor energy' (Wiener, quoted in Oeser, 1986). For present purposes, it is reasonable enough to adopt a pragmatic answer to the question, by viewing information as a meaningful entity which is passed on in communication: it is non-material but, nevertheless, it is bound to a material carrier.

These considerations argue for a four-sector model of economic activity, in which the tertiary sector encompasses personal and also materials-related services, whereas the quaternary sector consists of information activities. A number of reasons can be given for distinguishing the quaternary sector as a special category. Foremost is the practical issue that structural change can be more adequately described this way than it can be on the basis of the traditional three-sector model. Moreover, it is important to know which particular services - goods-related, person-related or information-related - are growing the fastest. This is important, especially for the purposes of labour policy and education planning. In a more abstract sense, it is interesting for social research to analyse how the informational 'meta-work' in society is developing, in comparison with all other activities, and thus to assess how far the 'abstraction of labour' has proceeded.

Information has some very special qualities as an economic entity. On the one hand, it is potentially multipliable and is without limits: information is passed from one communicator to another, but it, nevertheless, also remains with the first (Masuda, 1981). On the other hand, in order to be meaningful, information must be bound to a semantic context and can only be grasped by a cognitive structure, able to place it into its special context. It is useful for a receiver only when its context is comprehended and when the receiver also possesses sufficiently structured 'pre-information' to combine context and 'new information'. Production processes are, indeed, very different in information-related economic activities than in other branches: they depend much more on qualitative factors, such as intelligence, creative atmosphere, teamwork and continuous-learning capacity. Two further justifications for separate analysis of information activities and institutions in the quaternary sector are: firstly, the growing share of information labour in the employment distribution of advanced industrial societies; and secondly, the growing importance of information as an input in all spheres of the economy.

Also in its spatial behaviour and impact, the information industry has some special characteristics. The flow processes of information and its spatial movements are very different from movements of goods and people, and in many ways depend upon other factors. The essential issue relates not so much to actual passage through geographical space (using energy, time, money and labour), but, given that there is some kind of channel (face-to-face communication, mail service, telephone or wide-band digital electronic connection), it is much more a question of the common code of sender and receiver, and the necessary similarity of their cognitive structures. It is significant, too, that information and its functions have little demand on space for processing and storage. By concentrating information labour in high-rise buildings, the quaternary sector shows a potential for a high degree of contractability. On the other hand, because of the technical potentialities for information 'transport', information labour can theoretically also be highly dispersed in spatial terms. With the increasing division of labour in society, highly-specialised information institutions have developed. These include company headquarters, media houses, and research and development laboratories, which have attained spatial autonomy from other economic functions (particularly those involved in production), and can be located according to their specific informational requirements. This spatial autonomy is another important reason for the separate analysis of the quaternary (information) sector.

For research investigations on spatial patterns and trends of this particular economic sector, two types of statistical data can be used. One relates to the firm or institution, the other relates to individuals (with their occupations). The former discerns elements of the economy according to the output of productive units, the latter discerns them according to the output of individual employees. However, because of vertical concentration processes, it is becoming more and more difficult to work with firm- and institution-based data. Many different functions, including extraction, production, trade, public relations and management, can be performed by a single company. Today, therefore, studies of the quaternary sector usually have to work on the basis of occupational data.

The importance of the quaternary sector for spatial development

The quaternary sector has a decisive spatial role, simply because of its dynamics. To a much greater degree than occupations in tertiary services, those in information represent a dominant growth sector in modern economic development. A glance at the development of the sectoral distribution of occupations in West Germany during the period 1950-78 (Figure 14.1), confirms the strong decrease in primary sector (mainly agricultural, mining, and energy production) jobs. Since 1961, there has also been a steep decline in the share of secondary sector (mainly manufacturing) occupations. However, the proportions of the labour force in the tertiary and in the quaternary sectors continue to increase. The rise in the latter is considerably steeper; significantly, during the 1970s, the quaternary sector took the lead for the very first time. Forecasts of future trends in West Germany assume continued reductions in the numbers and proportional shares of primary and secondary jobs, a levelling-out of the rise of tertiary employment, and further gains in the quantity of information jobs (Rothkirch, 1985). Similar trends are occurring in most other economically-advanced countries. Such countries do, however, have differing proportions of information labour in their total workforce, partly due to differences in their occupational classifications.

287

Figure 14.1: Occupational change in West Germany, 1950-78

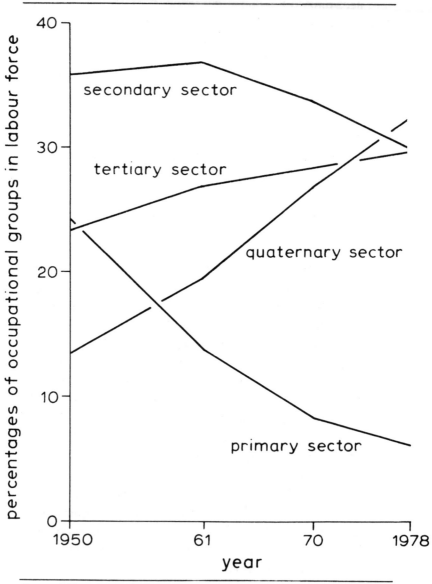

Source: Mikrozensus, 1978.

With its growing importance as a provider of new jobs, the quaternary sector will more and more determine the economic fate of regions and their spatial processes. Information increasingly becomes the dominating input factor in all areas of economic activity. Thus, cities and regions now depend heavily on the existence and growth of creative information employment and institutions which succeed in maintaining a high level of knowledge (about technology, markets and political decisions) and, at the same time, enlarge their fields of administrative control. The elite, highly-paid occupations, which are so characteristic of the information industry, accentuate this dependence. Another important effect is the pressure of quaternary functions on land use within growth regions. With their ability and readiness to pay enormous prices or rents for space, quaternary enterprises are very capable of pushing other potential users of land and buildings away to other locations.

Research on the spatial tendencies of quaternary functions stresses the importance of macrospatial concentration of information activities within growth-intensive metropolitan agglomerations (Kellerman, 1985). This is commonly attributed to specific locational factors, which tend to favour places which have good accessibility, intense information exchange, a high level of 'transactional performance', availability of skilled 'elite' labour, and living attractions, such as high-quality housing, good leisure facilities, pleasant natural landscapes, and amenable climate. It is also important to note that the locational processes of quaternary functions are, in many respects, self-reinforcing. Moreover, the concentration of quaternary institutions in certain specific regions and places is a circular and cumulative trend (Pred, 1977), which is in turn related to the fundamental principles of information. Thus, theories of circular-cumulative polarisation of economic activity find their most adequate application in the locational behaviour of the quaternary sector.

The quaternary sector in Baden-Württemberg

Data for empirical investigation

For the *Land* of Baden-Württemberg in south-west Germany, an empirical investigation of the growth and spatial distribution of information labour can be made on the basis of data compiled and published by the Statistisches Landesamt Baden-Württemberg (State Statistical Office); in particular the 1979 and 1988 *Kreis* level statistics of socially-insured employees. These statistics are based on the returns of the national social insurance scheme. Accordingly, payroll workers who are compulsory members are included in this system, but self-employed persons (including farmers), and also civil servants, are excluded. However, about 80% of the active persons are registered. The Baden-Württemberg statistics are available for this state's nine *Stadtkreise* and 35 *Landkreise*. The populations of each of these 44 districts average just over 200,000, ranging from under 50,000 in *Stadtkreis* Baden-Baden to over 500,000 in the capital city of Stuttgart. The first date for which the statistics are available is the registration of 1979; the most recent is 1988. Thus, trends over nearly a full decade can be measured.

Recent spatial developments in Baden-Württemberg

The spatial structure and development of urban settlement in Baden-Württemberg is dominated by the metropolitan areas. As shown in Figure 14.2, a regionalisation of the state, for the purposes of spatial analysis and regional planning, divides the urbanised parts into four *Verdichtungsräume* (urban agglomeration areas), which are surrounded by their *Randzonen um die Verdichtungsräume* (fringe zones around the agglomerations). The fringe zones around Stuttgart, Mannheim-Heidelberg and Karlsruhe merge into one extensive urbanised area, forming what may be described as the '*Randstad*' of north-west Baden-Württemberg.

Figure 14.2: Baden-Württemberg; regional framework

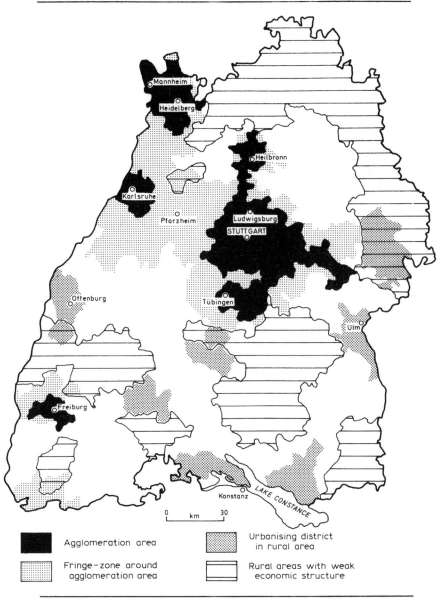

Agglomeration area

Fringe-zone around agglomeration area

Urbanising district in rural area

Rural areas with weak economic structure

Source: based on Borcherdt, 1983.

Beyond the agglomeration fringe zones, seven localised *Verdichtungsbereiche im ländlichen Raum* (urbanising districts within rural areas) have been demarcated. All of the rest of Baden-Württemberg is classified as *ländliche Raume mit Strukturschwächen* (rural areas with weak economic structures).

Recent development in Baden-Württemberg has strongly favoured the prominent, and centrally-positioned, Stuttgart region. Population and employment losses within the city itself are being more than compensated for by large gains in the surrounding *Kreise*. Thus, a major feature of spatial development in Baden-Württemberg is the 'metropolitanisation' process, which is focused on the Stuttgart metropolitan area and is accompanied here by suburbanisation and spatial extension of the urban agglomeration, especially towards the west. The smaller Mannheim-Heidelberg and Karlsruhe agglomerations in the north-west also show suburbanisation trends. However, losses from these cities are higher than the gains in their fringe zones. Hence, in overall terms, north Baden's share of Baden-Württemberg's population and employment is now declining. The state is, in fact, experiencing a general shift of employment and population from the north to the south, with major gains now in the Freiburg and Lake Constance areas. Stagnation and losses characterise the rural areas in the north-east, in parts of the Swabian 'Alps' to the south of Stuttgart, and in the Black Forest. In broad terms there is a marked contrast between the central growth region around Stuttgart and the rest of Baden-Württemberg. This is reflected not only in regional patterns of employment and population change, but also in spatial differences in income levels and unemployment rates (Münzenmeier and Walter, 1985).

Quaternary sector growth and its spatial distribution

With 7% more people employed in 1988 than in 1979, Baden-Württemberg, unlike many other parts of West Germany, has experienced a quite remarkable growth in employment during the past decade. Employment in the information sector, with a gain of 17.6% during the years 1979-88, has enjoyed a particularly strong increase; today it accounts for as much as 33% of the state's total insured employment. Baden-Württemberg's economy, therefore, is now becoming strongly information-based. However, it still cannot be described as being 'post-industrial', for manufacturing still employs nearly one-half of the labour force and more than one-third of the information workers. Interestingly, over the last decade, tertiary activities have also been growing strongly in Baden-Württemberg, a trend which is contrary to the hypothesis of *decreasing* service employment in an advanced 'self-service economy' (Gershuny, 1978).

The spatial distribution of quaternary employment reflects the strong position of Stuttgart and its surrounding *Kreise* (Figure 14.3). As much as 15% of Baden-Württemberg's information sector workforce works in this city, whilst a further 30% works in the rest of the middle-Neckar region (Stuttgart's four adjoining *Landkreise*, plus Göppingen). The two large urban centres in Baden (Mannheim and Karlsruhe) have substantially smaller shares, and so have their suburban fringe zones. The entire planning region around Mannheim-Heidelberg includes only 11.9% of Baden-Württemberg's information-based workers, whilst the Karlsruhe planning region accommodates only 10.1%. Outside the agglomeration areas and their fringes, a significant representation (over 1.8% of the state's total) of information workers is to be found in the Bodensee (Lake Constance) area and in the semirural districts of Ostalbkreis, Reutlingen, Konstanz, Schwarzwald-Baar-Kreis and Ortenaukreis. Areas with a poor showing of information employment are mostly in the weakly-structured rural regions, especially in north-eastern Baden-Württemberg, the rural districts of south Württemberg (Sigmaringen and Biberach in particular), and the southern part of the Black Forest.

Figure 14.3: Baden-Württemberg; percentage distribution of the state's information sector workforce, 1988

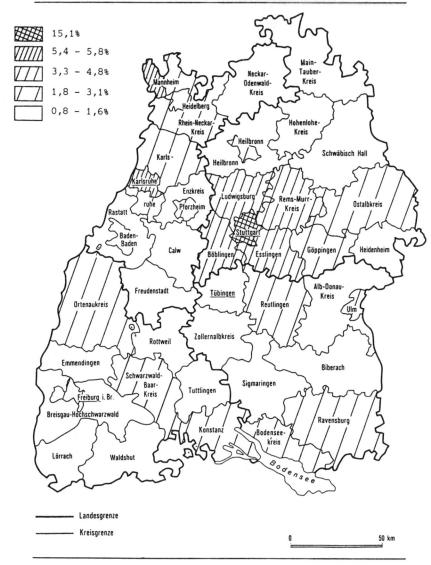

Note: the map also indicates the names of all *Kreis* districts.

Source: Statistisches Landesamt Baden-Württemberg, 1989.

Figure 14.4: Baden-Württemberg; location quotients of information sector workforce, 1988

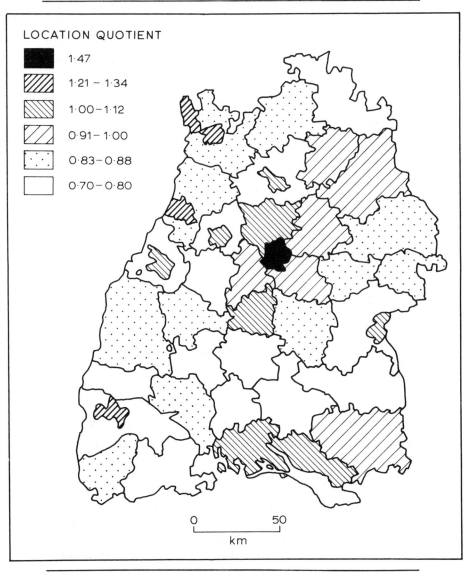

Note: see Figure 14.3 for names of *Kreis* districts.

Source: Statistisches Landesamt Baden-Württemberg, 1988.

Using the 'information location quotient' index (Figure 14.4), which relates to the importance of information-based jobs within the structures of local employment (in comparison to the Baden-Württemberg average), Stuttgart stands out even more clearly; and, with the notable exception of Freiburg, whose importance is enhanced by this index, the gap between Stuttgart and other Baden-Württemberg cities is noticeably greater than on the preceding map. Interestingly, four *Landkreise* (each with a quotient between 1.21 and 1.47) also stand out strongly in Figure 14.4. These are:

- Ludwigsburg, to the north of Stuttgart, which is important for trade and banking;

- Tübingen, to the south of the Stuttgart region, which is dominated by its university;

- Konstanz, in the Lake Constance 'sun belt' region, with its important media functions and university;

- lastly, Bodenseekreis (also adjoining Lake Constance), with its information-intensive manufacturing at Friedrichshafen.

Quite high quotients are also to be seen to the north-east of Stuttgart (Hohenlohekreis, Schwäbisch Hall and Rems-Murr-Kreis).

Figure 14.5, showing shifts in the spatial distribution of information labour during the period 1979-88, reveals a relative decrease of information employment within the main urban centres, and a relative increase within the suburban fringe-zone districts. Quite clearly, therefore, quaternary employment is being subjected to a pronounced centrifugal trend, from cities to their surrounding suburbanising zones. This spatial shift is a response to differences in growth rates, rather than a 'literal' process. Beyond the agglomeration areas and their fringe zones, the improved showing of districts such as Bodenseekreis, Hohenlohekreis, Ostalbkreis and Main-Tauber-Kreis, has come very recently and reflects a new trend of remoter rural areas becoming involved in the quaternary sector.

Figure 14.5: Baden-Württemberg; change of information sector workforce by districts, 1979-88

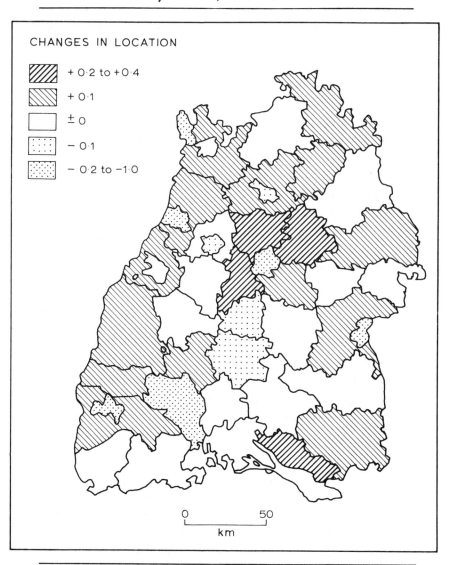

CHANGES IN LOCATION

+ 0·2 to +0·4

+ 0·1

± 0

− 0·1

− 0·2 to −1·0

0   50
km

Note: the changes refer to the changing *Kreis* share of Baden-Württemberg's information sector workforce (percentage points).

Source: Statistisches Landesamt Baden-Württemberg, 1980 and 1989.

The pattern of regional development in Baden-Württemberg during the last decade raises the important question as to whether or not the 'suburbanisation' of information employment makes up for losses within the central cities. In the Stuttgart region it certainly does, but in the Mannheim and Karlsruhe metropolitan areas it does not. In terms of regional shifts, the Stuttgart region and to some extent the southern 'sun belt', too, have to be seen as winners of spatial change in the quaternary sector. On the other hand, north Baden, and its older-industrialised urban centres, is very much the loser.

The strong growth of information functions within the centrally-situated Stuttgart agglomeration and its neighbouring districts, is largely due to the expansion of powerful administrative institutions and various functions concerned with information production and distribution. This region is by far the most important focus of industrial and commercial headquarters in Baden-Württemberg. Stuttgart, and nine other urban centres within the region, control about two-thirds of the total turnover of the state's 75 largest companies (Ellger, 1988). Among them is Daimler-Benz, which is now the largest enterprise in West Germany and (largely through takeovers) is still vigorously expanding into an enormous complex for car, aircraft and armament production. It is also strongly involved in technological development in electronics, engineering and various other fields.

Some of the headquarters which are based within the Stuttgart metropolitan area, for example IBM Deutschland, or Bosch, control nationwide, or even global, production operations. Accordingly, the expansion of quaternary activities within the Stuttgart region is, in many respects, an outcome of the ongoing process of economic concentration of control functions.

The other fields of Stuttgart's quaternary sector are linked to the city's function as the state capital of Baden-Württemberg. This means that not only governmental and legal institutions are located here, but also many other types of organisation, including the media and cultural associations. In contrast, in the Baden portion of Baden-Württemberg (the north-western, western and south-western parts), historical development did not produce a single major capital city. Instead former 'capital' functions tended to be dispersed amongst four cities, which today have to compete against each other for quaternary institutions: Heidelberg and Mannheim, which each took its turn to serve as the residence capital of the Palatinate, Karlsruhe (formerly the capital of Baden) and Freiburg (once a seat of Hapsburg provincial administration for their territories in south-west Germany). Thus, for historical reasons, a decentralised city system developed here, and the dynamics of the quaternary sector are threatened by a macrocentralisation process which is heavily focused on the much larger and centrally-situated city of Stuttgart.

In general, continuing change in the spatial distribution of quaternary functions plays a vital role in the unequal regional development of Baden-Württemberg and other West German *Länder*. 'Metropolitan centre'/'rural periphery' distinctions here are now much less significant than the selective dynamics in the urban system. Continuing concentration in and around Stuttgart, dominated today by the expansion of headquarters' functions and the proliferation of financial, insurance, media and public organisations, underlies what is still a notably strong metropolitanisation tendency within this affluent, but diverse, part of West Germany.

References

Abler, R., 'Effects of space-adjusting technologies on the human geography of the future', in Abler, R. et al. (eds.), *Human geography in a shrinking world*, North Scituate, pp. 35-56, 1975.

Borcherdt, C., 'Das Land Baden-Württemberg - ein Überblick', in Borcherdt, C. (ed.), *Geographische Landeskunde von Baden-Württemberg*, Schriften zur politischen Landeskunde Baden-Württembergs, Vol. 8, Stuttgart, pp. 21-80, 1983.

Browning, H.L. and Singelmann, J., 'The transformation of the US labor force: the interaction of industry and occupation', *Politics and Society*, Vol. 8, pp. 481-509, 1978.

Dicken, P. and Lloyd, P.E., *Modern western society. A geographical perspective on work, home and well-being*, Harper and Row, London, 1981.

Ellger, C., 'Informationssektor und räumliche Entwicklung - dargestellt am Beispiel Baden-Württembergs', *Tübinger Geographische Studien*, Vol. 99, 1988.

Gershuny, J., *After industrial society? The emerging self-service economy*, London, 1978.

Gottmann, J., *Megalopolis. The urbanized north-eastern seaboard of the United States*, New York, 1961.

Gottmann, J., 'Urban centrality and the interweaving of quaternary activities', *Ekistics*, Vol. 29, pp. 322-31, 1970.

Jones, B., *Sleepers wake! Technology and the future of work*, Melbourne, 1982.

Innenministerium Baden-Württemberg, *1986 Landesentwicklungsbericht für Baden-Württemberg, Tendenzen und Konsequenzen*, Stuttgart, 1986.

Kellerman, A., 'The evolution of service economies: a geographical perspective', *The Professional Geographer*, Vol. 37, pp. 133-43, 1985.

Machlup, F., *The production and distribution of knowledge in the United States*, Princeton, USA, 1962.

Masuda, Y., *The information society as post-industrial society*, Bethesda, USA, 1981.

Meier, R.L., *A communication theory of urban growth*, Cambridge, USA, 1962.

Münzenmaier, W. and Walter, I.A., 'Die Arbeitnehmer sowie ihre Löhne und Gehälter in den Stadt- und Landkreisen 1970 und 1980', *Baden-Württemberg in Wort und Zahl*, Vol. 33, pp. 182-88, 1985.

Oeser, E., 'Der Informationsbegriff in der Philosophie und in der Wissenschaftstheorie', in Folberth, O.G. and Hackl, C. (eds.), *Der Informationsbegriff in Technik und Wissenschaft*, Munich and Vienna, pp. 231-56, 1986.

Parker, E.B., *Social implications of computer/telecommunications systems*, Stanford, USA, 1975.

Porat, M.V., *The information economy*, Vol. 1, Stanford, USA, 1977.

Pred, A.R., *City systems in advanced economies. Past growth, present processes and future development options*, London, 1977.

Rothkirch, C.V. et al., *Die Zukunft der Arbeitslandschaft. Zum Arbeitskräftebedarf nach Umfang und Tätigkeiten bis zum Jahr 2000,* Nuremberg, 1985.

Statistisches Landesamt Baden-Württemberg, *Statistik der sozialversicherungspflichtig Beschäftigten,* Stuttgart, annual volumes.

Törnqvist, G., 'Contact requirements and travel facilities. Contact models of Sweden and regional development alternatives in the future', in Pred. A.R. and Törnqvist, G., *Systems of cities and information flows. Two essays,* Lund Studies in Geography B, Vol. 38, Lund, pp. 83-121, 1973.

Chapter XV

Wilfred Dege (Kommunalverband Ruhrgebiet)

Regional public relations for the Ruhr area; strategies and concepts

Introduction

A region's image is a vital factor in modern regional development. One's readiness to work in partnership and to collaborate with a region, the decision to select it as a location for a business enterprise or a place to live, and the willingness for bodies and people to invest, are all greatly influenced by personal appraisal. Accordingly, regional public relations is an important tool of regional policy.

It is widely known that the image of the Ruhr region is a poor one: it is ingrained with prejudice and cliched notions. This negative opinion has proved to be a significant restraint on economic development. There have been many instances of the region's bad image hampering, and in some cases actually preventing, the selection of the Ruhr as a business or residential location, or both. It is true, in this context, that regional public relations, cannot provide direct tangible measures to promote economic development. However, it is an aim of the Kommunalverband Ruhrgebiet (KVR), Department of Public Relations, to improve the situation by changing attitudes and reactions to this major industrial heartland.

It is not the purpose of this chapter to discuss questions of image and regional development at a theoretical level. Rather than this, it focuses on the pragmatic perspective of practical administration of concepts and strategies which the KVR have adopted to improve the Ruhr's evaluation. First of all, however, it is necessary to describe briefly the evolution of the KVR as a regional policy-making institution.

The Kommunalverband Ruhrgebiet

The Kommunalverband Ruhrgebiet is the successor of the former Siedlungsverband Ruhrkohlenbezirk (SVR), which was founded in 1920, with its headquarters in Essen. The functions of the old SVR extended to promoting 'all matters which foster settlement' in the Ruhr region. This included involvement in regional planning, encouraging industrial development and initiating infrastructural improvements. In 1979, the SVR was not only given a new name (the KVR), but its role was also altered. Today's KVR is a public services organisation which is financed by, and receives its policy guidelines from, its constituent (local authority) members. These members include 11 autonomous cities and four districts, with a total population of 5.2 million. On their behalf, it looks after regional services in the following fields:

- safeguarding open spaces and caring for the landscape;

- planning services, surveying and cartography;

- recreation;

- waste-disposal;

- public relations.

However, the KVR's functions do not extend to actual decision-making, as far as private investments are concerned.

The KVR'S statutory brief for public relations involves the provision of both regional advertising and regional information. These are inseparably linked and mutually influence each other. Experience showed that information on the region, and also on the changes that are taking place within it, was not reaching the public. In response to this problem, an offensive was launched in 1984 to improve the Ruhr's image. The underlying idea was to use a broad-based image campaign to focus public attention on, and stimulate interest in, positive developments within the region. A cornerstone of this policy was the provision of 'targeted' information in a broad range of media, ranging from publications to tour services.

The image campaign

An important feature of the planning of the concepts and strategies for the image campaign was a sociological investigation of the Ruhr's actual image, both within the region itself and elsewhere throughout West Germany. In this study, 2,000 households were interviewed in April 1985 and questioned on their attitudes to the region. The questions dealt with 14 image-building sectors, but two fundamental objectives stood at the centre of the analysis: firstly, identification of the Ruhr's negative-image features and, from this, a clarification of what the image campaign should really focus on; secondly, the scale of the discrepancies between the images of the Ruhr respondents and those of the external respondents. Assuming that the Ruhr inhabitants have more realistic ideas of the region, then the discrepancies can be used as some measure of the differences between images and realities. It only makes sense to invest in regional advertising and information, as a way of bringing the image into line, if it is actually shown to be considerably negative. The results of the 1985 analysis showed that this was indeed the case, in almost all of the image-building sectors considered.

The current image campaign, which has been running since the results of the investigation were known in September 1985, has been developed on this basis, and in consultation with the KVR's local authority members. An advertising agency was also called in, and the costs of the campaign are about DM 4 million per annum. The basic aim remains the same: that is to focus interest on the Ruhr region, particularly among a target group of decision- and opinion-makers. The campaign, however, has expanded to include 70 designed image 'motifs', each of which is reproduced in double-page advertisements in important national magazines. With their printer's marks, slogans and typography, the advertisements have a homogeneous appearance, which is re-used in all the public relations media as a form of corporate identification. The motifs appear as a photograph, combined with an unusually striking headline. This is quite deliberately meant to serve as a 'stopper', to arouse interest in the text which appears on the same page. The motifs consistently show verifiably special features of a Ruhr city, especially on themes of trade and industry, the cultural and scientific scene, the environment and recreation and, last but not least, the local people.

The response to the image campaign has been very satisfactory. The KVR, in 1987 and 1988, received about 4,300 requests for further information: of these, 51% came from the *Land* of North Rhine-Westphalia, 16% from elsewhere in northern Germany, and an encouraging 29% from southern Germany.

Publicity publications

This demand for information on the Ruhr has been satisfied through the publication of a series of publicity pamphlets, dealing with the following topics: trade and industry, culture, sport, research, transfer agencies, education, further training, and even gastronomy. Future pamphlets will include topics such as traffic, the environment, housing and recreation facilities. An important supplementary medium of information is *Treffpunkt Ruhrgebiet,* a quarterly journal which provides information on high-ranking cultural and sporting events within the region.

These publications represent the middle level of the KVR's public relations work. They normally consist of three to five pages, and each topic is dealt with more diversely and in more depth than is possible in the image campaign, both textually and cartographically. The last page of each pamphlet is reserved for addresses where interested readers can direct requests for further information. Here again, there is an invitation to dialogue. The pamphlets have a close connection with the image campaign in their external design and, through this, present a continuous corporate identity. On the one hand, this is achieved by means of a standardised typography and, on the other, by using photographs from the image campaign as title pictures which facilitate quick recognition.

Specialist publications

There is an increasing need for the KVR to meet the information needs of policy- and decision-makers, especially in the fields of politics, administration, industry and science. This need is being met by the KVR's specialist publications, which contain basic statistical data on the Ruhr region, and also expert opinions compiled by the association's specialist departments and by outside experts. Individual topics from the fields of trade and industry, the environment, planning, recreation and culture are dealt with. However, the topics which are pursued are not always suitable for the general information needs of some specialists. Some do require a more comprehensive and factually differentiated overview of certain regional and local issues.

An initial step forward was taken in this direction in 1988 at the Systec fair in Munich, where the KVR combined with transfer agencies to make a joint presentation in the form of a 64-page brochure. This publication, which was distributed to visitors to the fair, was designed to highlight current research on the Ruhr region and, most notably, the work on computer-integrated manufacturing (CIM) within the locality. The brochure, which was fully financed by the proceeds of company advertisements, also included articles on other local research projects and descriptions (with addresses) of important Ruhr research institutes.

Other publicity/publication ideas are now being considered. One strong possibility for the future is the setting up of electronic data bases for regional statistics; another is the compilation and publication of short analyses and comments on topics of current interest in the Ruhr region. However, the situation at the moment is still such that a large proportion of the requests for in-depth and specialist information can only be answered individually, or passed on to other information outlets. These services, provided by the KVR public relations department will, of course, continue, but, in order to make the answering of queries more efficient, there needs to be more standardisation of factual information material.

Within the spheres of regional information and regional advertising, questions concerning the relationship between image and reality invariably arise. Here the KVR adheres to a code of principles: in all of its publications, attention is paid in the finest detail to the correctness and verifiability of the information. The credibility of statements is based on their factual authenticity and, at the same time, is a precondition for their effectiveness. Viewed as such, public relations, at all levels, is a matter of regional information. However, the actual selection of topics and issues for publicisation is guided by the principle that positive developments in the region should be publically documented. Moreover, public relations is also a matter of regional advertising. This is a legitimate approach, although it should not preclude middle and lower levels of discussion of the region's structural problems as, for example, in the information pamphlet on trade and industry.

Trade fairs and exhibitions

Publications provide only one basis for the KVR's public relations work: others are trade fairs and exhibitions, including involvement in tour arrangements. The presentation of the Ruhr region, at trade fairs and other important events, covers a wide spectrum. It ranges from image presentations, in the form of large-sized photographs, to information stands illustrating the Ruhr's top sporting and cultural events. These now commonly feature at prestigious trade fairs, including the annual international tourism fair at Berlin. Here, the emphasis is mainly laid on the Ruhr's cultural attractions, in presenting the region as a destination for urban tourism.

The KVR recognises that primary contacts are the most direct and effective way of providing information on the region, and thereby changing the Ruhr's image. Accordingly, the association pursues a policy of presenting topic-orientated educative tours, each designed to provide its participants with an insight into the Ruhr area. These have met with very positive responses, ever since their inception a decade ago, but, time and again, it has been shown that the biggest problem is that of building up the initial motivation of people to visit the region for tourism purposes. Because of this, the KVR recently initiated a second 'tour' concept - the pleasure tour - which is aimed at those people who would, in fact, probably contemplate visiting the Ruhr in the first place. In these cases the KVR's service extends to planning excursions through the Ruhr area (and providing an excursion guide), in conjunction with the specific wishes of the group organisers.

Information for teachers and schoolchildren

Schools and the education industry in general, are considered by the KVR to be a special target for regional publicity. This growing sector of public relations assumes that opinions and prejudices tend to be ingrained in people during their childhood and youth. Recognising this, the KVR began with a scientific analysis of the actual situation. Every school textbook published in West Germany, dealing with the subjects of geography, history, politics and sociology, was examined to see how the Ruhr was presented. The results of this investigation indicated that, despite the efforts of the writers to present matters objectively, texts in many cases were incorrect, outdated and even included unmistakeable distortions.

A broad range of public relations activities, in connection with school textbooks, has developed from the results of this analysis. These activities include:

- presentation of conferences as part of further training of teachers. This is done mainly in co-operation with partners in school administration.

- Presentation of specialist symposia on topics related to the Ruhr. A major example was the KVR's first geography symposium (under the title of 'structural change'), held in the autumn of 1988 and attended by 350 participants. Another geography symposium on 'the environment' is being planned for the near future.

- Co-operation with publishers and authors in the compilation of school textbooks and other forms of classroom media. Here, the publishers themselves sometimes approach the KVR, either for information, or to submit manuscripts for scrutiny.

- Establishing a 'school textbook information service' for the Ruhr region (1988). This includes the distribution (three issues per annum) of information pamphlets to textbook publishers and authors. Each pamphlet consists of a short portrait of a specialist department of the KVR, or other regional association, detailing its range of activities, its specific information services, a comprehensive article on a Ruhr topic, and up-to-date short regional new items.

- Participation at educational and other specialist congresses. An important case in point is the presentation of an exhibition stand by the KVR for the 1989 German Geographers' Congress at Saarbrücken.

Conclusion

Public relations work, aimed at improving the image of the Ruhr region by means of advertising and information, is a lengthy process: results can not be seen in a short time, and there have been some setbacks. The Ruhr's economic problems, especially those which relate to the crises in the coal and steel industries, still remain, and the reporting of these is still often one-sided. Nevertheless, there have been some major improvements in the region's image during the last few years. There is a more optimistic atmosphere in the area, particularly in the cities of Dortmund and Duisburg. This is producing much more favourable media reports and outside impressions than could ever have been contemplated only a decade ago.

Chapter XVI

Christopher Law (University of Salford)

Planning for urban revitalisation in a capitalist framework: issues and conflicts

Introduction

Compared with previous Conservative administrations, Mrs Thatcher's government has proved to be very radical. It aspires to what might be called a classical capitalist economy, in which market forces are dominant and the role of public sector expenditure and intervention is reduced. In spite of a decade in office (at the time of writing), these aspirations have yet to be realised fully. This is, in part, because when the government came to power, there was no blueprint of how the country should be changed and plans for many activities are still being evolved (with the help of 'right-wing think-tanks'). In part too, it reflects the fact that Mrs Thatcher has an intuitive awareness of the limits of practical politics. In effect, this means that change takes place in small steps, with the government hoping to be able to prepare public opinion for further changes. In this chapter, I shall be considering some of the implications of the government's philosophy on inner-city policy, and illustrating the argument by reference to the Manchester-Salford area.

Town and country planning in Britain

For most of the postwar period, town and country planning has been part of the accepted consensus in Britain. Planning was perceived as necessary to achieve an efficient city, which might not happen if market forces reigned supreme. Thus, there was an obvious need for planners to design an effective motorway network to facilitate flows of traffic. Planning was also necessary to achieve community objectives, whether these were economic, social or environmental. Accordingly sites and premises could be provided to stimulate job creation, housing and community facilities, to assist the poorer members of society, whilst open space could be designated as an amenity for all. Finally, planning is a way of resolving conflicts between different interest groups in society. These objectives could be achieved through plans, development control and public expenditure. For most people in Britain (over the age of 25), these statements may be regarded as unexceptional, and are only worth mentioning as a context to the 'New Britain' which is emerging today. There is not the space here to discuss all the changes in town and country planning during the last decade; instead the focus of this chapter is on planning in the inner city.

British inner-city problems and policies

The situation in the inner-city areas in Britain is probably more comparable to that in the United States than in many continental European cities (Law, 1988a). The decentralisation of people, accompanied by smaller household size, has left a reduced and poorer population in the inner city. In Manchester and Salford, the population of the officially-defined inner-city area (Figure 16.1) declined drastically, from 620,000 in 1951 to 297,000 in 1981. There has also been a decrease and dispersal of jobs, particularly in manufacturing and wholesaling. In the Manchester and Salford inner-city area, plus Stretford (containing the Trafford Park industrial estate), the number of jobs fell from 402,000 in 1971 to 298,000 in 1984: this included losses in the city centre. During the 1970s, the problems of British inner cities came to be recognised by the government, and were perceived in terms of poverty, high unemployment, decayed buildings and poor infrastructure. In 1978 the Labour government passed the Inner Urban Areas Act and increased funds available through the 'Urban Programme'.

313

Figure 16.1: Inner Manchester and Salford

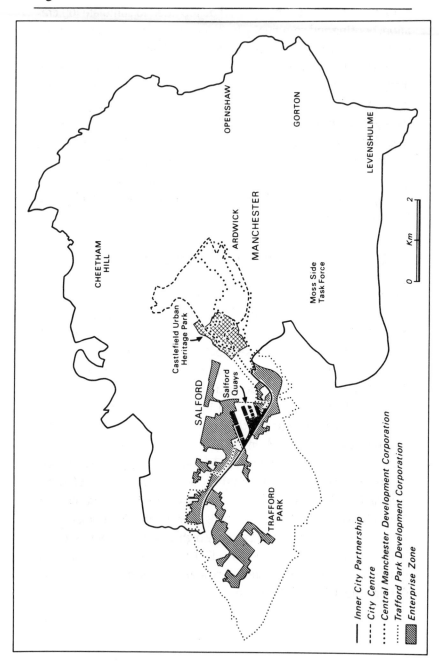

For large cities, like Manchester and Salford, an 'Inner City Partnership' was established, that is, a partnership between central and local government, through which the latter could bid for funds to undertake economic, environmental, social and housing projects. The objectives of these policies were expressed in terms of helping local people to obtain jobs and housing, and to have a better environment and better community facilities.

Conservative inner-city policies since 1979

For many commentators, the continuation of inner-city policies under Mrs Thatcher has been surprising. Their predicted eclipse has not occurred and, indeed, their significance has repeatedly been emphasised, most notably on the night of the June 1987 election results, and later with the publication of a government document, 'Action for Cities', in March 1988. There has been speculation on the reasons for this support, whether it be for electoral purposes, or out of concern for the people of the inner cities. However, Conservative inner-city policy has evolved and, over time, has become significantly different from that envisaged by the last Labour government (Lawless, 1988; Stewart, 1987).

Various shifts can be noted, all of which reflect the basic philosophy of the government. Most important has been the emphasis on economic regeneration, which means in effect that social and, to a lesser extent, environmental objectives have been downgraded. Whilst economic regeneration will no doubt involve job creation, the importance of the latter has been subtly reduced. Economic regeneration frequently refers to land development, and in particular the bringing back of vacant and derelict sites into commercial use. Since 1982, the 'Derelict Land Grant' programme has been used increasingly in urban areas. Within this scheme, potential projects are classified as either 'hard' (i.e. likely to lead to economic development) or 'soft' (i.e. non-economic, simply concerned with environmental improvement). Civil servants are instructed to favour the former. Economic regeneration will occur as firms grow, and to encourage this, 'Enterprise Zones' (EZs) were created in the early 1980s. These were given the benefits of freedom from local taxes, 100% capital allowances for taxation, and simplified planning procedures.

A second trend of note concerns the function of local authorities. As part of the general objective of reducing the role and expenditure of the public sector, the activities of local government have been restrained. This can be illustrated in many ways, but perhaps most notably with the curtailing of public-housing construction and the opening to tender of many of the services previously provided 'in-house' by the councils. Furthermore, the government perceives local authorities as inefficient, wasteful and attempting to undertake activities which are not part of their real role. The actions of about 25 'left-wing' councils, mainly representing inner-city areas, have enraged the government and provided it with arguments with which it can attack other local authorities. This displeasure with local government has expressed itself in various forms. The rate-support grant for inner-city councils, for example, has been cut back; for Manchester City Council, it fell in real terms from just over £120 million in 1980/81 to under £90 million in 1984/85 (Kitchen, 1986). 'Urban Programme' funds have also been cut back, initially in relative terms and, more recently, in cash terms.

In order to bypass local authorities and achieve the objectives of inner-city policies, 'Urban Development Corporations' (UDCs) have been established, with powers to purchase land, grant planning permission, and use government funds. The first two UDCs were created in 1981 for the London and the Merseyside docklands; in the eyes of the government, these have been so successful that the concept has been extended to eight other areas. In the Manchester-Salford area, the Trafford Park Development Corporation was established in 1987, with £160 million to spend over 10 years, on reviving the industrial zone (Figure 16.1). Subsequently, in 1988, the Central Manchester Development Corporation was established, with £15 million to spend over five years, on regenerating the southern and eastern parts of the city centre. The alleged advantage of the UDCs is that, being single purpose (and undemocratic), they are able to proceed quickly and efficiently with environmental and infrastructural projects, which will bring back vacant land into economic use. However, in effect they are another means by which the central government ensures the supremacy of economic over social objectives.

Constraints have also been placed on the way in which local authorities use funds provided by central government in inner-city projects. 'Derelict Land Grants', and some 'Urban Programme' finance, can only be used to encourage private sector development. The latter is another emphasis of government inner-city policy. To encourage projects by the private sector, grants have been provided to assist schemes which otherwise might not be viable. In 1982, 'Urban Development Grants' (UDGs) were introduced: in these the government provided 75% of the grant, and the sponsoring local authority provided the remaining 25%. The UDGs did not prove very successful, as allocated funds were never fully used and there were wide variations in uptake between areas, suggesting that some councils gave low priority to the programme. Accordingly, in 1988, UDGs were replaced by the 'City Grant', in which the private sector applicant goes directly to the government, which then may supply the whole grant.

In assessing the use of public funds and the involvement of the private sector, the concept of 'leverage' has been used. This idea, borrowed from the United States, stresses that public funds are there to 'lever' private sector investment. The 'leverage ratio' is the balance of public to private investment, and the government's target is 1:5. This target puts pressure on the public sector to gain as much private sector activity as possible, even if this weakens other objectives.

The limits of inner-city policy

These shifts in policy have significantly moved inner-city planning away from the pre-1979 situation. Social objectives have been downgraded; economic regeneration, usually meaning land and property development, has supplanted the objective of creating jobs for local people. There is very little targeting of new jobs with the needs of local residents. The link between policy and the local area is only maintained through the unproven idea of 'trickle-down' effects. The objective of improving housing has been changed to 'widening housing choice', which may be a euphemism for gentrification. The objective of providing community and leisure facilities is made more difficult to achieve, as local authority funds are being cut back and projects must involve the private sector (which is unlikely to see profit in serving low-income social groups). Indeed, commercial recreation facilities may be deliberately aimed at a non-local market. Using the private sector to fund public transport improvements will also have implications (Lane, 1989): only heavily-used and profitable routes will be enhanced. Other lines, which are either not profitable (although fulfilling social objectives), or where the justification is in terms of reductions in road transport, will not be improved.

One interesting dilemma concerns the provision of open space. Most commentators would agree that many inner-city areas require more open space, whether it be in large parcels, small parcels or green strips. This would be both an amenity for local people and, at the same time, improve the general environment to such an extent that it would be more attractive to visitors and investment. In this sense, green spaces are a positive externality, but, as with other externalities, there is the question of who pays. Private landowners will be reluctant to provide such space and forgo the profit arising from development. Moreover, since green spaces will need to be widely scattered, without a proper plan the individual landowner will not know how his contribution of a small parcel will significantly contribute to the general improvement of the area. The obvious answer is for public bodies to plan and provide open spaces. But this means using public funds (which they may not have) to purchase land or, if they do have the funds, these are supposed to be used to lever private investment.

Is there a way out of this situation? One solution is to use the idea of 'planning gain', or 'linkage', as it is called in the United States (Boyle, 1989). Under Section 52 of the 1971 Town and Country Planning Act, local authorities can extract a benefit for the community before granting planning permission. This can take the form of infrastructural improvements, such as road widening, provision of open space, and a requirement to use local labour, or finance, for an identifiable object, such as affordable housing. This method is possible when and where the private sector is pressing to be allowed to develop land. However, in many inner-city areas there is no pressure for development, and any conditions might drive companies away. Local authorities can also form joint companies with the private sector, to develop sites and incorporate facilities which meet with social objectives.

An example: the redevelopment of Manchester Docks

The construction of the 56km Manchester Ship Canal, opened in 1894 to link Manchester with the Mersey estuary, was one of the great enterprises of Victorian Britain. Until the early-1970s, the upper reaches of the canal were busy. Manchester Docks, which are actually located within the jurisdictions of Salford and Trafford, handled about 2 million tonnes of cargo a year. Then, within the duration of just a decade, the trade of the docks almost completely disappeared, as a result of the combined effects of containerisation, the increasing size of ships (and their inability to use the canal), the general shift of trade from the west to the east coast, and the development of the national motorway network which undermined an inland port. Consequently, the Manchester Ship Canal Company (MSCC), and the two local authorities, were left with a problem of what to do with the redundant docks (Law, 1988b).

Figure 16.2: The Manchester Dock system

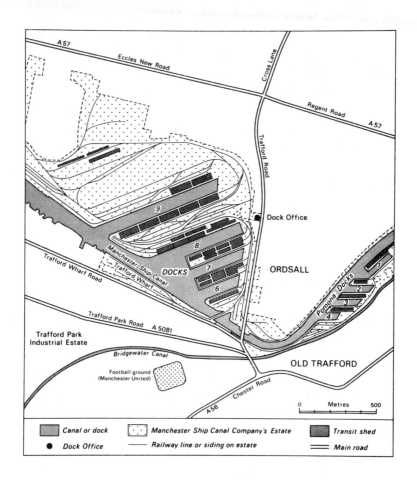

The Manchester Docks consisted of three parts, namely Pomona Docks, Salford Docks and Trafford Wharf (Figure 16.2). In addition, the MSCC owned land to the north of 'Dock 9' which had been kept in case there was a need for further expansion of the dock system. On the south side of the docks lay the pioneer Trafford Park Industrial Estate (developed from 1896), where employment fell from 52,000 in 1965 to 24,000 in 1985. Elsewhere, the docks were surrounded either by working-class housing (as in Ordsall), or industrial areas.

In the late 1970s, with the rundown of trade, parts of the Pomona Docks were filled in. In 1980, when the government announced the concept of Enterprise Zones, the City of Salford and the Metropolitan Borough of Trafford successfully sought designation for parts of the docklands and the surrounding area. By 1988, over 7,000 jobs had been created within the two parts of the Enterprise Zone, with significant proportions of the new employment being in service activities and in new locations. Development in the Salford part of the EZ had been encouraged by the opening of the M602 motorway extension in December 1982. However, in the early 1980s, the core of the Salford Docks lay outside the EZ, and it was unclear as to what form future development should take here. At this time, when there was still a deep economic recession and the successes of dockland redevelopment schemes elsewhere had not yet been realised or made known, the MSCC did not think that an investment in the clearance of buildings and the construction of a new infrastructure would be profitable. Therefore, it sold most of the Salford Docks to the City Council for the reputed sum of £1.5 million. At this stage, the main objective of the City Council was to bring back derelict land into use. In 1985 a redevelopment plan was published, the scheme involving the damming of dock basins and the construction of spinal roads, to produce a high-quality environment with public access to the waterfront. Government funding was successfully sought, with £25 million being offered over five years, but conditional upon private sector involvement.

Although the economy was still sluggish and there was yet no evidence on the ground of the new 'Salford Quays', a local firm, Urban Waterside, contracted to develop the southern end of the docks. By 1987, the first fruits of redevelopment were beginning to be seen in a multiplex cinema, an hotel, offices and up-market housing. While the scheme was far from nearing completion, it began to be hailed as a successful example of inner-city regeneration, and received much publicity. But now the context of the scheme began to change: the inhabitants of Salford started to ask: what was in it for them? On the surface, the answer appeared to be little, since the new houses were expensive and the new jobs were becoming increasingly white-collar. About the same time, the MSCC was taken over by a local entrepreneur, John Whittaker, whose aim was to exploit the land of the company for property development. On the southern side of the canal, the newly-formed Trafford Park Development Corporation sought to redevelop the 'Wharfside' area for commercial actvities. Finally, at this time the demand for office space in the Manchester area increased substantially, making new development profitable once again, with the waterfront areas of Salford Quays and Wharfside being perceived as prestigious locations. By early-1989, there were outline proposals for over 300,000m^2 of offices.

The scene has now been set for a clash of objectives. The local authority is seeking to introduce more social objectives into the redevelopment process. A revised strategy for Salford Quays (Salford City Council, 1988) sought to include leisure facilities and affordable housing on Pier Number 8. But how will these be funded? Would a private sector watersports centre be profitable in the area and, if so, would it not charge prices too high for local residents? Would the private sector be interested in providing a cultural centre? There may even be difficulty in bringing in a housing association to provide affordable housing. It would be very easy to sell the land for office development against these problems. One solution, therefore, might be to use the idea of 'planning gain', and exact facilities from developers, which have now become part of the social objectives of the scheme. In December 1988, the site at the head of Dock 9 was leased to AMEC Properties for a £50 million project, involving about 25,000m² of offices, with the company paying a premium of £3.9 million. However, press reports (March 1989) suggest that instead of using this project to fund other schemes in the Quays, it has been used to keep the rates down for 1989-90.

Elsewhere in the docklands, a tourism study (English Tourist Board, 1989) has suggested creating more open space along the river Irwell, including the area within, and opposite, the Pomona Docks. This would improve the environment and make the area more attractive for residents, visitors and economic activities. However, on the day before this plan was announced, the MSCC, clearly aiming to maximise its returns, proposed a large scheme for the Pomona Docks, involving 56,000m² of offices and 250 new dwellings. With land now being so valuable in the area, will the public sector have either the authority to refuse large-scale development schemes, or the finance to purchase the sites for open space?

Conclusion

The purpose of this chapter has not been to decry all current inner-city policy. There is much that is good happening today in this field. Inner cities desperately need economic development, and a wider choice of housing and gentrification is also desirable. However, it is to be wondered whether the pendulum has swung too far towards market forces and too far away from the social objectives of local government. Councils have, in fact, played a major role in inner-city regeneration, and their role is generally welcomed by private developers. There must be a mechanism through which local needs can be expressed, whether they be those of the local population, or those of the business interest. Co-operation is essential, and the anarchy of free market forces is no substitute.

References

Boyle, R., 'Missing links with States experience', *Planning,* Vol. 801, pp. 16-17, 1989.

English Tourist Board and Land/Design Research, *Manchester, Salford, Trafford - Strategic Development Initiative: a framework for tourism development,* English Tourist Board, London, 1989.

Kitchen, T., 'Inner-city policy and practice 1975-1985', in Willis, K.G. (ed.), *Contemporary issues in town planning,* Gower, Aldershot, 1986.

Lane, R., 'Light rail encounters a blockage on the track', *Planning,* Vol. 809, p. 16, 1989.

Law, C.M., *The uncertain future of the urban core,* Routledge, London, 1988a.

Law, C.M., *The redevelopment of Manchester Docks,* Discussion Paper No. 13, University of Salford, Department of Geography, 1988b.

Lawless, P., 'British inner-urban policy: a review', *Regional Studies,* Vol. 22, pp. 531-42, 1988.

Salford City Council, *Salford Quays: the development plan for Salford Docks,* Salford, 1985.

Salford City Council, *Salford Quays: development strategy review,* Salford, 1988.

Stewart, M., 'Ten years of inner-city policy', *Town Planning Review,* Vol. 58, pp. 129-45, 1987.

Chapter XVII

Hans-Werner Wehling (Universität
Gesamthochschule Essen)

The crisis of the Ruhr: causes, phases and socioeconomic effects

Introduction

For more than three decades the Ruhr has been experiencing a continuous decline of its traditional industrial base. The crisis began in 1957 when a worldwide surplus of oil, together with comparatively lower costs for imported coal and changes in furnace processing, began to reduce the market outlets of the Ruhr mining industry. This was answered at first by the closure of smaller mines within the southern and central parts of the Ruhr, and by an increase in mechanisation, with a drastic reduction in numbers of miners from 374,748 in 1960, to just 140,536 in 1980. By 1973, on the eve of the oil crisis, there was confidence that these measures were sufficient to prepare a new future for Ruhr coalmining (Hommel, 1988). This process of consolidation in the coal industry was, however, being overshadowed by a steepening crisis in the region's steel industry, induced partly by an international surplus of steel capacity, and partly also by a distortion of competition caused by subsidies granted to steel production in other European countries. As was the case in the coal industry, the numbers of producing units were reduced and rationalisation programmes were vigorously promoted. However, due to the close connections between these basic industries and many other economic activities in the Ruhr, a structural crisis developed in the entire regional economy. Between 1975-87, a total of 112,456 jobs were lost in the Ruhr's manufacturing sector, a loss which was not compensated for by expansion in the region's few prosperous industrial branches, such as chemicals and electrical-energy production.

Figure 17.1: Regional subdivisions of the Ruhr

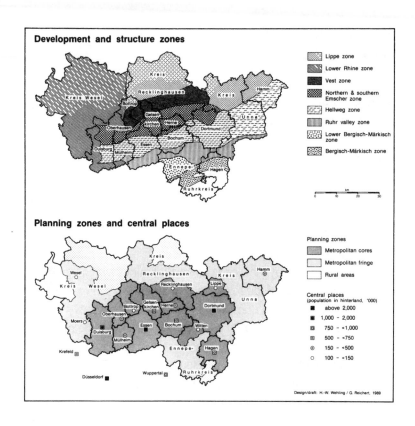

Source: Ministerpräsident des Landes Nordrhein-Westfalen, 1979.

The decline of the steel industry caused further reduction in the markets for Ruhr coal and ushered in the second phase of the coal crisis. From 1981-7, several more mines were closed in the central Ruhr ('Emscher zone'), and a further 22,317 mining jobs were lost. The markets for Ruhr coal continued to contract, and dependency on the electricity-generating industry continued to increase. This time, the hope of a recovery in coalmining was unrealistic. Today, the unrelenting decline in coalmining comes at a time of intensifying reductions in the steel industry.

A direct consequence of the job losses in the basic industries of the Ruhr has been the heavy out-migration of people away from the region. During the period 1961-88, the Ruhr witnessed a massive 550,832, or 9%, population reduction. Up to 1980, the outflow of people was accompanied by some substantial core-to-periphery movements within the region itself. The main cause of these intraregional shifts was the strong dissatisfaction with the poor form of urban development and bad environmental conditions that had to be endured by the inhabitants of the central parts of the Ruhr. In many cases, these localities were characterised by an unco-ordinated mosaic of residential and industrial areas, and also by generally high levels of environmental stress (Wehling, 1984).

During the 1980s, the various zones of the Ruhr were affected differently by the socioeconomic consequences of the structural crisis. Figure 17.1 illustrates two commonly-used frameworks of regional subdivision. The first, which carries the title of 'development and structure zones', relates to the historical northwards progression of different forms of economic and urban development. Within this primarily south-north pattern of regional subdivision, some less well-defined, secondary west-east zones can also be distinguished, mainly on the basis of their degrees of involvement in basic industries. In the Hellweg zone, the old-established cities of Duisburg, Mülheim, Essen, Bochum and Dortmund (each of which had been a small urban centre before the industrial expansion of the nineteenth and twentieth centuries) became major foci for strong urban growth during the industrial age after circa 1850. Along the Emscher valley, however, there emerged a patchwork of incompatible land uses which was adjusted to the infrastructural needs of only the basic industrial activities. The second framework of regional subdivision is described in Figure 17.1 as 'planning zones and central places'. In this, the Ruhr region is divided into three major types of area:

- firstly, the 'metropolitan cores', stretching from Duisburg to Dortmund, and including both the Hellweg and Emscher zones;

- secondly, the surrounding 'metropolitan fringe';

- thirdly, the 'rural areas', which are situated within the extreme north and south of the region.

Elements of both frameworks are combined for the purposes of the analyses presented in Figure 17.2. Here, demographic changes since 1975 are represented for each of four 'hybrid' zones - 'northern and western fringe', 'Emscher zone', 'Hellweg zone' and 'southern fringe'. In response to some improvement in the regional economy, and in qualities of local infrastructures (especially urban renewal), all parts of the Ruhr saw reductions in the numbers of out-migrants during the years 1976-80. However, as the graphs indicate, the years 1981-5 brought a new wave of rising unemployment and heavy migration losses. This short, but eventful period, represented the second phase of the Ruhr's structural crisis.

Since the mid-1970s, manufacturing employment has decreased in all parts of the region, but most strongly in the Hellweg zone, where the long-lasting decline in the steel industry has had pronounced negative effects. The coal industry, which has likewise been in long-term decline within the Hellweg, is still important in some of the local economies and labour markets of the Emscher zone and the 'northern and western fringe'.

Figure 17.2: Socioeconomic effects of the crises in the Ruhr, 1975-87

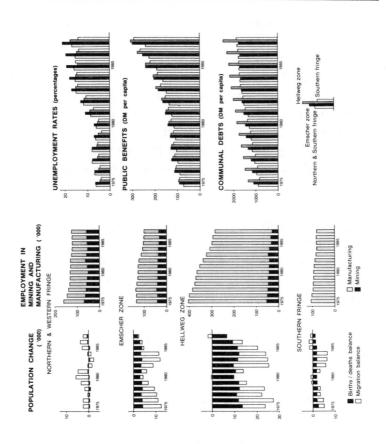

Source: KVR, annual volumes, 1976-88.

For employment in retailing and services, some reliable information can be obtained from the 1987 Census. Data from this shows that employment in the service sector in the Ruhr region has increased by 16.2% since 1970, and now accounts for 59.7% of all jobs, but there are some remarkable subregional differences. Even if the dominating influence of mining and manufacturing on the labour markets of the Emscher towns and cities could be overcome (Wehling, 1987), their service sectors are still much smaller and less varied than those of the Hellweg cities, especially Essen and Dortmund. However, even in the Hellweg, the increases in service sector employment have not been sufficient to offset properly the huge losses of local industrial jobs. Consequently, the second phase of the crisis served widely to increase unemployment rates well above national levels in the Ruhr regions (Blotevogel, Butzin and Danielzyk, 1988). The rates exceeded 14% in all four zones after 1982, and exceeded 20% in the Emscher zone after 1985.

Long-term unemployment on this scale eventually leads to a dependency on social benefits. Since 1975, the amounts of communual expenditure for these purposes within the Ruhr, rose by as much as 335%. Increasingly, therefore, these costs became major burdens on local authorities, especially those in the greatly depressed Emscher zone.

Changing patterns of industrial sites

The postwar period to 1980
The economic crises, and the measures taken to overcome them, have not only had very significant socioeconomic effects, but have also had major impacts on urban patterns, particularly the distribution and usage of industrial sites. These changes can be illustrated by reference to what has happened within the example cities of Essen (Hellweg), Oberhausen (Emscher) and Gelsenkirchen (Emscher).

Figure 17.3: Industrial sites and derelict industrial land in Essen, Oberhausen and Gelsenkirchen

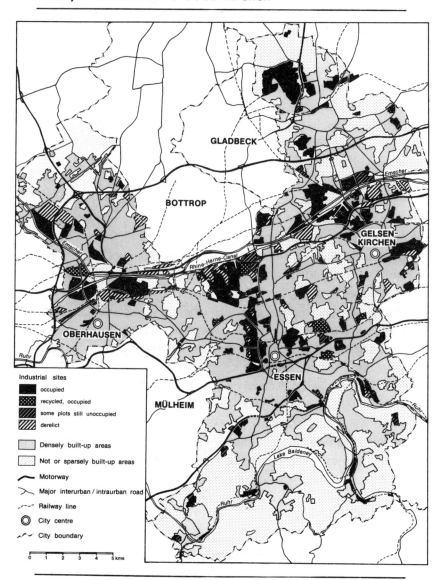

Source: Stadt Essen, 1986; Stadt Oberhausen, 1987; Stadt Gelsenkirchen, 1987; also personal field survey.

To a large extent, the distribution of industrial areas in these cities (Figure 17.3) still reflects the industrial heritage of the Ruhr. In the southern parts of Essen, overlooking the valley of the river Ruhr, the industrial sites are small and diffuse; most are more than a century old. The central parts of Essen, which are in fact within the Hellweg zone, have, in addition to the extensive area of the former Krupp works, various scattered, medium-sized industrial plants. The northern districts of Essen, together with the cities of Oberhausen and Gelsenkirchen, lie in the Emscher zone. Here there is a pronounced linear concentration of large industrial sites, following the river Emscher and the Rhine-Herne canal. This 'Emscher axis' was the location of the Ruhr region's highest industrial production throughout the long period from the end of the nineteenth century up to the 1950s.

More recently, local economic development policies and land use planning have exerted a major influence on the distribution and form of industrial sites. During the postwar reconstruction of the Ruhr, the aim was simply to rebuild old works as quickly as possible. Due to the restrictions of the Allies on steel production, the city of Essen was placed in a special position: unlike other cities (for example, Dortmund and Duisburg), where it was not until much later in the postwar period that steel sites became derelict, the major part of the giant Krupp area became available for conversion as early as the 1950s. Within other cities, particularly those of the Emscher zone, the tendency at that time was for traditional industries to be rebuilt on their traditional sites. Here, expansion of established firms and also the setting-up of new plants, could only be achieved by planning new suburban industrial sites. These developments, particularly those which came to be involved in the environmentally-damaging chemicals industry, proved to be large consumers of former agricultural land.

When the economic and demographic effects of the first phase of the structural crisis became apparent in the Hellweg cities, overall conditions and planning concepts changed quite abruptly. In Essen, the sites of 22 closed collieries became available as a major, and much-needed, land resource. At the same time, people were becoming increasingly unhappy with local housing and general environmental conditions, and responded by migrating from this city in substantial numbers. Accordingly, new objectives for a comprehensive improvement of Essen's urban environment were initiated. These were designed to increase the numbers and size of recreation areas, and also to disintegrate the existing prevalence of undesirable land uses. As a major part of the new policy, derelict mining sites in the southern and central parts of Essen were not converted for new industrial development; instead, some were incorporated into large 'green' land use zones with recreation functions, whilst others were designated for a mixture of residential development and smaller green spaces.

The Emscher cities of Oberhausen and Gelsenkirchen experienced a markedly different type of development during the 1960s and early-1970s. The productivity of their coal industry had been so high that most local collieries were able to survive the first mining crisis; only three collieries (all in Oberhausen) were closed, their sites in each case being redeveloped for housing and recreation. Most of the development land within and around these two cities was taken by steel companies which, as in other parts of the Ruhr, pursued a policy of 'hoarding' industrial land. Because they were the biggest local taxpayers, and had an enormous impact on the labour market, they were able to maintain pressure on local and regional authorities. They withheld large quantities of derelict and undeveloped land, partly in the hope that the economic situation of the steel industry would eventually improve, and partly with a speculative intention.

As a consequence, urban planning in the Emscher cities became greatly constrained by acute shortages of development land. Planning, here, could not properly promote a strategy of economic, let alone environmental and infrastructural, improvement, since the local authorities here were unable to offer suitable sites to prospective new firms (or even to established firms wishing to expand within the locality). The only realistic means of escaping from this dilemma was for the Emscher cities to designate new industrial areas within their outer districts. Accordingly, in the southern suburbs of Oberhausen, for example, 88 hectares of new developmental land was allocated for industrial uses. This was so attractive that, by 1979, every single plot had already been taken up (Stadt Oberhausen, 1987).

By the mid-1970s, a general shortage of industrial land had also become apparent within Hellweg cities such as Essen, where companies which had settled during the 1960s and early-1970s had built up private stocks of development land. By that time, only a few small non-hoarded sites were still available for industrial development. Local planning, therefore, had to be redirected into the preparation (for industrial usage) of derelict colliery land, a process which involved land reclamation, construction of new access roads and finally, the provision of green spaces and tree belts to shield the sites from adjacent residential areas. At present, five of these colliery sites have been recycled in Essen, at a combined cost of DM 83.4 million (Stadt Essen, 1988). The new roads and green landscaping account for as much as 40% of the area, but this 'loss' of potential new industrial land is compensated for by the enhanced attractiveness of the development estates.

From 1980 to the present

The situation changed sharply when the second phase of the structural crisis affected collieries and steel works in the Emscher zone. This was also a time when the *Deutsche Bundesbahn* closed several railway lines, sidings and stations that had formerly served the industries and working populations of this central part of the Ruhr. The 1980s, in fact, saw the disintegration of the monolithic 'palaeindustrial' axis of heavy industry that had lined both sides of the Rhine-Herne canal. Here, many extensive derelict industrial sites suddenly became available.

Figure 17.4: Industrial sites and 'status' of derelict industrial land in Essen, Oberhausen and Gelsenkirchen

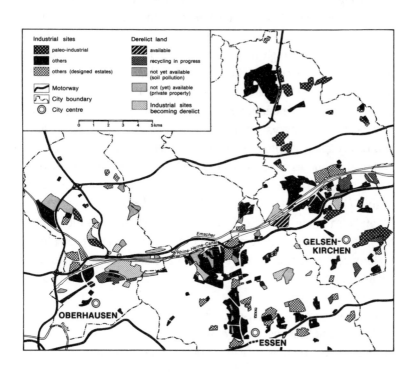

Source: Stadt Essen, 1986; Stadt Oberhausen, 1987; Stadt Gelsenkirchen, 1987; also personal field survey.

Emscher cities, which had previously suffered from shortages of developmental land, now found that they had large potential surpluses (Figure 17.4). At the same time, however, they were facing low points in their own financial resources, as the accelerating decline of their basic industries brought not only a decrease in local taxation revenues, but also high unemployment and consequent increased expenditures on social benefits. Faced with these rising financial difficulties, the Emscher cities were unable even to contemplate purchasing some of the derelict sites, let alone to afford the high extra cost of demolishing vacant plants, decontaminating polluted soils and landscaping. Appropriate planning organisations and additional financial resources were clearly essential. They were eventually provided for by the creation of the partnership, property-dealing, pools of the 'Grundstücksfond Ruhr' and the 'Landesentwicklungsgesellschaft Nord Rhein-Westfalen' (LEG). On application to a local authority, the LEG can acquire a derelict industrial site and promote its reclamation, preparation and eventual sales of revitalised plots. The profits from the sales then flow back into the LEG pool for the financing of further projects.

In Oberhausen and Gelsenkirchen, it is considered that as much as 89% and 56% respectively of the acquired industrial land would not have been revitalised, had it not been for the property-pool involvement. There is now a high demand for the prepared plots; several, in fact, have been resold and have increased in value. This is markedly different from the situation in the Hellweg city of Essen. Here the recycling of old industrial sites has continued to be promoted, mainly by the city on its own, and there is an acute shortage of good quality development land suitable for new industrial development. A recent survey (Stadt Essen, 1986) indicated that planning restrictions alone are responsible for making as much as 35.5% of this city's 214 hectares of derelict industrial space unavailable. Most of the land which is available, is being taken up by established locally-based industrial companies, rather than by new inwards-moving firms.

Structural effects of economic development

The potential surpluses of development land in the Emscher cities and its shortage in Hellweg cities, such as Essen, pose important questions concerning the demand for industrial sites. Only 25.2% of firms in the study area were new enterprises. This small proportion of new firms, and the corollary predominance of established companies, is typical of the Ruhr. Many of the latter do, in fact, expand, or even relocate, within the region, usually in order to broaden their production. However, figures for Essen show that as much as 30.6% of such expansions and relocations would not have occurred had it not been for the availability of revitalised old colliery sites (Stadt Essen, 1988). Most of the companies involved in this were engaged in the manufacturing sector, with small- and medium-sized firms prevailing.

Faced with such tendencies, and also the competition of other Ruhr cities, the aim to settle more new firms will not be discarded, but the activities of municipal economic development departments will now concentrate more on encouraging existing firms not to leave. This policy will involve improved consultation, the supply of expansion land on properly designed and equipped industrial sites, and the relaxation of planning controls on changes to established industrial premises. For legal reasons, direct financial support, such as subsidies, tax reductions and low-interest credit, are not included. To have suitable development sites readily available is regarded as the main priority; in Oberhausen and Gelsenkirchen the estimated demand for new industrial land is about 10 hectares for each city. The problem, however, is much worse in Essen, which needs as much as 297 hectares of prepared land for a present-day demand in which services, retailing and workshop activities also seek a substantial share. Even if the regional economy moved more quickly towards the service sector, demand for this type of land would not decrease. On the contrary, although industrial production (and its spatial needs) is stagnating, there is now a fast-increasing land market for such

337

growing functions as offices and research institutions (Henckel et al., 1984). Interestingly, the Essen survey also showed that the majority of relocated enterprises moved to the northern districts of the Emscher zone, but are now again looking for new sites, this time in the southern periphery of the Ruhr where there are much better environmental conditions.

Planning perspectives

By the end of the 1980s, it became very apparent that changing economic structures and changing directions of planning policy had progressed through different phases, each of which had affected the core zones of the Ruhr region in a markedly different way. To keep sufficient quantities of suitable development land available will continue to be a major aim of the local authorities. With the changing economic background, however, this will not only become a quantitative problem in the near future, but will also have a qualitative component: new planning concepts, therefore, are now required. As a first step, companies with similar types of production, services and research activities, and consequently with similar infrastructural demands, are now being grouped into single estates. In 1985 the 'Essener Technologie- und Entwicklungs-Centrum' (ETEC) was founded, as a centre for the development of energy and environmental technologies. It includes small firms, as well as the research departments of Essen University and some large industrial firms. For these institutions, basic facilities are provided for common usage. The success of the ETEC encouraged the application of this concept, not only to high-tech enterprises, but also to certain low-tech firms. Plans for technology parks, workshop parks and industrial parks were initiated. Unlike the industrial sites of the previous era, a key feature of these 1980s' parks is the ample provision of green spaces, not just as additive features, but also as constitutional components.

Figure 17.5: Major investment projects in Essen, Oberhausen and Gelsenkirchen

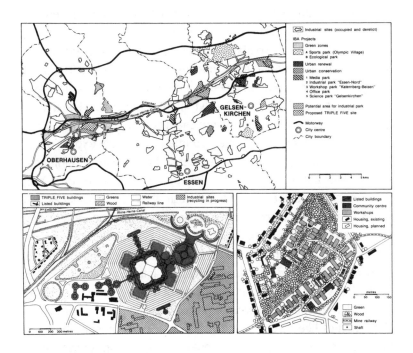

General location map (top); 'Triple Five' project (bottom left); IBA 'Katernberg-Beisen' project (bottom right).

Source: Stadt Essen, 1988.

This refined concept of 'working in the park' will eventually be integrated into the major project of 'Internationale Bauausstellung Emscher-Park' (IBA). The large derelict sites along both sides of the Rhine-Herne canal cannot be so easily revitalised and integrated into existing urban structures. The IBA project (Figure 17.5), therefore, aims at a new form of spatial integration of housing and industry, as well as a comprehensive economic and ecological revitalisation. It also provides for recreational needs and for social and cultural infrastructure. The scheme aims to resolve latent conflicts between overall urban renewal and local economic change.

Within the Ruhr region the suburban-orientated expansion of housing and industry, which characterised the urban development of the 1960s and 1970s, is now being redirected into a restructuring of the inner parts of the cities. More industrial parks will be developed in the near future, incorporating urban and landscape designs that serve not to document continuing regional decline, but to promote progress and the will to invest (Ganser, 1987). Even if some of the prepared industrial development plots are left unsold, at least their ecological value will remain - the banks of the river Emscher and the Rhine-Herne canal are to be transformed into linear recreation zones. Within cities like Essen, Oberhausen and Gelsenkirchen, there are now plans for further urban renewal and urban conservation schemes, and also a greater variety of industrial parks, some with special objectives. An interesting example of one of the new proposals is the workshop park of 'Katernberg-Beisen' (Figure 17.5), part of which will be developed on the site of a derelict colliery. This park will consist of preserved colliery buildings, as well as new workshops, each embedded into an attractively-designed parkland landscape and each equipped for a small- or medium-sized enterprise.

While the IBA was being scheduled, the city of Oberhausen proposed a development which, in scale and potential impact, will surmount any other planned project in the Ruhr region. The promoters (the international 'Canadian Triple Five Corporation') plan to use a 100 hectare site of derelict industrial land for the construction of a

'Euro Mall' (Figure 17.5), which will incorporate as many as 800 shops and 100 catering establishments, together with hotels, a cinema, a marina and various sports facilities. The CTFV Corporation envisages that the scheme, when complete, will provide a total of 15,000 jobs on the site. However, initial enthusiasm about this proposal is now being cooled somewhat by opposition from neighbouring local authorities, which fear that the mall will exert an adverse effect on their own city centres. They also argue that for every job created in the mall, two others will be lost elsewhere. The final decision of whether or not to give the go-ahead to the CTFV is still pending.

Conclusion

The Euro Mall proposal, with its foreign involvement, and the IBA project, indicate that structural change in the Ruhr has now entered a new phase. In the 1970s, economic regeneration was largely confined to the Hellweg cities, where the first wave of the closures of mines and steelworks meant that many industrial sites became available for revitalisation earlier than was the case further north in the Emscher zone. At that time, the Emscher cities were still strongly committed to these basic industries; until recently, therefore, they could make only very small steps towards the restructuring of their urban land uses and the broadening of their local economies. A major regional contrast was created within the Ruhr region.

During the 1980s, it was the turn of the Emscher cities to face a massive economic crisis. This, 'the second structural crisis' of the Ruhr, has meant that new perspectives on regional and local planning have had to emerge, but these can only be positively pursued with comprehensive support from outside the Ruhr.

If ecological and economic revitalisation can be properly achieved, urban structures could be developed in the Emscher zone that are sufficiently varied to form attractive contrasts to those of the Hellweg cities. Well-designed new residential areas and industrial parks on revitalised sites may not only reverse the migration flow of population, but may also create a new competition (between Emscher cities and Hellweg cities) on the industrial property market. It could well be the case that industrial sites converted in the Hellweg cities in the 1970s will eventually be subject to their own economic decline, and will require a new cycle of regeneration. If so, the existing regional contrast within the Ruhr, between the broader-based local economies of the Hellweg cities and the heavily-industrialised Emscher zone, will assume a new form. There is a distinct possibility that the communities of the Emscher zone will change from their traditional reliance upon their basic industries, to an economic and political dependence on government subsidies.

The industrial cities of the Ruhr cannot survive without comprehensive economic and ecological revitalisation. But it is questionable as to how far the planned economic aims can be achieved within the optimistic timescale that is envisaged for the region. Doubts do arise: firstly, from the likelihood that the pace of overall regional economic development will continue to be slow and, secondly, because there are now indications of the beginning of yet another phase of colliery closures and consequent job losses. The spectre of high unemployment rates may well appear again and, in spite of all the progress that has been made during the last two decades, the easing of the Ruhr region's damaging negative national image may well be reversed.

References

Blotevogel, H., Butzin, B. and Danielzyk, R., 'Historische Entwicklung und Regionalbewußtsein im Ruhrgebiet', *Geographische Rundschau,* Vol. 40, pp. 8-13, 1988.

Ganzer, K., 'Erneuerung von Gewerbegebieten', *Stadtbauwelt,* Vol. 94, pp. 907-9, 1987.

Henckel, D., Nopper, E. and Rauch, N., 'Informationstechnologie und Stadtentwicklung', *Schriften des Deutschen Instituts für Urbanstatistik,* Vol. 71, Kohlhammer Verlag, Stuttgart/Berlin/Köln, 1984.

Hommel, M., 'Das Ruhrgebiet im siedlungs- und wirtschaftsgeographischen Strukturwandel', *Geographische Rundschau,* Vol. 40, pp. 14-20, 1988.

Kommunalverband Ruhrgebiet, *Statistische Rundschau Ruhrgebiet,* annual volumes, 1976-88.

Schöller, P., 'Städte als Mobilitätszentren westdeutscher Landschaften', *Verhandlungen des Deutschen Geographentages,* Vol. 32, pp. 158-66, 1960.

Stadt Essen, Amt für Wirtschaftsförderung, *Gewerbeflächenpolitik in Essen,* Essen, 1986.

Stadt Essen, Amt für Wirtschaftsförderung, *Wirtschaftsförderung in Essen 1987-1988,* Essen, 1988.

Stadt Gelsenkirchen, Amt für Stadtentwicklungsplanung, *Gewerbeansiedlung in Gelsenkirchen. Standortvorteile und Entwicklungschancen für Investoren,* Gelsenkirchen, 1978.

Stadt Gelsenkirchen, Amt für Stadtentwicklungsplanung, *Wirtschaftsförderung in Gelsenkirchen. Standorte, Förderprogramme, Zukunftschancen*, Gelsenkirchen, 1987.

Stadt Oberhausen, Amt für Liegenschaften und Wirtschaftsförderung, *Strukturwandel in Oberhausen. Chancen und Möglichkeiten*, Oberhausen, 1987.

Wehling, H-W., 'Wohnstandorte und Wohnumfeldprobleme in der Kernzone des Ruhrgebietes', *Essener Geographischer Arbeiten*, Vol. 9, 1984.

Wehling, H-W., 'Jüngere wirtschaftsstrukturelle und funktionale Veränderungen in den Städten des Ruhrgebietes', in Klasen, J., Nebel J. and Pletsch, A. (eds.), *Der Städtische Raum in Frankreich und in der Bundesrepublik Deutschland*, Georg Eckert Institut, Brunswick, 1987.

Chapter XVIII

Robert Bennett (London School of Economics)

Local taxation and local economic development incentives in Britain and Germany

Introduction

Local economic development policy must consider both the costs and benefits to the firm of any public sector activities. On the cost side are to be set local taxes, fees, charges and any special costs arising from public utilities or other public trading operations. On the benefit side are a variety of possible actions, ranging from information and advice, through land preparation, site and rental support, to workspaces, equity and grant finance.

In two projects supported by the Anglo-German Foundation for the Study of Industrial Society, the author has been examining these two aspects jointly with Günter Krebs (London School of Economics), and Horst Zimmermann (Universität Marburg). This paper summarises some of the main findings to date, and their implications. One element of our analysis of the tax aspect has been developed using a tax comparison model which will not be discussed here, but which is important for understanding our work further (for a full discussion of this model, see Bennett, 1987, and its development from the work of King and Fullerton, 1984).

Local taxes and businesses

Formal incidence

The work on local taxes in Britain and Germany presents the first systematic analysis for both countries of the formal incidence of local business taxes, the ranges of their tax rates, and the impact of burdens in different locations. The aggregate assessments of effective tax rates are themselves a major step forward in allowing the burden of these taxes to be assessed, over time, between local authorities and between economic sectors. The 'costs of capital' tax model allows the analysis to include an assessment of the impact of tax rates within the total tax system, and by sources and owners of sectors. The result is an analysis at the local and the macroeconomic level, within a total budgetary framework.

For Britain, the results show wide ranges, between localities, of required rates of return. These ranges, as expected, are widest for building assets, since non-domestic rates are primarily a tax on buildings. Ranges of required rates of return are 2.0-3.6% between 1960 and 1986. Plants and machinery bear burdens which range from 0.1-0.3% between 1960 and 1986. Sources of finance and ownership of assets experience only small variations in required rates of return, although there is a slightly wider range of effects for tax-exempt institutions. For industrial sectors, commerce consistently experiences the greatest level in burdens, followed by industry, and then by other industry. This is to be expected, given the differences in absolute burdens and ranges of burdens evident for commerce. The ranges are 1.3-1.9% (commerce) and 0.8-1.1% (manufacturing) for 1960 to 1986. Tax exhaustion increases these ranges where there is no profit against which to offset local tax costs. In general, burdens increase markedly after 1979, particularly over the period 1982-5. This is due to a combination of low profitability in recession, declines in central government tax rates (and hence in the benefit of deductibility), and rapidly-increasing real local tax rates in some localities in the 1980s.

For Germany there are four local taxes: property tax, capital assets tax, profits tax, and (up to 1980) payroll tax. The widest range of tax-rates impacts between localities in recent years is for machinery assets in manufacturing, which are financed by equity or retentions. The largest ranges overall are by source of finance. These results contrast with earlier years, where building assets in other industry, financed by equity, have the greatest ranges. The decline in the im-

346

portance of the property tax has been the main factor underlying this change. Overall, the range of the tax system has stayed roughly constant over time, but the distortions between sectors have changed substantially. For the 'tax exhausted' case, ranges of burdens increase in all cases. The effect of payroll tax gives only small additional burdens in aggregate, and only in payroll tax-levying communities; but for some businesses and some communities the payroll tax burden can be quite extreme.

When we compare the tax system of the two countries, we find a general decline in local tax burdens in Germany, compared with Britain. In Germany, over time, effective tax rates have declined somewhat overall; and variability, although it increased up to 1979, has decreased markedly (during the years 1979-84) since then. These decreases are due, in part, to the erosion of the valuation base of the property tax, but chiefly they arise from the abolition of the payroll tax which, particularly for tax-exhausted firms, has considerably reduced the overall variability of the local financial system. In aggregate, German total business taxes are generally more burdensome than those in Britain. However, for the impact of local business taxes, recent decreases in burdens in Germany and recent increases in burdens in Britain have resulted in the British system becoming much more burdensome since 1979, whereas the two systems are comparable for earlier years. Under the standardised assumptions (presented in Table 18.1), the German system has an effect of decreasing overall investment rates of return as a result of local business taxes; by 0.6% in 1960, 0.6% in 1970, 1.0% in 1979, and 0.8% in 1984, compared with 0.6%, 0.7%, 0.8% and 1.1% in Britain at the same dates. For the tax-exhausted case, however, the German local tax system is, and always has been, more burdensome: 2.2% in 1960, 2.0% in 1970, 1.6% in 1979, 1.7% in 1984, compared to Britain with 1.1% in 1960, 1.4% in 1970, 1.0% in 1979 and 1.3% in 1984. The lighter burden of local business taxes in Germany applies only to fully-taxed firms, and is largely the result of the offsetting effect of local tax from federal tax through deductibility.

347

The results demonstrate the strong effects in both countries of local business taxes or distortions between assets, economic sectors, owners and sources of finance and, for Germany, between compacts and non-corporate business. For both countries, too, there are strong differences between 'tax-exhausted' and fully-taxed firms. The main results are summarised in Table 18.2. For a fuller discussion of these results, see Bennett and Krebs (1987 and 1988) and also Bennett and Zimmermann (1986).

Table 18.1: Differences in fiscal wedge between Britain and West Germany

| | Britain | | Germany | |
	fully-taxed	tax-exhausted	fully-taxed	tax-exhausted
1960	0.7	1.4	0.6	1.1
1970	0.8	1.3	0.5	1.9
1979	0.8	1.3	0.9	1.4
1984	1.0	1.3	0.8	1.5

Note: The differences in fiscal wedge (pre-tax minus post-tax real rate of return) are as a result of addition of local taxes to national tax system averaged over all sectors. This is a comparison of zero local taxes with mean local tax rates. The Germany analysis is made directly comparable with Britain by using UK weights for asset ownership and sources of finance, UK depreciation rates and a standard inflation rate of 0%. It includes property, profits and assets taxes, and payroll tax up to its abolition in 1980.

Source: Bennett and Krebs, Tables 2 and 7, 1987c.

Table 18.2: Fiscal wedges in different local authorities in Britain and Germany

| | Britain | | | | Germany | | | |
	mean	min	max	diff	mean	min	max	diff
asset:								
machinery	3.3	3.3	3.4	0.1	4.3	4.1	4.5	0.4
buildings	5.0	4.5	7.3	2.8	4.1	4.1	4.1	0.0
inventories	-	6.7	-	0.0	5.8	5.6	5.9	0.3
industry:								
manufacturing	3.8	3.6	4.6	1.0	4.7	4.5	4.8	0.3
other	5.3	5.2	5.8	0.6	5.6	5.4	5.7	0.3
commerce	5.9	5.6	6.8	1.2	4.3	4.2	4.3	0.1
sources of finance:								
debt	1.5	1.3	2.5	1.2	-0.7	-0.6	-0.7	0.1
shares	3.7	3.4	4.5	1.1	6.3	5.8	7.7	0.9
retentions	5.3	5.2	6.1	0.9	9.0	8.7	9.3	0.6
owner:								
households	6.3	6.1	6.9	0.8	7.0	6.9	7.2	0.3
tax exempt	1.5	1.3	2.5	1.2	0.4	0.3	0.5	0.2
insurance	6.0	5.8	6.7	0.9	-0.7	-0.9	-0.6	0.3
Total	4.5	4.3	5.3	1.0	4.7	4.5	4.8	0.3
'tax-exhausted'								
total	1.9	1.6	2.9	1.3	4.1	3.7	4.8	0.6

Note: German estimates are not standardised to be directly comparable with Britain and include all local taxes as in Table 18.1.

Final (post-shifting) incidence

Our work on local taxes has also been extended to give the first large-scale systematic attempt, for Britain, to appraise the incidence of the non-domestic rates and, for Germany, to appraise the incidence of its wider range of local business taxes. The specification is explicitly a short-term model; it withholds from general equilibrium analysis, and is developed in a format in which prime and explicit emphasis is given to the local variability of the tax (and/or benefit) impacts of local government activity. This means that the assessments are of differential incidences between localities. This emphasis is borne of the assumption that shifting of local taxes can only be analysed in a specification which allows flexible treatment of local market conditions, non-competitive markets and decision-making in the firm. For both countries, the available data limit the analysis in a number of crucial directions, particularly with respect to the definition of variables which would be desired in an ideal world (especially with respect to wages, rents and profits), the absence of measures of capital assets, and the limitations on the accuracy of disaggregating for economic sectors, or for different types of business, particularly in Germany. These constraints restrict the results to being indicative, rather than definitive.

For Britain, despite the strong constraints on the analysis, due to poor data a surprisingly strong consistency of results has been obtained over a very wide range of alternative specifications over the two years 1979 and 1981. In particular, the basic model is surprisingly robust to alternative specifications. In aggregate, the results for Britain suggest that the non-corporate sector has a slightly greater capacity to shift prices than the corporate sector. Within these groups, corporate industry has a generally higher capacity to price shift than has corporate commerce. Not too much weight can be placed on these sector comparisons, however, given the inadequacies of the data and the limitations on disaggregation. The general conclusion is a very low price impact of rates in the short term. If we also conclude that, in the short term, influences on wages and employment must be small, we can estimate the main residual burden to be borne by profit at a level of 80-90%.

For Germany, again, despite all the limitations of data, there is considerable consistency of conclusions to be drawn from alternative specifications. The general conclusion is that the incidence of both local business taxes is on profits: mainly in the range of 14-57%, in the case of the local profits tax. The results contrast with the conclusions of Roskamp (1963 and 1965) on the general incidence of the federal corporation tax, as well as with his conclusions on the local profits and property taxes. This conclusion is also somewhat in contrast to more general opinions in this field, which have seen the *Gewerbesteuer* as a tax which is designed to be shifted (because of its deductibility from its own tax base, and from the federal corporation tax). The results of our analysis indicate little price shifting, but can be seen only as indicative of this conclusion, not definitive. Further research is clearly necessary.

Local economic development benefits for businesses

Our analyses have attacked these problems at various levels:

- firstly, local tax expenditures;
- secondly, local general expenditures;
- thirdly, regional policy effects;
- fourthly, local government-specific economic development functions.

Our present main work on the fourth aspect is the subject of a paper by Krebs and Bennett (1989); accordingly, this chapter will focus on the first three.

Local expenditures and tax expenditures

We have extended our final incidence model to assess also the incidence, after possible shifting, of local government general expenditures (Bennett and Krebs, 1988). This is the first such analysis, and again, we do not wish to be too firm in conclusions. But some important implications can be drawn.

For Britain, the effect of local expenditures may either increase or decrease local business profitability, depending upon how these ex-

351

penditures are spent. Our estimates suggest that local authority aggregate expenditures normally decrease profitability in the corporate sector and, through the influence of only small price shifting in the short term, this profit reduction can be recouped slightly through forward shifting to prices. The results of negative profit impact could suggest either 'physical' or 'financial' 'crowding-out'. Alternatively, the effects represent subsidies to the non-business sector of local authority activity. Both explanations are in line with the theoretical position on local tax benefits developed by Mieszkowski (1976) that:

'the benefits of public expenditures for industrial purposes will be imperfectly related to the property tax on industrial capital. And this will be true even if the taxes imposed on the industrial sector are not used to finance household public goods'.

This conclusion depends upon recognising: firstly, that property-tax payments are financed very differently in non-domestic and domestic sectors and, secondly, that different mixes of domestic and non-domestic sectors locally result in arbitrary differences in expenditure relationships. Hence, an industrial property tax can, at best, be a very imperfect benefit tax, and is not likely to induce any straightforward benefit offsets. The results of the present analysis suggest very strongly for the corporate sector in Britain, that there is either 'crowding-out' and/or that business subsidises non-business sectors. As a result, local expenditures have generally negative consequences for profitability. For the non-corporate sector, however, there is some evidence to suggest that a limited level of benefit offsets may apply. Further credence for the low estimates of the benefits of local expenditures can be drawn from the only other analyses of British property-tax incidence undertaken to date (Bennett and Fearnehough, 1987; Mair, 1987; Damania, 1986; Blair, 1989).

For Germany, the analysis contrasts with that for Britain in the influence of local expenditures. In the British case, benefit offsets do not generally occur but, instead, local expenditures relate to non-business service provision, with negative consequences for business profitability. In Germany, however, all expenditure estimates suggest positive (and mostly fairly large) influences of local government benefit provision on business. This contrast in the effect of local authority service activity in the two countries, is in line with the conclusions of many other analysts who have discussed the local government-business relationship in the two countries. In Germany, both local government and business see their actions as ones of 'partnership' in which they need to remain interested in one another (Bennett and Zimmermann, 1986; Zimmermann, 1987). In contrast, in Britain, there has been a mutual suspicion, and frequently a lack of regard by local government, for the needs of business (Webb, 1986). These conclusions have led us to make different suggestions for the policy debate for the two countries.

Regional policy

We have also analysed and compared regional policy in the two countries (Bennett and Krebs, 1989). Regional policies of various forms have been employed in most European countries, both as means of stimulating investment in 'problem regions', and as an attempt to limit the pace of industrial contraction. We have demonstrated that pre-tax real rates of return, and fiscal wedges between pre- and post-tax real rates of return are affected very markedly by these incentive packages. In Britain, fiscal wedges of 3% derive from regional policy up to the late 1970s, but decline to 1.6% in the mid-1980s. In Germany, fiscal wedges increase from 3.0 to 3.5% over the same period (on a standardised basis of comparison). Thus, declines in the significance of regional policy in Britain are to be contrasted with continued expansion in Germany (Table 18.3).

Table 18.3: Comparisons of the most important regional policy incentives between Britain and Germany on a standardised basis

	Britain			Germany (ZBA A-Centres)		
	1970 DAs	1979 SDAs	1985 DAS	1972	1980	1985
asset:						
machinery	5.2	5.2	2.9	5.6	6.3	6.2
buildings	1.9	1.7	0.9	2.3	2.8	2.9
inventories	0.0	0.0	0.0	0.0	0.0	0.0
sector:						
manufacturing	3.6	3.5	2.0	3.6	4.0	4.0
other industry	7.2	7.3	4.0	1.1	1.2	1.2
commerce	0.0	0.0	0.0	0.0	0.0	0.0
finance:						
debt	2.7	2.6	1.6	2.5	2.7	2.7
equity	3.6	2.9	1.6	3.3	3.3	3.4
retentions	3.2	3.1	1.7	3.6	4.1	4.0
investors:						
households	3.3	3.0	1.7	3.1	3.5	3.5
tax exempt	3.1	3.0	1.7	2.8	3.3	3.2
insurance	3.1	3.0	1.6	2.8	3.2	3.2
Total	3.1	3.0	1.6	3.1	3.5	3.5

Note: Estimates of the differences between assisted and non-assisted areas in the fiscal wedges between pre-tax and post-tax real rates of return of 5% by sector and area, 1970-85.

This Table compares the areas receiving the strongest level of support in the two countries. The figures can be compared with those in Tables 18.1 and 18.2, which both use the same definitions and are standardised in the same way, using our tax comparison model. This comparison shows the leverage of regional policy to be considerably greater than that of local tax policy in both countries for most years.

The ratio is about three times as significant in both cases. However, for Britain in the 1980s, the decline in importance of automatic regional policy grants has brought the level of regional tax incentives approximately in line with the general policy of the Thatcher government of reducing tax burdens in total, reducing distortions in the taxation of different sectors, and shifting from general automatic subsidies to selective regional assistance.

Conclusion

This paper has been able to do no more than summarise the results of a long period of intensive comparative research between the two countries. We commend the model of comparative research to others to follow. The results presented are also preliminary, since a considerable amount of further work is still to be completed.

References

Bennett, R.J., 'A general accounting model of intergovernmental tax and benefit effects on business', *Environment and Planning A*, Vol. 19, pp. 1495-1510, 1987.

Bennett, R.J. and Fearnehough, M., 'The burden of the non-domestic rate on business', *Local Government Studies*, Vol. 13, pp. 23-36, 1987.

Bennett, R.J. and Krebs, G., 'Die Wirkung Kommunaler Steuern auf die Steuerliche Belastung der Kapitalbildung', *Studien zur Finanzpolitik*, IFO-Institute für Wirtschaftsforschung eV, Munich, 1987.

Bennett, R.J. and Krebs, G., *Local business taxes in Britain and Germany*, Nomos, Baden-Baden, 1988.

Bennett, R.J. and Krebs, G., 'Regional policy incentives and the relative costs of capital in assisted areas in Britain and Germany', *Regional Studies*, 1989.

Bennett, R.J. and Zimmermann, H. (eds.), *Local business taxes in Britain and Germany: conference report*, Anglo-German Foundation, London and Bonn, 1986.

Blair, P., *Non-domestic rates and business location*, Ph.D., University of Cambridge, 1989.

Damania, D., *The incidence of the non-domestic property tax*, Ph.D., University of Glasgow, 1986.

King, M.A. and Fullerton, D., *The taxation of income from capital: a comparative study of the United States, United Kingdom, Sweden and West Germany*, Chicago University Press, 1984.

Krebs, G. and Bennett, R.J., *Local economic development initiatives in Germany*, Research Papers, Department of Geography, London School of Economics, 1989.

Mair, D., 'The incidence of the non-domestic rates: preliminary estimates', *Government and Policy: Environment and Planning C*, Vol. 5, pp. 99-103, 1987.

Mieszkowski, P., 'The distributive effects of local taxes: some extensions', in Grieson, R.E. (ed.), *Public and urban economics*, Lexington Books, Lexington, USA, 1976.

Roskamp, K.W., 'The distribution of tax burdens in a rapidly growing economy: West Germany in 1950', *National Tax Journal*, Vol. 16, pp. 20-35, 1963.

Roskamp, K.W., 'The shifting of taxes on business income: the case of the West German corporations', *National Tax Journal*, Vol. 18, pp. 247-257, 1965.

Webb, A.J., 'Business taxes: the views of British industry', in Bennett, R.J. and Zimmermann, H. (eds.), *Local business taxes in Britain and Germany: conference report*, Anglo-German Foundation, London and Bonn, 1986.

Zimmermann, H., 'British and German local business taxes under criteria for a 'good' local tax', *Government and Policy: Environment and Planning C*, Vol. 5, pp. 43-52, 1987.

Chapter XIX

Jürgen Oßenbrügge (Universität Hamburg)

Impacts of environmental protection on regional restructuring in northern Germany

Introduction

Recent regional and urban development of urbanised societies is characterised by the following interrelationships:

- selective de-industrialisation and reindustrialisation of local and regional economies;

- geographical decentralisation and recentralisation of production and management activities within growth sectors of the economy;

- lastly, the peripheralisation of social issues and the internationalisation of capital

(Castells, 1983; Leborgne and Lipietz, 1988). Within these basic sociospatial processes, environmental issues have assumed a strategic position, not only because environmental concern is growing in society, but also because environmental protection has become a new field of regulative policy in a period of general deregulation in most western industrialised countries. The implementation of higher standards of air-pollution control and waste-water handling (and other important controls) can change the existing structure of production and intensify the quantitative importance of environmental technologies. Within a framework of a cause-effect chain, this chapter summarises the results of investigations which attempt to integrate regional, environmental and economic policies.

Conceptual reflections on environmental improvement and regional change

The following conceptual outline for analysing the complex interrelationships between economic and environmental development within regions, distinguishes between an 'autonomous' and an 'induced' type of change (Figure 19.1). A structural change of the regional system, caused by determinants of the market economy, will be called autonomous. This is the case if changes in supply, demand, or foreign trade exert durable effects which modify and reduce levels of pollutive emissions into the air, water or soil. Such processes can result from the introduction of new technologies and, because of the rise in the service economy and changing spatial divisions of production, also from a shift to non-polluting industrial activities. As long as the environment belongs to the category of 'public goods', relieving the effects of autonomous factors are of an accidental nature. In other words, a reduction of emission levels is only a side effect.

Induced changes derive from the political regulation of economic production processes. In West Germany, for example, the *Immissionsschutzgesetz* and the *Technische Anleitung Luft (TA Luft)* specify how much pollution industrial plants may emit. The more control which governments exert through strict regulations, the greater the changes will be at the regional level. Furthermore, a government can perform as an 'economic actor' by spending public money on infrastructure and equipment to handle waste water, waste disposal, derelict land and nature conservation. Emissions from private consumption processes can be managed by government institutions or government-owned enterprises. In this way the state is directly able to affect the quality of the environment and the economic process.

Figure 19.1: Determinant factors for regional change

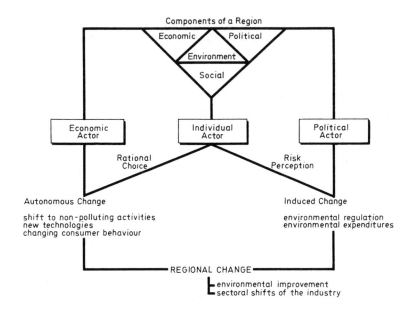

The personal level may be seen as a determinant factor too. On the one hand, changing consumer behaviour affects industrial production, especially so within the consumer goods and food-processing sectors. Recent product innovations are, to a large extent, a reaction to the growing environmental concern in society. It is assumed that at least one-third of private households in West Germany belong to a consumer group in which a consciousness of the environment influences the purchases that they make (Adlwarth and Wimmer, 1986). On the other hand, people are political subjects who, in democratic societies, have the ability to use their own voices to influence political decision-making (Hirschmann, 1970; Dear and Long, 1978). The importance of environmental groups in West Germany is well established and well known. They have been the forerunners of the recent general debate on environmental issues in the political arena.

From the cause-effect chain, presented in Figure 19.1, a whole range of geographical perspectives can be derived. These are notably:

- different ecological carrying capacities for mass production and mass consumption;

- varying social and political perceptions of environmental risks;

- spatial divisions of labour in areas of 'clean' and 'dirty' industrial production;

- different environmental regulations;

- lastly, uneven environmental expenditures.

Two particular perspectives - the effects of environmental expenditures on regional labour markets, and new possibilities of interregional competition - will be discussed in more detail later in this chapter, in association with a hierarchical diagram of technological changes.

361

A new growth sector of the political space-economy: the environmental industry

'Environmental protection creates new sources of employment and economic growth'

(Brunowsky and Wicke, 1984). This has been one of the main arguments used to promote more activities, stricter legislation and more expenditure, in respect of environmental improvement. The earlier emphasis of research investigations in West Germany on the 'job-killing' character of environmental policies, has now been replaced with attention to the 'job-creating' aspect. Today there is scientific and political interest in the flow of money spent, directly and indirectly, on the environment by public bodies and industrial companies. Some general statistics for this are available, which have been used in early studies of the spatial effects of environmental investments on regional economies (Ullmann and Zimmermann, 1981; Sprenger and Knödgen, 1983).

As shown in Table 19.1, in West Germany most of the government money (nearly 90%) is spent on local community, or *Gemeinde*, services. Of the DM 3,683 million contribution to the industrial sector, the raw-material processing and chemical industries account for more than 50% of the expenditure; energy and water provision account for a further 30%. As far as demand is concerned, if all private expenditures (including those from activities not listed in Table 19.1) are allowed for, the total quantity of money needed would now be over DM 40 billion. Recent estimates for the 1990s expect this figure to rise by more than 10% per annum to reach a total of more than DM 100 billion before the end of the century (Commerzbank, 1988; *Wirtschaftswoche*, 1988). The ability of expenditure resources to meet this huge demand will depend very much upon the collective financial situation of the local *Gemeinde* authorities.

Table 19.1: West Germany: expenditure on environmental protection in the industrial sector, 1983

	expenditure in DM million					
	waste water	waste disposal	air protection	other sectors	cons servation	total
ADMINISTRATIVE LEVEL						
Federal	-	-	-	376.6	-	376.6
Land	499.6	311.2	-	303.7	69.0	1,184.4
Gemeinde	7,639.3	3,008.9	-	697.2	-	11,345.4
Total public	8,138.9	3,320.1	-	1,3775	69.0	12,906.5
%	63.1	25.7	-	10.7	0.5	100.0
INDUSTRIAL SECTOR						
Energy & water	213.0	75.2	762.8	36.4	-	1,087.3
Raw materials	157.5	30.1	618.6	68.2	-	874.5
Chemicals	381.1	56.3	461.4	96.4	-	684.0
Other industries	360.5	119.2	461.4	96.4	-	1,037.5
Total industries	1,112.1	280.8	2,067.3	223.2	-	3,683.3
%	30.2	7.6	56.1	6.1	-	100.0
TOTAL	9,251.0	3,600.9	2,067.3	1,601.4	69.9	16,589.8
%	55.8	21.7	12.4	9.7	0.4	100.0

Note: Construction industries are excluded; 'other sectors' include such activities as noise reduction, and road cleaning; *Gemeinde* expenditures include *Zweckverbände* (co-operations between *Gemeinden*).

Sources: Statistisches Jahrbuch, 1986; Essig, 1985.

Figure 19.2: Recipients of public and industrial expenditures for environmental improvement in West Germany

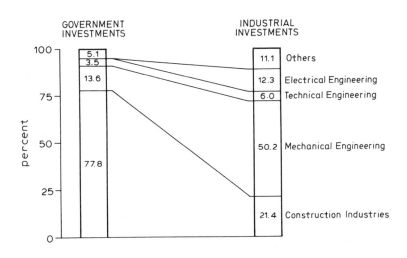

Source: personal analysis of information in Sprenger and Knödgen, 1983.

The general increase of expenditure has led to a reinterpretation of the financing of environmental protection in West Germany. Today, a broader definition of the multisectoral environmental industry is used. The broadly-categorised recipients of expenditures are shown in Figure 19.2.

While public efforts to improve the environment indirectly tend to give strong support for construction activities, expenditure from private industry is more diversified. The supply side of the environmental market is very heterogenous; many different types of economic activity are involved, including construction plants, infrastructural establishments for handling waste water and waste disposal, medium- and high-tech firms, and some research and development concerns (Zimmermann, 1981).

Environmental technologies

There are four basic levels of environmental technologies. First and foremost, there are the innovations and technologies with respect to products and processes. The function of changing consumer behaviour today is a shift to products with only minimal effects on the environment during their life cycle. A general evaluation of how far emissions from production processes have been reduced by new technologies is difficult to make, on account of a paucity of sufficiently detailed statistics. An early long-term analysis by Ullmann and Zimmermann (1981) calculated that the demand for primary energy in the manufacturing sector in West Germany was only one-half as high in 1980 as it would have been had the same technology of 1960 still been in use. During the period of rising energy costs in the 1970s, there were some successful attempts to reduce the amount of primary energy usage. However, the question as to whether or not the quantity of emissions decreases, per unit of production over time, can be answered by referring to the information presented in Table 19.2.

Table 19.2: Industrial origins of waste in West Germany, 1977-84

	i	ii	iii	iv	v	vi	vii
INDUSTRIAL SECTOR							
Elect., gas & water	+22.9	12,346.7	275.6	230.6	34.0	81.0	72.0
Chemical industry	+17.7	11,263.7	133.9	115.3	4,455.0	185.2	182.6
Food processing	+15.6	10,947.7	132.2	119.9	37.0	97.4	91.1
Building materials	-6.5	9,271.8	86.5	89.0	19.0	6.9	7.2
Iron and steel	-12.3	6,769.3	114.1	115.5	1,734.0	100.9	105.7
Mining	-17.7	4,080.7	87.5	96.6	76.0	133.3	131.0
Paper products	+40.9	3,657.7	291.0	217.3	804.0	149.4	123.4
ALL SECTORS	+16.4	82,486.1	122.0	113.4	10,703.0	144.0	138.4

Key to vertical columns:

 i change of the index of production, 1976-84.
 ii industrial waste, 1984 (in thousand tonnes).
iii change in quantity of industrial waste, 1977-84 (1977=100).
 iv change in quantity of industrial waste per unit net production, 1977-84 (1977=100).
  v high-toxic waste, 1984 (in thousand tonnes).
 vi high-toxic waste, change 1977-84 (1977=100).
vii change of unit net production, 1977-84 (1977=100).

Source: Statistisches Bundesamt, *Fachserie 4* and *19*.

This shows that in growth sectors of West Germany's industrial economy (especially electricity, gas and water, paper products, chemicals, and food processing), expansion of production during the period 1977-84 was certainly accompanied by an increased output of waste materials. Particularly disturbing is the fast overall growth (an increase of 44%) in the amount of high-toxic waste.

The second level consists of those environmental technologies which are used to recycle raw materials and energy. Such technologies had a boom period during the 1970s, when it was perceived that there limits to general economic growth were emerging, and when there also occurred a sharp rise in energy prices. Recycling methods are, in turn, often connected with the third level of environmental technologies. Labelled as 'end-of-pipe' technologies, these serve for the extraction, collection, reduction and deposition of waste. Their functions are to control and to minimise the diffusion of dangerous elements into ecological circuits. However, if these are unsuccessful and certain amounts of toxic elements do accumulate, a fourth level of environmental technology is needed. This is directed at repairing environmental damage, preventing human risks and preparing and recycling contaminated and derelict land.

Integration of environmental and regional policies

Although there have been some successes, the environmental situation in West Germany has not changed in a really positive way: emissions have not yet been greatly reduced, nor have the incidence of dangerous accidents and the accumulation of problematic elements in ecological circuits (Umweltbundesamt, 1986; Hübler, 1987). One way forward is to integrate regional economic and environmental policies by using the environmental industries to reduce regional economic and ecological problems (Zimmermann and Nijkamp, 1986). Perspectives on this will now be outlined within a background of the basic components of regional restructuring. Stressing the respective core of argumentation, the political synthesis between environmental improvement and regional development will be distinguished within a neo-liberal concept of an ecological market society, and a Social Democratic programme of creating new jobs that are ecologically-orientated and demand-sided.

Ecological market society
An approach to integrate regional, economic and environmental policies can be derived from an export-base model, in which the evolution of environmental industries is seen as a new field of tech-

nological innovation that can effectively strengthen regional economies within a climate of interregional and international competition. According to this view, an invention of a particular environmental technology (or an early adaption of an environmental innovation), on account of resulting comparative advantages, can have the strategic function of stimulating regional growth. The logic of this approach has been underlined by empirical studies, which have demonstrated that regions already plagued by environmental problems, especially the heavily-industrialised agglomeration areas, are, in fact, attractive as locations for all types of enterprises of the environmental industry (Ullmann and Zimmermann, 1981). Given this situation, it is only a small step further to recommend an environmental regional policy for old- and heavily-industrialised regions, because these 'offer' intensive environmental problems, a skilled labour force, existing investment in environmental improvement, and little productive investment in their traditional industries.

The view that environmental industries do contribute to regional economic growth has gained considerable ground recently; it owes much to the general upturn of West Germany's industrial economy since the early 1980s. Today, firms with above-average involvement in the environmental sector tend to regard their economic situation as 'good', but other firms more commonly regard it as only 'satisfactory' (Oßenbrügge, 1988). There is much justification, therefore, for the application of political strategies which try to stimulate new investments in a region, by using environmental protection as an economic tool. In a personal unpublished survey of 165 firms in northern Germany in 1988, it was found that as many as two-thirds were willing to invest in this way.

Environmental industries are primarily located in the urban agglomerations, either in the cores or in the surrounding fringes (Table 19.3). It is, however, not clear whether the decisive locational factors here are the high environmental problems themselves, or whether they relate to urbanisation economies.

Table 19.3: Turnovers and employment in different types of area in northern Germany

	% turnover		% employment	
regional type	all industry	environmental industry	all industry	environmental industry
urban agglomerations				
cores	45.8	34.1	30.5	38.2
fringes	15.3	32.8	17.6	21.2
intermediate area				
towns & small cities	9.3	16.3	12.6	21.7
rural areas	20.4	12.6	27.7	13.6
peripheral rural areas	9.2	4.2	11.6	5.3
ALL AREAS	100.0	100.0	100.0	100.0

Source: personal survey of 165 enterprises in northern Germany, 1988.

Qualitative growth, environmental protection and new sources of employment

The spatial coincidence of areas of old-industrialisation and structural decline on the one hand, and areas of expansion of environmental industries on the other, has provoked suggestions for qualitative-growth and regional-employment strategies from both Social Democratic and trade unionist political bodies. But the underlying logic is rather different. A special programme of public investment should create new jobs first and foremost in those regions which suffer from heavy employment. Such programmes now exist for the Saarland, North Rhine-Westphalia and parts of the coastal belt (Wand, 1986). Earlier demand-sided regional policies were dominated by the creation of economic and social infrastructure, especially new roads, schools, hospitals and leisure centres. Today, however, changed attitudes encourage proposals to intensify public expenditure, especially at the local level, primarily for environmental improvement.

It has been estimated recently that about 300,000 people, representing 3% of West Germany's industrial workforce, are engaged in activities concerning the environmental market (Umweltbundesamt, 1986). This small proportion, however, does not take into account the important indirect effect of the environmental sector on the security of other forms of employment and occupation. Indeed, its impact on the stabilisation of established jobs and the maintenance of local industrial employment, especially within the old-industrialised urban agglomerations, may well be of greater quantitative significance than its role as a job creator.

Conclusion

The principles of an efficient economy and a diversified ecology will always be antagonistic. Environmental industries and technologies do not build a harmonising bridge, but they do have the ability to reduce pollution production and consumption processes, and thereby to reduce environmental costs in the long term. Over the last decade there have been certain successes in West Germany in the introduction of environmentally-sound process technologies and the development of recycling methods. However, in spite of these achievements, the country still suffers from a continuing high quantity of pollutant emissions. The management, and eventual reduction, of these must be the function of the environmental industry. There are opportunities to link this obligation with counterstrategies, which can work towards the easing of regional imbalances. In particular, de-industrialising regions and agglomeration areas stand to gain the most benefits from this mode of ecological intervention.

References

Adlwarth, W. and Wimmer, F., 'Umweltbewutßsein und Kaufver-halten - Ergebnisse einer Verbraucherpanel-Studie', *Jahrbuch der Absatz- und Verbrauchsforschung*, Vol. 2, pp. 166-92, 1986.

Bonkowski, S. and Legler, H., *Umweltschutz und Wirtschaftss-truktur in Niedersachsen*, Pilotstudie im Auftrage des Niedersächsi-schen Ministers für Wirtschaft und Verkehr, Hanover, 1986.

Brunowsky, R-D. and Wicke, L., *Der Öko-Plan. Durch Umwelt-schutz zum neuen Wirtschaftswunder*, Munich and Zurich, 1984.

Castells, M., 'Crisis, planning and the quality of life: managing the new historical relationships between space and society', *Society and Space*, Vol. 1.1, pp. 3-21, 1983.

Commerzbank, 'Umweltschutz: Wachsende gesamtwirtschaf-tliche Bedeutung', *Bericht der Abteilung Volkswirtschaft*, Vol. 18, 1988.

Dear, M. and Long, J., 'Community strategies in locational con-flict', in Cox, K.R. (ed.), *Urbanisation and conflict in market societies*, London, pp. 113-27, 1978.

Essig, H., 'Erfassung öffentlicher Umweltschutzausgaben und -einnahmen durch die Finanzstatistik', *Wirtschaft und Statistik*, Vol. 12, pp. 957-66, 1985.

Härtel, H-H. et al., *Zusammenhang zwischen Strukturwandel und Umwelt, Spezialuntersuchung im Rahmen der HWWA-Strukturbe-richterstattung*, Vol. 2, Hamburg-Weltarchiv,1987.

Hirschmann, A.O., *Exit, voice, loyalty*, Cambridge, 1970.

Hübler, K-H., 'Wechselwirkungen zwischen Raumordnung-spolitik und Umweltpolitik', *Forschungs- und Sitzungsberichte*, Vol. 165, pp. 11-43, 1987.

Kunzmann, K. et al., *Regionale Auswirkungen der Umweltpolitik auf die Beschäftigtensituation in Rheinland-Pfalz*, Dortmund, 1985.

Leborgne, D. and Lipietz, A., 'New technologies, new modes of regulation; some spatial implications', *Society and Space*, Vol. 6, pp. 263-80, 1988.

Oßenbrügge, J., 'Regional restructuring and the ecological welfare state - spatial impacts of environmental protection in West Germany', *Geographische Zeitschrift*, Vol. 76, pp. 78-96, 1988.

Sprenger, R-U. and Knödgen, G., *Struktur und Entwicklung der Umweltschutzindustrie in der Bundesrepublik Deutschland*, Umweltbundesamt, Berlin, 1983.

Ullmann, A.A. and Zimmermann, K., *Umweltpolitik und Umwelt-schutzindustrie in der Bundesrepublik Deutschland - Eine Analyse ihrer ökonomischen Wirkungen*, Umweltbundesamt, Berlin, 1981.

Umweltbundesamt (ed.), *Daten zur Umwelt*, Berlin, 1986.

Wand, K., 'Beschäftigungspolitische Initiativen in der norddeutschen Küstenregion', in Fricke, W. et al. (eds.), *Mehr Arbeit in die Region*, Neue Gesellschaft, Bonn, pp. 76-89, 1986.

Wirtschaftswoche, 'Spezial: Umweltschutz', *Wirtschaftswoche*, March, 1988.

Zimmermann, K. and Nijkamp, P., 'Umweltschutz und regionale Entwicklungspolitik - Konzepte, Inkonsistenzen und integrative Ansätze', in Zimmermann, K. et al. (eds.), *Umwelt-Raum-Politik*, Berlin, pp. 19-101, 1986.

Chapter XX

John Hall (London Boroughs Association)

Implications of 1992 for London government

Introduction

This chapter is written by an academic geographer turned policy analyst. Such a transformation remains surprisingly rare, for Britain's employers, and even employees, in the private and public sectors show little interest, as yet, in furthering mobility between the academic, business and government spheres. Moving from university to local government in the late 1980s brings few culture shocks, however: both institutions have traditionally recruited staff with a commitment to public service; both have witnessed radical restructuring during the 1980s; many individuals and corporate bodies in both feel less in control of their destinies, misunderstood, undervalued even, and less able to command the resources necessary for doing their jobs properly. But, simultaneously, restructuring is bringing new approaches and practices and a desire to experiment.

The chapter will indicate some of the ways in which local authorities in the London region might be affected by a further wave of restructuring associated with the cumulative adoption of European directives and regulations now widely known in Britain as the '1992' package, and as '1993' in some other member states of the European Community. Although much of the narrative relates to London, the themes also relate to other regions and to the discussion of national responses to problems and policies in what on these western shores of Europe is seen as an economic heartland (the Federal Republic of Germany) and an economic periphery (the United Kingdom).

What is '1992'?

The expression '1992' refers to the European Council meeting in Luxembourg in 1985 at which the EC heads of state resolved to create a proper internal market without frontiers by 31 December 1992. The related 'Single European Act' came into force on 1 July 1987, 30 years after the Treaty of Rome had established the original European Community of six member states, which was enlarged to nine in 1973 (including the United Kingdom), 10 in 1981 (the addition of Greece), and 12 in 1986 (the addition of Spain and Portugal).

The original Rome treaty had sought to create 'an area without internal frontiers in which the free movement of goods, persons, services and capital is ensured'. Nevertheless, this has not been achieved, and some 300 measures have been tabled subsequently, in order to remove fiscal, physical and technical barriers to trade.

Viewed from Britain, and more to the point the Treasury, the principal objective of the Single European Act is to weld the individual markets of member states into one growing and flexible market, in which resources are used to greatest economic advantage. The market will comprise some 325 million consumers, exceeding that of the USA (250 million) and Japan (125 million). According to the much-quoted report by Cecchini et al. (1988), dismantling the barriers might add about 1% to each member state's gross domestic product. The economic boost is viewed as an amalgam of the removal of frontier barriers affecting production, together with gains from economies of scale and intensified competition. Nevertheless, such growth might reinforce the economic core area of the Community, and even nudge it from north-west Europe towards the Alps. Because of this prospect, support for disadvantaged and frontier regions is to be offered during the transitional period to the mid-1990s.

As has become apparent during the recent 1992 fervour, different member states of the Community give emphasis to different parts of the Single European Act. The British Prime Minister, Mrs Thatcher, has been vigorous in her defence of national monetary and political

375

sovereignty. A government white paper on 'releasing enterprise' (1988) asserts that 'the key must be liberalisation, not harmonisation for its own sake'.

Others put a different gloss on 1992. Those on the political left may condemn it as a charter for a 'businessmen's Europe'; those on the right may be wary of the formalisation of a 'social Europe'; yet others espy cultural and educational opportunities which may weld a broader appreciation of a 'citizens' Europe'. The process of liberalisation will doubtless precipitate all of these - and 1992 is a process, rather than a destination. The measures required by the Single European Act have been called 'the end of the beginning'.

How does 1992 affect British local authorities?

Many groups, notably employers, professions, and trade unions, are assessing the likely impact of 1992 on their activities and members, and are arranging conferences, courses and publications. Local authorities across Britain are now showing a quickening interest in 1992.

Within the United Kingdom as a whole, government spending in the financial year 1988-9 was 39.5% of the gross domestic product, compared with 47% six years earlier. The estimated public expenditure outturn for 1988-9 comprises £114.4 billion by central government and £42.9 billion by local authorities. Thus, local authorities remain significant for their volume of spending, although their capital expenditure continues to decline and is strictly controlled by central government. Local authority employment, which in England and Wales is about 2,050,000 people (one-half of whom are in education), has remained almost constant over the last decade.

The likely effects of 1992 on local authorities are being investigated by individual local authorities and by their associations, which in England represent the 39 'shire' counties, the 296 county districts, the 36 metropolitan districts (in the now abolished 6 metropolitan county areas), and the 32 London boroughs, plus the City of London. The associations are also supported by the Local Government International Bureau, which is Britain's local government conduit to the European Community, to the Council of Europe and the Council of European Municipalities and Regions, and to the International Union of Local Authorities. Indeed, in 'Eurospeak', local authorities, together with central government, employers, trade unions and the voluntary sector, are expected to function as the partners in the implementation of Community policies within member states.

Newcomers to European affairs soon learn about the complexities of influence and decision-making within the Community institutions. Likewise, newcomers to local government soon learn about the complex division of functions between central government departments. Within England, the Department of the Environment is in overall charge of relations between central and local government; other government departments take the lead in the negotiation and administration of sectoral policies, as indicated in Table 20.1.

Of particular immediate concern to local authorities are the new European Community directives about public purchasing, relating to supplies and works. These, possibly excepting energy, telecommunications, transport and water, will require the publication of tenders throughout the Community. And, given the scale of many local authorities' involvement in promoting economic development (Church and Hall, 1989), there is concern about the extent to which local incentives might be declared inadmissible distortions of the free market. Will national governments, indeed, still be able to operate national, or regional, preference in their procurement of defence equipment? This is now recognised as a potent force for maintaining regional economies.

Environmental issues, covering product and food standards and hygiene and pollution, are also of growing concern throughout the Community. Interestingly, it is the consumers who are seen to be in the driving seat, forcing national governments to respond to new concerns about the health of nations, and even the well-being of the planet.

Table 20.1: Selected effects of 1992 on English local authorities

function of local authority	supervision by central government
FINANCE:	
assistance to industry & commerce	Department of the Environment
public purchasing & contracts	Treasury
GRANTS FROM STRUCTURAL FUNDS:	
European Social Fund	Department of the Environment
European Reg. Dev. Fund	Department of the Environment
EAGFF	Ministry of Agriculture
EMPLOYERS OF PROFESSIONALLY-QUALIFIED PERSONS:	
qualifications	Department of Trade and Industry
training	Department of Employment
PUBLIC SAFEGUARDS AND STANDARDS:	
consumer protection	Department of Trade and Industry
environmental policy	Department of the Environment
food regulations	Ministry of Agriculture
trading standards	Department of Trade and Industry

Note: The Welsh Office, Scottish Office and Northern Ireland Office exercise separate powers.

How is London governed?

In 1889 the London City Council came into being, following an Act of Parliament of the previous year. It provided services across an area of 311 km^2, which at that time accommodated about 4 million people. A rationalisation of lower-tier government came in 1899, when 28 metropolitan boroughs were formed within the LCC area. This two-tier division continued, with the enlargement of the upper tier in 1965 into a new Greater London Council area of 1,580 km^2, embracing over 7 million people, and the amalgamation of boroughs and adjoining municipalities into 32 London boroughs, each with an average population of about 250,000: the historic City of London remained intact at the core of the metropolis.

In 1986 the GLC was abolished, leaving its Londonwide functions to be shared among the constituent boroughs, or to be given to either ad hoc authorities or absorbed by central government departments. Table 20.2 summarises the distribution of powers and functions before and after the abolition of the GLC. (For a fuller description of bodies and functions, see Hebbert and Travis, 1988.) Note also that the remaining larger-than-a-single-borough elected authority (the Inner London Education Authority, which inherited the LCC's education functions and its boundary), is also abolished. In the case of education, however, schools will be empowered to 'opt out' of local authority control. This is part of a wider movement of allowing hospitals and hitherto mainly public services, such as urban passenger transport, to be managed independently, or even privatised.

Before 1986, the GLC would have been active in investigating the Londonwide implications of 1992 on London's interests. That task now falls to the individual boroughs, and to the two associations that serve them: one being the the exclusively Labour representation of the Association of London Authorities (formed when the abolition of the GLC was under way), including 15 boroughs and the ILEA in its membership; the other being the original London Boroughs Association, which is Conservative-controlled (but with Liberal/Democrat and Labour boroughs in membership) and represents 18 boroughs, plus the City of London. Each Association's specialist committees will be considering how 1992 is likely to affect their member authorities and Londoners themselves in various categories. In this discussion, I will concentrate on the broader impacts that are likely to be felt across London and in the south-east region.

Table 20.2: The functions of London local government, 1965-90

TWO-TIER GOVERNMENT, 1965-86:

GLC AND BOROUGHS JOINTLY:

Planning	(GLC strategic; boroughs local)
Roads	(GLC strategic; boroughs local) and traffic management
Housing	(GLC estates transferred to boroughs, 1981)
Refuse	(boroughs collect; GLC disposes)

Arts, culture, entertainment, parks, recreation, historic buildings

GLC SEPARATELY:
London Transport (until 1984, when LRT came under Dept. of Transport control)
Thames flood prevention and land drainage
Fire service
Information, research and scientific services

BOROUGHS SEPARATELY:
Environmental services and consumer protection
Personal social services
Libraries and swimming pools

EDUCATION AND THE CAREERS SERVICE:
ILEA serves (until 1990) inner boroughs and the City of London
20 outer London boroughs are each separate education authorities

Successor authorities to the GLC since 1986:

Road planning	Department of Transport
Strategic planning advice	London Planning Advisory Committee - guidance issued by DoE
Fire service	London Fire & Civil Defence Authority
Floods and drainage	Thames Water Authority
Research	London Research Centre
Survey of London	English Heritage

Boroughs singly: arts, archives, building control, coroners, entertainment licensing, trading standards, recreation and parks, rights of way, tourism

London Boroughs Grants Committee: gives grant aid to the voluntary sector (Richmond-upon-Thames acts as 'lead borough')

London Residuary Body: winds up affairs of the GLC (and from 1990, of the ILEA)

London in the European context

The geometry of south-east England

From time to time newspapers carry articles lamenting the fact that Britain's capital city (Scots, Welsh and Northern Irish might well suggest 'England's' capital) is eccentrically located in the south-eastern corner of mainland Britain. The Romans can take the blame, since London was positioned within Britain's least rebellious zone and was close to already-conquered Gaul. This situation is now again proving convenient, as Britain's overseas trade becomes increasingly dominated by the European Community: one-third of UK exports were to the EC in 1972, and the proportion had risen to one-half by 1987. So the south-east, London included, is once again being seen as the 'gateway' to and from mainland Europe.

There is a certain resentment in the north of England, and in Wales, Scotland and Northern Ireland, of the favoured situation of London and the south-east. After all, this region is also the part of Britain which is the most prosperous, the most dominated by growth industries, the least afflicted by unemployment, and (many would now say) the most troubled by congestion - a congestion which has been created by its own success. Northern firms fear that much more production in the near future will be relocated to the south-east, maybe to northern France, in order to take advantage of easier access to the mainland European market.

Those jealous of the south-east's advantages are told to think nationally: if London and the south-east region cannot thrive, what hope is there for the rest of the country, in the face of any possible further southwards march of the EC's centre of gravity? What hope is there of countering further international penetration of our economic strongholds, and of competing against globalised production?

Figure 20.1: Projected high-speed railway networks in Britain and mainland Europe

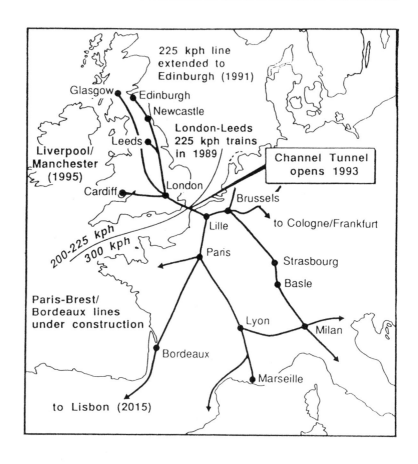

225 kph line extended to Edinburgh (1991)

Glasgow
Edinburgh
Newcastle
London-Leeds 225 kph trains in 1989
Liverpool/ Manchester (1995)
Leeds
Cardiff
London
Channel Tunnel opens 1993
Brussels
to Cologne/Frankfurt
Lille
200-225 kph
300 kph
Paris
Strasbourg
Basle
Paris-Brest/ Bordeaux lines under construction
Lyon
Milan
Bordeaux
Marseille
to Lisbon (2015)

The physical impact of the Channel Tunnel fixed link

The advantage to south-east England of the country's geometry, in relation to mainland Europe, becomes even more apparent when the physical and psychological impacts of the Channel Tunnel are considered. Once 1992 becomes accepted as an inexorable tightening of the harmonisation ratchet (if not a fully-completed process), then press attention will be given to 1993 - the target year for the opening of the rail tunnel between France and Britain. At present, British Rail is intending to build the principal passenger terminals at two existing London rail termini: Waterloo on the south bank of the Thames, and King's Cross to the north of the City.

Later in 1989, British Rail will be presenting a bill to parliament to authorise construction of the new rail line through Kent to London. A preferred route was announced in March 1989, 37 km of which, out of a total length of 109 km between London and Folkestone, are to be tunnelled. Further modifications to the preferred alignment can be anticipated, although, as published, it follows the M20 motorway transport corridor for part of the route. Tunnelling was adopted as a means of reducing the hostility of Kent residents to the alternatives presented in 1988 and early 1989.

Passenger-traffic forecasts (made when only a single London rail terminal was proposed), suggested that by the year 2003 the hourly service to Paris and Brussels would be used by some 13 million rail passengers. One reason for choosing Waterloo was spare capacity on intersecting underground lines, given an anticipated 4.5 million additional tube trips a year through that London main-line railway station.

Patently, the impact of 'tunnel' rail traffic on London - freight as well as passenger - will be given more detailed attention in the near future. Although the London Planning Advisory Committee, on which all boroughs are represented, is considering the tunnel's impact, there is little likelihood of a thorough environmental impact assessment being undertaken along the proposed London approaches and around the chosen London termini. East London boroughs, Newham especially, had wanted Stratford, just to the north of the Docklands, to be designated as a rail interchange for the tunnel. To have done so would have been a clear gesture of support for the generally less-favoured east side of London. It would also have been cheaper to build there than at King's Cross, and easier to accommodate significant volumes of freight.

Economic position of the City of London

Will the City of London be able to retain its dominance as the capital of finance within the European Community? Today there are reports of the Amsterdam *Bourse* wishing to expand its influence, and Dublin is seeking to augment its role as a financial trading centre. For those who equate height with importance, the *Messeturm* in Frankfurt is now hailed as western Europe's highest building (overtaking the towers proposed for Canary Wharf in the London Docklands).

For the time being, London certainly ranks alongside New York and Tokyo as one of the three principal world finance centres. It has about 400 foreign banks and accommodates as much as 25% of the international banking market, which is more than New York and Tokyo's combined 24% (Marshall, 1988). But, in stock market capitalisation, Tokyo exceeds London and New York together. The recent growth of financial services in the City of London is clearly expressed there by the current wave of new building and refurbishment, notably the virtual forest of tower cranes in the vicinity of London Wall and Bishopsgate. Canary Wharf has been marketed as an extension of the City of London in the London Docklands; the Docklands Light Railway makes both a symbolic and physical link between the City of London and the quickly-filling Enterprise Zone on the Isle of Dogs.

Estimates by the Institute of Manpower Studies (Rajan with Fryatt, 1988,) have suggested that during the period 1987-92, employment in the City of London may rise by 11,000 in banking (from a base of 114,000), 5,000 in insurance (from 45,000), 9,000 in accounting and management consultancy (from 25,000) and 8,000 in software services (from 18,000).

Exactly what has caused the growth of producer services is still very much in debate. In London's context, the labour market effects must be stressed. There are particular difficulties for City firms seeking to recruit suitably-qualified staff. Hitherto, City of London employers have captured staff by, in effect, 'vacuum cleaning' national and, indeed, international labour markets. The extent to which they can continue to do so, while the school and college leaving-age cohorts decline, relates, in part, to the whole package of job opportunities and working and living conditions (and costs) in London, compared with elsewhere. One implication of the opening up of European markets is the wider availability of knowledge about other places. How does the London package of remuneration and daily living conditions, including the strains of the housing market and irritations of travelling to work, compare, not just with other British cities, but - for those internationally-mobile workers with language competence - with mainland European cities, such as Frankfurt and Paris?

In addition, although London may retain its preeminence in the several European markets for money, shares, commodities and insurance, it has not been able, as a latecomer to the EC club, to attract a fair share of institutional headquarters. Will new small- and medium-sized enterprises want a London, or a European mainland headquarters? If large British firms are involved in mergers and takeovers, will they retain London-based headquarters?

Tourism in London

In respect of tourism flows within the European Community, Britain exhibits an adverse balance of tourists. More particularly, the British Tourist Authority has remarked that, whereas in 1986 a total of 4.62 million visitors came to Britain from our near neighbours (France 1.76 million, West Germany 1.60 million, Netherlands 0.77 million and Belgium 0.50 million), nearly double that number of British people (8.1 million) visited these same countries. Bravely, the BTA views this lopsided pattern as a 'challenge' for those marketing Britain in mainland Europe.

385

Yet the Channel Tunnel might conceivably make things worse. Having crossed the Channel, Britons can then fan out across the whole of mainland Europe from their point of entry in northern France. Conversely, a cross-Channel trip from France to Folkestone, or to London, enables the traveller to fan out across only a single kingdom.

As to the London effects, the London Tourist Board is reasonably optimistic. The important business-travel market is likely to favour London at the expense of other regional centres in Britain. Moreover, if mergers continue apace within the Community, then headquarters' functions within London may be reinforced. But other countries are not standing still, most notably France, which is pushing the further development of Charles de Gaulle Airport in Paris as a major European interchange.

Should London receive ERDF financial support?

To this picture of a booming London, overflowing with tourists, money market players and company headquarters, can be added a more sombre scene: a London in which seven inner east London boroughs, including the three Docklands boroughs of Tower Hamlets, Newham and Southwark, saw their industrial component in their local employment structures fall from 36% to 23% between 1971-84, and (during the period 1975-81) a total loss of 57,400 manufacturing jobs. These same boroughs house one-third of London's unemployed; their unemployment rates in 1987 were nearly double those of the Community average, but have fallen since.

Armed with facts such as these, a delegation from the Labour Association of London Authorities and also from London's Labour members of the European Parliament, argued the case for these boroughs to be made eligible for support under the Community's reformed Structural Funds. The case was taken up by central government's Department of Trade and Industry (DTI) and pressed consistently up to the spring of 1989. Seven inner east London boroughs, now known at the 'London City Action Team Priority Area', were not on the list of areas eligible for European Regional Development Fund support (so-called 'Objective 2' regions in the new EC Structural Funds). However, they are expected to receive a modest level of support for innovatory projects supported by the ERDF. London's case has highlighted the plight of inner-city areas in respect of unemployment, training and infrastructural needs; these and other inner London boroughs will continue to seek appropriate European Social Fund support, which is itself greatly overshadowed by UK government incentives. The 'London City Action Priority Area' example also serves as a useful demonstration of the political and analytical impetus behind the 'inner urban areas versus traditional problem regions' debate.

Conclusions

This chapter has presented a number of loosely-drawn outlines, for the details are to be filled in over the next two or three years. If one stands back from the legitimate concerns of the London boroughs about their powers, duties and available resources, one can glimpse rather a European Community in which old patterns are reasserting themselves. For just as British de-industrialisation has seemingly led to the reassertion of the south as the centre of wealth within the United Kingdom, so, in the enlarged Europe, trade routes would now seem to favour the traditional crossroads nations, not least Germany (West and East), which forms a fulcrum between maritime and continental Europe, and between between the Baltic and Mediterranean lands. Indeed, German colleagues will no doubt recognise the possible rediscovery of that old regional geography chestnut, known as *Mitteleuropa*.

Students of an earlier generation, when Britain still saw itself as a world power, were brought up with a school geography which gave a world view. How do the present generation of school children in the different parts of the country view Britain in relation to mainland Europe? The committee charged by the Department of Education and Science with examining geography for the country's first national school curriculum will have this question in mind.

Because local authorities are responding to their own perceptions of the European challenge of 1992, and also because local authorities are education authorities, their elected members and officers have a particular opportunity to make EC development more comprehensible than have national politicians and interest groups. Local authorities, not just in London, are, in fact, gearing up to this challenge.

References

Cecchini, P. et al., *The European challenge to 1992: the benefits of a single market*, Wildwood House, 1988.

Church, A. and Hall, J.M., 'Local initiatives for economic regeneration', in Herbert, D.T. and Smith, D.M. (eds.), *Social problems and the city: new perspectives*, Oxford University Press, 1989.

Hebbert, M. and Travers, T. (eds.), *The London government handbook*, Cassell, 1988.

HMSO, *Reclaiming enterprise*, HMSO, Cm 512, paragraph 1.9, 1988.

Marshall, J.N., *Services and uneven development*, Oxford University Press, 1988.

Owen, R. and Dynes, M., *The Times guide to 1992: a complete handbook to Europe without frontiers*, Times Books, 1989.

Rajan, A. with Fryatt, J., *Create or abdicate: the City's human resource choice for the '90s*, Witherby & Co, 1988.

Chapter XXI

Trevor Wild and Philip Jones

Conclusion: common problems, policies and questions for British and West German society

Common processes

The chapters in this volume have demonstrated that, in a general way, both the onset and the course of de-industrialisation in Britain and West Germany have followed similar paths. In detail, there are salient differences in the experiences of the two countries, but these are not of sufficient magnitude to prevent us from recognising the importance of common components in economic and spatial development. In particular, regions severely affected by the crises of de-industrialisation appear to suffer from combinations of structural, organisational, and technological weaknesses.

Structural weaknesses stem from an overdependence on inappropriate and outdated industries and economic activities. The most typical areas are the old textile manufacturing districts and the 'rust belts', with their concentration on resource extraction, metal production and metalworking industries. A feature of such regions is their limited degree of compensatory new economic growth, particularly in the key sectors of high-tech industries and quaternary activities. This deficiency accords with the Schumpeterian notion of 'shifting industrialisation', in which the location of new forms of economic development, unless directed by planning intervention, tend to avoid the old-industrial heartlands.

This, in part, reflects the second characteristic deficiency, which is the weak organisational basis of many industrial branches in declining regions. A paucity of headquarter-control establishments, and a low degree of involvement in high-level decision-making are common disadvantages, which further hamper industrial restructuring of these regions. It also results in a generally-lower quality of employment, with insecure assembly-line production being much more prevalent than such elite occupations as research and product development, information processing, and marketing. Consequently, while these regions still have large concentrations of human capital, they are now being depleted by large-scale movements of people to more prosperous regions. Moreover, as Fothergill and Guy (Chapter VII) have demonstrated in their analysis of branch plant closures in British peripheral regions, there is a high degree of external dependency in most of the new manufacturing industries which have been attracted recently by government policies. They stress that the vital consideration in a plant's future is neither the location, nor the product itself, but the plant's role in the overall organisation of the firm's activities. There are close parallels in West Germany, in that older industrial regions such as the Ruhr, west Münsterland, Hamburg and Rhine-Neckar are witnessing a steady increase in the proportion of externally-controlled jobs in the manufacturing sector.

The third common weakness of old-industrial regions is the dominance of older technological modes of production, in which the giant plants of the Fordist type, with their assembly-line output of standardised products, is the predominant type of factory. In both Britain and West Germany, and particularly in their northern regions, it is precisely this outdated Fordist model which is in fast retreat. It should also be stressed that it is difficult to apply new technology to this production format without incurring a large corresponding loss of jobs; the iron and steel industry is an outstanding instance in both countries, and it is clear that other manufacturing industries, such as motor vehicles, are following this trend.

From the evidence of the contributions, it is also clear that the path of de-industrialisation in particular industries and in particular regions is extremely difficult to reverse. Nuhn's analysis of the Hamburg shipbuilding industry is particularly pertinent in this respect. It illustrates that a well-organised industry, with a worldwide reputation for quality products, proved ultimately unsustainable in the face of global competitive pressures. The remaining shipbuilding industry is now a shadow of its former self in the halcyon years of the 1950s and early-1960s. Industrial regeneration within declining regions has to be grounded upon the introduction and/or attraction of new industries, making new products with new technologies. The British and West German experiences amply illustrate the hard truth of this statement, which has to be faced by both local and national policy-makers. How to achieve this goal is the crucial issue.

Problems of change

In both countries the fact that de-industrialisation and new industrialisation have different spatial emphases has enhanced regional imbalances. In the old-industrial regions, the problems are those associated with economic decline - high levels of unemployment, deteriorating social and economic capital, outdated infrastructures, scarred environments, and negative images. Newly-industrialising spaces, however, are also not without their problems, although these are of a different kind. For example, economic expansion generates demand for jobs which often outruns local labour markets, stimulating substantial population in-migration, which in turn intensifies pressures on housing, health, education and transport facilities.

Regional imbalances are undoubtedly stronger in the United Kingdom, with its immensely sharp and still-diverging north-south divide, accompanied by acute local-scale differences. Within the context of retreating regional policy and increasing emphasis on market forces during the 1980s, there has been a substantial shift to an unregulated, laissez faire approach to such economic divergence. As well as the familiar entrenchment of social and economic difficulties in the north, there has been substantial regional 'overheating' in the growth arena of the south. As expansion in the latter has accelerated, so attendant diseconomies have emerged - congested roads, overcrowded public transport, a remarkable upward spiral of house prices, and intense local-scale land use planning conflicts. The desperate shortage of affordable housing in the south-east is, perhaps, the most critical problem of all, since it underlies a proliferation of local-scale conflicts over building-land in environmentally-sensitive locations, and generates social stress through the imposition of ever-lengthening journeys to work. This intensely competitive atmosphere is not conducive to the development of community-oriented life-styles.

Before leaving this point, however, it is perhaps pertinent to indicate that the 'new' regionalisation of decline and expansion is not necessarily permanent. To imply this state is to ignore Schumpeter's central thesis of 'creative destruction'. Nothing is permanent: today's problem industrial regions were yesterday's cores of prosperity. To the discerning observer, there are already some pointers to checks on growth in the south-east, such as the 'post-crash' (1987) loss of more than 30,000 jobs in the financial sector of the City of London, and increasing doubts, which have been expressed in many quarters, concerning the long-term viability of the ambitious office and other property schemes in London Docklands. For example, the government is now coming under severe pressure from property developers to provide further massive funding for additional public transport infrastructure in London Docklands, particularly an extension of the Jubilee line, which they claim is vital for the continued viability of the whole scheme (*Independent*, 5 August 1989). Moreover, Wood (Chapter XIII) raises the even more fundamental issue of whether or not London will retain its current role as western Europe's primary financial centre into the next century.

In West Germany, the dispersion of major nodes of prosperity reduces the risks of such large-scale regional overheating. There is simply no parallel here to the scale and extent of the metropolitan concentration process that is taking place in Greater London and the adjoining counties of south-east England. The quantity and forms of new economic activity and investments, which are essentially the prerogative of this 'favoured' part of Britain, although certainly showing something of a southern tendency, are spread out among several individual city systems in West Germany. The pacesetters here are undoubtedly Frankfurt, Munich, Stuttgart, Düsseldorf-Cologne, and Hamburg - the so-called 'Big Five'. It is noticeable that their representation straddles the West German north-south divide.

Policies and their influence

With the evidence of such substantial regional imbalances in economic growth and consequent problems, there is clearly much scope for the application of policies of different kinds - industrial, economic, environmental, and social. However, before commenting upon those policies which have been examined, it should be appreciated that there are distinct caveats to what they can achieve in a basically market-orientated economy, however well regulated. Within a capitalist economy, the ultimate arbitration of the market place has to be recognised. Even within the fastest-growing branches of industry, there will inevitably be unsuccessful 'players', with corresponding negative job impacts on some locations. Likewise, as we have seen, the combined efforts of firms and government cannot prevent the continuing decline of jobs in structurally-weak industries. Nuhn's analysis of Hamburg's shipbuilding industry and Hauff's examination of the west Münsterland textile industry, provide two characteristic examples.

A further underlying principle is that, despite the existence of interventionary policies, the role of the individual entrepreneur and his 'bottom-up' initiatives, cannot be easily institutionalised. There is argument, indeed, that public intervention in the field of entrepreneurship can, in some ways, deter this style of individualistic involvement, through imposing often-stultifying procedures of bureaucracy. While the presence of numerous entrepreneurs and their financial supporters is apparently effortless and endemic in growth regions, leading to a flourishing proliferation of small- and medium-sized enterprises, as Keeble demonstrated (Chapter II), such economic effervescence is unfortunately difficult to replicate in old-industrial areas. Yet outstanding exceptions do occur, in the form of individuals who possess special qualities of enthusiasm, perseverance and aptitude. These individuals are capable of surmounting some of the most formidable local difficulties, in order to lay the foundations of self-sustaining economic regeneration (Spooner, Chapter VI).

A reading of the contributions suggests that, as far as policy initiatives are concerned, the differences between West Germany and Britain are greater than the similarities. This derives from the different ethos underpinning their political economies. West Germany is committed to the principles of the social market economy, while Britain now leans heavily towards the 'enterprise culture'. West Germany, as stated in the *Bundesraumordnungsgesetz* of 1965, has a constitutional requirement:

'to create, safeguard and continue to develop healthy living and working conditions, as well as balanced economic, social and cultural opportunities in all parts of the Federal Republic of Germany'.

There is no such explicit policy objective in Britain, but rather an ultimate reliance upon the 'trickle-down' mechanisms created by market-led forces.

These attitudes are reflected in quite considerable national contrasts in the extent of financial and political resources devoted to regional policy initiatives, and also in profound differences in the strength and continuity of local and regional administrative structures. In Britain, the 1980s have seen the deliberate weakening of local democratically-controlled administrative structures, accompanied by deregulation and loosening of planning controls. West Germany has retained its tiers of Federal, *Land* and *Gemeinde* structures, as well as introducing further regional-level bodies. Consequently, the spirit of regionalism and localism in West Germany is being maintained.

Despite these major differences in approach, similar problems are encountered in attempting to stimulate local and regional economic regeneration. As well as the obvious priority of encouraging the growth of new economic activities, there is also the need to achieve an interconnected and parallel improvement in the environment, modernisation of infrastructures, and transformation of the external image of declining regions. A further area of difficulty concerns the development of effective means of balancing necessary 'top-down' policies, such as labour retraining and the development of technical skills in the labour force, with the mobilisation of 'bottom-up' initiatives. It is widely acknowledged that West Germany has an elaborate (indeed, many would say superlative) range of policies which are essentially of a top-down nature, creating firm foundations for the best-equipped, best-educated and most thoroughly-trained human capital in the European Community. It is the exemplar in this respect. In the United Kingdom, the emphasis is now on designing policies to encourage local private enterprise, which is, in essence, 'bottom-up'. The energies of policy-makers, together with public financial resources, have been directed to this end. Ideally, a blend of the two models is required, combining the strength of the technically-oriented, regulated West German system, with the fluidity and experimental character which is potentially provided by the British 'enterprise' model.

A further common policy weakness, which appears to some extent under both systems, is a lack of forecasting mechanisms to recognise and avoid the onset of new regional crises. Diagnostic forecasting techniques and anticipatory planning have been neglected in the past, yet adequate forewarning and quick remedial action should facilitate the task of economic restructuring at local and regional scales. Too much of the planning that occurs is concerned with responding to already-developed crises, and too little resources are directed to strategies which could head off incipient crises. This is especially the case in Britain, which lacks the more holistic and better-informed perspectives and also the continuity of basic approach which is characteristic of regional and local planning in West Germany.

Questions for British and West Germany society

The fundamental question that must be asked in concluding this volume is: what do these two advanced industrial societies want for the future? We consider that the following considerations must be made in any evaluation of the answer:

- there are important decisions to be made regarding the balance between economic regeneration and restructuring on the one hand, and the attainment of social objectives on the other. It is not sufficient to view job creation in terms of head-counts, but cognisance must be taken of the quality of employment, the quality of life, and the security of economic recovery. We have seen that economic crises create inevitable losers, for example, the *Gastarbeiter* of Gronau, the redundant steelworkers of Scunthorpe, and the former dockworkers of East London. We are not convinced that these very losers are the immediate beneficiaries of the new schemes that have replaced their former factories and facilities. Surely more consideration needs to be given to achieving a more harmonious social outcome.

- A crucial and growing issue is the need for greater regulation and protection of the environment. This is in conflict with the general deregulatory economic climate which is becoming more influential in the European Community as 1992 approaches. There has been an upsurge of consumer interest in 'green' issues which, whilst still in an early, politically-immature stage, is nevertheless a countercurrent which cannot be ignored. Is it too fanciful to see the priority of the creation of economic wealth being eventually supplanted by the more idealistic vision of the ecological market society, as Oßenbrügge postulates?

- To many eyes, the spectacular landscapes created by recent, property-led regeneration in both countries possess an inherent vulnerability and impermanence. They symbolise the divorce between the making and circulation of money, and the making of tangible, marketable products. This divorce is particularly pronounced in Britain, whose national economic recovery in the 1980s has been led by the financial and business services sector. Alternatively, will the sheer suddenness of its emergence be replaced by an equally rapid deflation? There are significant signs emerging from London Docklands to make us pose this question.

- The clarity of the north-south divide in Britain, where market forces have been accorded their maximum freedom, and regional interventionist policies have been most weakened, inevitably leads us to suggest that more consideration should be given to the reintroduction of active regional development policies. The north-south divide (or, to be more accurate, north-south 'gradient') in West Germany, is less apparent and less profound. At the same time, the complexities of the regional problems within declining industrial regions are such that a return in Britain to the old-style regional policies, which placed undue emphasis upon sheer numbers of jobs at the expense of other, more qualititative economic considerations, would clearly be inadequate. Any reinvigoration of regional policy should, therefore, be within a more comprehensive and sensitive mould.

- A Europeanwide perspective is needed in planning for the future of both countries, especially for 1992. Indeed, this should not just be confined to the nations within the European Community, but to the likely development of closer links with East European countries within the framework of an enlarged 'European home', as President Gorbachov has recently intimated.

Concluding remarks

This volume has clarified common trends of de-industrialisation and new industrialisation within the two countries. Important differences in scale, durability and public policy have emerged. Britain's de-industrialisation has been faster and more enduring, and its social cost has been more profound; regional imbalances, especially the north-south divide, are much harsher. New science- and technology-based enterprises are also less linked to a productive economy than in the case of West Germany. Britain experiences greater 'economic turbulence', yet has arguably seen a stronger, if more regionally-constrained, emergence of a new form of service and information economy, predicated on a more deregulated economic environment. West Germany's transition from an industrial to a postindustrial society has been more cautious, and more accommodating in its social priorities. It has been more consistently committed to stronger public control of the market economy, as is prominently displayed by its continued retention of regulations on quality of production and environmental protection. The two countries are converging in some important respects; but will the markedly different living standards and levels of human welfare, experienced by the large majority of their peoples, continue to diverge?